Postmodern marketing

How can postmodernism throw light on the theory and practice of marketing?

Stephen Brown guides the reader through the postmodern debate with great clarity, showing how important the questions raised by postmodern thinking are for marketing theory and research.

With typical postmodern panache, Stephen Brown traces the development of 'modern' marketing, describes the characteristic features of the 'postmodern condition', identifies the manifestations of postmodernism in contemporary marketing practice, and assesses the implications for marketing theory and research.

Controversial at times, *Postmodern Marketing* is an entirely accessible account of postmodern theory in a marketing context that will be gripping reading for all those who are interested in marketing and postmodernity, whatever their personal standpoint.

Stephen Brown is Professor of Retailing at the University of Ulster.

Postmodern marketing

Stephen Brown

INTERNATIONAL THOMSON BUSINESS PRESS
I ⓉP® An International Thomson Publishing Company

London • Bonn • Boston • Johannesburg • Madrid • Melbourne • Mexico City • New York • Paris
Singapore • Tokyo • Toronto • Albany, NY • Belmont, CA • Cincinnati, OH • Detroit, MI

Postmodern Marketing

Copyright ©1995 Stephen Brown

 I**T**P
A division of International Thomson Publishing Inc.
The ITP logo is a trademark under licence

British Library Cataloguing-in-Publication Data
A catalogue record for this book is available from the British Library

First published 1995 by Routledge
Reprinted by International Thomson Business Press 1997 and 1999

Typeset by Florenctype Ltd., Stoodleigh, Devon
Printed in Croatia

ISBN 1-86152-483-8

International Thomson Business Press
Berkshire House
168–173 High Holborn
London WC1V 7AA
UK

http://www.itbp.com

Are you with me?

Age cannot wither us, Noodles

Do you have a problem with this, pretty boy?

Round up the usual suspects

There are few more blood-curdling sights in the management literature than books which commence with a quotation from, or allusion to, the work of a distinguished philosopher. A philosophical epigraph not only marks the author out as a pretentious pseudo-intellectual, someone who endeavours to bolster the paucity of his or her own paltry thoughts with the reflected gravitas of a 'genuine' thinker, but it also indicates that we are in the presence of a proud possessor of the *Oxford Dictionary of Quotations* rather than a properly educated mind. Such blatant displays of non-erudition are a grisly signifier that reading the material to follow will be an excruciatingly painful experience akin to having bamboo shoots inserted under one's fingernails, attending BTEC examination board committee meetings or watching a compilation video of Charlie Chaplin shorts.

I'm telling you all this not because I have eschewed the option of a philosophically informed preface. As you'll shortly come to realise from my citation of several celebrated philosophers – continental philosophers at that – I am the owner of a well-thumbed *ODQ* and Blackwell's *Dictionary of Philosophical Quotations*, for good measure. Nor is this a devious attempt to circumvent the pseudo-intellectual charge by drawing attention to it and thereby reducing the likelihood of condemnation. On the contrary, as a mere tyro-pseudo-intellectual, I aspire to the dizzy heights of full pseudo status. The real motive behind these, somewhat unusual, prefatory remarks is simply to get you into the postmodern mood, to give you a sense of the wry, ironic, reflexive, self-referential intellectual milieu that you are about to experience at first hand. Consider them the convoluted postmodern equivalent of 'once upon a time' or 'are you sitting comfortably?'. They also mean that I am able to quote continental philosophers without fear of censure, but that's neither here nor there.

In a wonderfully inventive essay entitled 'Outwork', the redoubtable French philosopher-cum-literary theorist, Jacques Derrida, discusses the nature of prefaces and analogous prefatorial remarks (forewords, prologues, acknowledgements, prolegomena, abstracts, etc.) found in almost every work of literature. He notes that although these introductory artefacts are placed at the beginning of the volume, they are invariably written last of all. What is more, they attempt to say what the book says before it says it and seek to give a sense of unity to the work of which they are both a part and apart. Conversely, it can be contended, *pace* Kierkegaard, that prefatory comments may well be written last but they prey on the author's mind throughout the book-writing process and, hence, when it comes to penning the preface etc. 'for real' not only have they already been 'written' hundreds, possibly thousands, of times before, but the final version is also a pale shadow of its prototypes because the author's creative energies have been sapped in the interim.

Indeed, it is arguable that prefaces, forewords and the like have already been written in another sense. As their form and content are bound by tradition, and rigidly circumscribed, they offer little or no opportunity for authorial innovation or invention. Acknowledgements, for example, *must* include expressions of undying gratitude to ever-understanding family and friends; egalitarian or jocular references to the tireless endeavours of support staff; admissions of minor personal failings, preferably atrocious handwriting; and, most importantly of all, some sort of indication that the author has a sense of humour (which leads inexorably to Brown's (1992) Law of Academic Acknowledgements – that there is an inverse correlation between an author's sense of humour and their use of exclamation marks!!!). Consider, moreover, the consequences of failing to include a list of personal acknowledgements. Readers will conclude that the author is either an egomaniac, labouring under the delusion that he or she has done it all unaided, or infer the presence of a sad and lonely individual, an obsessive with no life or companions to speak of. Clearly, the latter is true by definition and, after mulling over this question for some considerable time, I have come to the inescapable conclusion that the people mentioned in acknowledgements *do not exist* (well, have you ever heard of any of them?). They are figments of the author's imagination, (literal) figures of speech, vain attempts to make us believe that he or she is a fully-rounded, well-adjusted individual (though by far the saddest cases are those who actually *dedicate* their work to one or more of these fantasy figures). Now, some of you may be questioning the logic of this argument, but let me place a simple, albeit paradoxical, pedagogic conundrum before you. Why is it, when it comes to supervising undergraduate dissertations, that the students who place enormous demands on your time – and whose research you virtually end up writing for them – never bother to acknowledge your contribution, whereas the ones who don't show up, those you first encounter when they are submitting their projects, invariably express their fulsome thanks for the extensive encouragement, guidance and succour that you have generously extended to them throughout the ordeal? Am I right or am I right?

The foregoing ruminations may strike you as somewhat bizarre – eccentric even – but you may as well know from the outset that they are just the sorts of things that postmodernists ruminate about. Some scholars concern themselves with perturbations in the perihelion of Venus; others concentrate on the search for non-existent subatomic particles; yet others deal with the extent of desertification in sub-Saharan Africa; and, some even devote their lives to structuralist-syntagmatic analyses of the narrative of *Coronation Street*. But postmodernists address the really important things in life like prefaces, acknowledgements, footnotes and ellipses. As this book shall endeavour to demonstrate, however, they also have some interesting things to say to marketers. Honest!

Ever since I let it slip that I was writing a book on postmodern marketing, I have frequently been collared at conferences, dinner parties and public houses by people who feign interest in my work and who ask for a quick synopsis of what it's all about. Fool that I am, I have actually tried to explain, though the glazed expressions, furtive glances over my shoulder and rapid discoveries that drinks needed replenishing, soon made me realise that I was wasting my (and their) time. Accordingly, I have adopted a synoptic strategy of cryptic one-liners such as 'postmodernism has been described as "contrived depthlessness" and books don't come much more contrived and depthless than mine', or, 'postmodernism is characterised by style rather than content . . . my book is just like postmodernism, except without the style'. Indeed, in my more pretentious moments I have even made comparisons between Derrida's *sous rature* (a textual technique, derived from Heidegger, where a ~~word~~ is crossed out but remains visible, meaning that it is inadequate to the task of description yet remains necessary as there is no superior alternative) and my own ~~book~~. As my institution's remuneration committee continues to point out, academic research is vitally necessary but, in my case, remains hopelessly inadequate. More recently, I have simply taken to describing my endeavours as 'gonzo scholarship', though I'm not sure Hunter S. Thompson would approve, and I invariably respond to the invariable question (which is invariably posed in an exaggeratedly exasperated voice), but what *is* postmodernism?, with the definitive answer: postmodernism *isn't*!

Be that as it may, the time for synoptic circumlocutions has now passed, the final countdown has begun and it may be worth while making a number of small but important points before lift-off commences. First, I'll be using the term 'postmodernism' in an all-encompassing sense. Some commentators restrict 'postmodernism' to a latter-day artistic and cultural movement (in architecture, theatre, dance, music, etc.), but others treat it more loosely. The family of postmodern terms will be explained as the essay proceeds, but for our present purposes 'postmodernism' covers everything pertaining to the postmodern moment. A second, and closely related, point is that this monograph will be dealing with phenomena which, if

I were to itemise them now, would appear to have nothing whatsoever to do with marketing. All I ask is that you bear with me, as the relevance of these topics should again become apparent as the narrative unfolds. Third, you'll notice that I occasionally refer to 'mainstream' marketers and marketing researchers. I fully appreciate that this can be construed as gross stereotyping – something postmodernists go to great pains to avoid – but it reflects my personal sense of where the marketing discipline is at, at present. It is derived from reading the journals, attending conferences, reviewing books and manuscripts, etc., and while I recognise that my perceptions are distorted, I suspect we are all slightly guilty in this respect. Fourth, I have attempted to keep the number of citations within reasonable bounds. In the past, I have often been accused of including references for effect (though, as the first footnote will reveal, there are very important reasons for this personal failing). On this occasion, I have endeavoured to desist despite the enormous temptations that postmodernism places in the path of citaholics like myself. Fifth and finally, don't worry if you are still slightly confused by the unconventional style of these prefatory remarks. Just as Hegel warns of the dangers of getting into the water before being able to swim, so too you can rest assured that this preface will seem perfectly normal – once you have finished reading the book.

Now, some of the more observant among you may have noticed that we are rapidly coming to the end of this metapreface, that acknowledgements are conspicuous by their absence and, therefore, that the author is a sad and lonely egomaniac. Lest you reach this (in)correct impression, let me just concoct a number of postmodern subject positions without whose tireless and unstinting help this volume would never have been written. Patrick Butler, David Carson, Anne Marie Doherty, Richard Elliott, Paul Freathy and Rhona Reid kindly took the time to read through and comment constructively on the draft manuscript, as did Russell Belk of the University of Utah and Morris Holbrook of Columbia University Business School. I am deeply indebted to them all. Gordon Foxall's constant encouragement, especially at a time when my spirits were at a particularly low ebb, proved nothing less than inspirational. Avril McNamee skilfully typed the tables, despite the handicap of my execrable handwriting (yes!), Sharon Dornan was responsible for the excellent diagrams and Tony Feenan the first-class plates. Butterworth-Heinemann, the Chartered Institute of Marketing, Columbia Records, Harvey Nichols, MCB Press, *The Observer*, Open University Press, Panasonic, Robson Books, Toyota, Gilbert Adair, A. Fuat Firat and John Saunders gave permission for the reproduction of copyright material. Francesca Weaver, the business and management editor at Routledge, was a tower of strength and pillar of perseverance. Last but not least, I would like to acknowledge the constant vocal encouragement of my little postmodern multitude, Madison, Holly and Sophie (well, I assume it was encouragement – it was certainly loud enough), and above all else the unstinting support of my wife, Linda, who fought a valiant but ultimately futile rearguard action to control my spending on books which pertained, however remotely, to postmodernism.

This book is dedicated to Alan Smithee. Thanks Jim.

Stephen Brown
Coleraine, September 1994

1 You talkin' to me?

I do not like buying new shoes: there is the bit where you walk up and down the window outside gazing at the gleaming ranks of these somewhat comic things and vainly attempting to imagine them poking out of the end of your trousers, there is the bit where you enter and engage in the unsettling intimacy of being unshod by someone you have never met, there is the bit where the shoes come out of their boxes and you limp up and down in one of them, very carefully so as not to crack it and therefore totally unnaturally and therefurtherfore totally uselessly for assessing its comfort, and there is the bit where you go out of the shop carrying the only pair of shoes you hated when you first saw them in the window.

Since all these bits precede the bit where you get them home and try walking about in them the way you normally walk about, only to discover that they seem to be made of teak, you will understand why I hang on to the old ones.

The Age of Innocence

Ten years ago, I managed to bluff my way into gainful employment as a marketing research executive for a leading firm of management consultants. After working on two projects as an assistant to the senior marketing research executive, I was allowed to 'go solo', for the first time. The research project pertained to the market for men's shoes and, like the enthusiastic, thrusting and young(ish) executive I then imagined myself to be, I diligently scoured the sources of secondary data, organised, assembled and led a series of four focus groups, unobtrusively observed the in-store behaviour of prospective shoe purchasers, and developed, pilot-tested and conducted a detailed questionnaire survey of several hundred good men and true (well, many of them were telling fibs, but that's another story).

Yet despite these endeavours, a reasonably satisfied client, suitably impressed employers – though they were less than happy when I quit not long after to take up an academic position – and my subsequent attempts to keep my hand in, so to speak, on the shoe trade, I can honestly say that the above quotation provides a better insight into and, frankly, says more about male shoe-buying behaviour than all the results of my secondary research, focus groups, observation exercises and questionnaire surveys put together.

The foregoing quotation, however, is not extracted from a market research report, nor from the transcript of a focus group led by a moderator much more skilled than I in the black art of group discussions. It is from an article entitled 'Your feets too big' by humourist, newspaper columnist, *Through the Keyhole* panellist and self-styled Sage of Cricklewood, Alan Coren (1991, pp.179–80). Indeed, as the lead quotations in each chapter of this book demonstrate, Coren often waxes lyrical on what are essentially marketing phenomena – supermarkets, new products, high streets, the service encounter – and in the process often provides incisive insights into the nature and characteristics of consumer behaviour.

Coren, moreover, is not alone. The world of literature, and the arts generally, is replete with depictions of marketing artefacts. These range from F. Scott Fitzgerald's (1934) astonishing encapsulation of compulsive consumption in his description of Nicole Diver's shopping expedition to Paris, Zola's masterful *fin de siècle* summation of the department store experience (see Bowlby 1985) and David Lodge's (1988) celebrated deconstruction of a Silk Cut cigarette advertisement, to Jeffery Archer's (1991) inadvertent articulation of the 'wheel of retailing' theory in his best-selling novel on the rise and demise of a retailing dynasty (as for the 'sex 'n' shopping' sub-genre, suffice it to say that exhaustive/ing research (Brown 1994a) is currently being undertaken). However, the epitome of this 'marketing orientation', to coin a phrase, is arguably *Generation X* by Douglas Coupland (1992), which contains a chapter entitled 'I am not a target market'. So accurate, apparently, is Coupland's summation of America's 25–35-year-old blank generation, those aware of and hostile to the machinations of marketing, that marketing practitioners and researchers now employ the term 'Generation X' to describe this particular cohort of consumers.

Traditional, died-in-the-wool marketing academics and practitioners, especially the Kotler *über alles* militant tendency, are likely to respond with disdain (or at best with public reserve and private ridicule), to the suggestion that marketing has much to learn from literary and artistic endeavour. Where, they may well ask, is the rigour, the proof, the reliability, the generalisability, the internal and external validity, the representative sample, the replicability, the statistical significance, the, in short, 'scientific' basis for such a suggestion? Surely this represents a return to the discredited 'art or science' debate, a regression to marketing's infantile 'artistic' pretensions long since abandoned for the maturity of the 'scientific' method, which, according to Baker (1983, p.19), enables us to 'persuade our critics that marketing is a subject worthy of serious study'. Why risk marketing's hard-won respectability as an honourable profession and a legitimate social science for the sake of 'fictional' knowledge? What, in Shelby Hunt's (1994, p.17) scholarly and magnanimous phrase, can possibly be gained from the pursuit of 'postmodern episto-babble'? Would our time not be better spent testing, refining and extending the marketing principles we have rather than trying out the latest and, frankly, soon to be forgotten, intellectual fashions from Paris?

Although such sentiments are eminently understandable, they are seriously misplaced. They are seriously misplaced for several important reasons.

- First, it is mistaken to dismiss literary, artistic and cultural artefacts as uninsightful or degraded sources of data. On the contrary, many philosophers maintain, in a sophisticated variant of the 'life imitates art' aphorism, that aesthetic accomplishments represent a privileged form of knowledge. Artistic artefacts, furthermore, are often used as raw material by academic disciplines that are much older and longer established than marketing, though such data sources are not without their shortcomings (Schama 1988; Haskell 1993).
- Second, the picture of 'science' that continues to pervade the marketing literature has been scrutinised by sociologists and philosophers of science and found wanting. The extensive SSK (sociology of scientific knowledge) literature reveals that science is largely the expression of social, political and professional interests, which insinuate themselves into and taint scientific practice at every level. The 'scientific method', in short, is a fiction in itself (Woolgar 1988; Pickering 1992).
- Third, it is debatable whether marketing practitioners have actually abandoned the bad old 'artistic' ways in favour of the certainties of marketing science, as propounded by their academic brethren (Gummesson 1987; *The Economist* 1989). Indeed, if Tom Peters and analogous best-selling management gurus are to be believed, marketing managers would be much better off relying on their intuition and innate creative skills than the non-insights that emanate from the principal business schools.
- Fourth, marketing's hard won professional and academic respectability is by no means universally acknowledged. True, the prevailing view of marketing practice may be a world away from F.R. Leavis's celebrated 1930s summation, 'unremitting, pervasive, masturbatory manipulations' (see Table 1.1), but marketing practitioners are still regarded with a degree of suspicion, particularly by those on the left of the political spectrum. Marketing scholarship and education, moreover, continue to occupy a fairly lowly position in the academic firmament, as does

Table 1.1 F.R. Leavis on advertising

Background:

For F.R. Leavis, professor of English literature at Cambridge and founder (1932) of the influential journal *Scrutiny*, the twentieth century was characterised by a serious decline in social and cultural standards. The traditional 'organic community' of the seventeenth and eighteenth centuries, which was cohesive, ordered and stable, was being rapidly swept aside by a combination of industrialisation, suburbanisation and the debasements perpetrated by popular cultural forms. Romantic novels, motion pictures, the wireless, popular newspapers and, above all, advertising were to blame for this increasingly sorry state of affairs. In order to help stem the tide of decline, and thereby save English civilisation, Leavis wrote a series of pamphlets on the perils of popular culture, *Mass Civilisation and Minority Culture* (1930) and *Culture and Environment* (1933) being the most important. Aimed at schoolteachers (plus fifth and sixth formers), *Culture and Environment* comprised a series of examples and exercises designed to help pupils better understand the insidious pervasiveness and sheer vulgarity of advertisements, cheap novels and the mass media.

Example: An advertisement for Two Quakers tobacco, plus questions

'THE TOBACCO OF TYPICAL TWIST

"Yes, it's the best I've ever smoked. But it's deuced expensive."
"What's the tuppence extra? And anyway, you get it back – an' more.
Burns clean and slow – that's the typical twist – gives it the odd look.
Cute scientific dodge. You see, they experimented . . ."
"Oh! cut the cackle, and give us another fill. You talk like an advertisement."
Thereafter peace and a pipe of Two Quakers'

(i)   Describe the type of person represented.
(ii) How are you expected to feel towards him?
(iii) What do you think his attitude would be towards us? How would he behave in situations where mob passion runs high?

Exercises:

Approximately one-third of *Culture and Environment* comprised suggested class exercises. For example:

   2. 'I consider that advertising is a great profession, and as such it should be judged from the highest literary and artistic standards.'
       (a) What do you think of the attitudes to advertising, literature and art exemplified here?
       (b) How does this pronouncement condemn itself?
   7. 'Some advertisers aim at creating the illusion of "personal" relations between themselves and their prospective customers.'
       Give examples. When were you last taken in?
  17. 'Advertising created the cigarette habit.' Think of others.

Table 1.1 Continued

---

31. 'Modern publicity debases the currency of spiritual and emotional life generally.'

    Discuss and illustrate.

33. 'It is not merely phrases, speeches and slogans that are demanded of advertising men; rather it is *truth, philosophy,* and *vision.*'

    Why do you feel embarrassed when you find yourself using these words in the advertising way?

40. 'Advertising is the new world force lustily breeding progress. It is the clarion note of business principle. It is the bugle call to prosperity. But great force as it is, advertising must seek all aid from literature and art in order that it may assume that dignity which is its rightful heritage.'

    Comment on the ideas of progress, literature and art expressed here.

46. 'Sir William Crawford is reported to have said that advertising teaches people to think.'

    Given this fact, what effect would you expect advertising to have on the standard of living?

Conclusion:

It goes without saying that Leavis's élitist project was doomed to inevitable failure. Not only was it predicated on a mythical, totally imagined past of 'organic communities', but it assumed that English literature and education alone could prevent the inexorable slide into perdition. As Eagleton (1983, p.34) caustically notes 'The whole . . . project was at once hair-raisingly radical and really rather absurd . . . the Decline of the West was felt to be avertible by close reading.'

Source: Adapted from Leavis and Thompson (1933)

business studies generally, having recently been described as 'impoverished reductionism', 'pseudo-scientific determinism' and 'too crude to deal with the complexities of the post-industrial, post-Cold War world' (*The Higher* 1993, p.13).

- Fifth, the fact of the matter is that marketing cannot choose to ignore postmodernism, Hunt's 'episto-babble' admonition notwithstanding. At a time when all manner of academic disciplines are examining the implications of the postmodern condition, dismissing it out of hand only serves, ironically, to reinforce marketing's reputed lack of scholarly sophistication (it is doubly ironic that Hunt, someone who takes enormous care to position marketing thought in relation to positivism, should have issued such a blanket dismissal). To caricature it as an ephemeral intellectual fashion overlooks the fact that the concept has not only conspicuously failed to fade from the agendas of other academic disciplines, such as sociology and politics, but their experience suggests that 'serious' research programmes cannot resume until the questions posed and problems raised by postmodernism are addressed

Figure 1.1 Marketing as a co-ordinating function

Source: Brown (1987)

Quarterly Review of Marketing, Spring/Summer 1987, Vol. 13, © 1990 The Chartered Institute of Marketing. Used by permission. All rights reserved.

(e.g. Shapiro 1992; Squires 1993). Most importantly perhaps, and as this monograph will seek to demonstrate, the pursuit of the postmodern is not time wasted. Quite the reverse.

Postmodern marketing, of course, is not simply concerned with culling the literary, artistic and cultural canon for references to marketing or consumption-related phenomena – what Hollander and Rassuli (1993, p.xxxi) term the 'marketing in Shakespeare' approach – though is it undeniable that most postmodernists would be more sympathetic to such endeavours than the latest LISREL-based model, or multi-attribute attitude analysis, of buyer behaviour. Nor is it true to imply that marketing is methodologically monolithic, the last refuge of positivist perspectives or indeed that all practitioners and academics are recalcitrant, mealy-mouthed marketing 'scientists'. On the contrary, marketing has been more than open – some say too open – to exogenous concepts and methodologies. It has long regarded itself as an integrative business philosophy, a co-ordinating function within the firm, and a bridge discipline between ivory-tower esoterism and the real world of the practising manager (Figure 1.1). Last but not least, marketing has by no means ignored postmodernism – a small but rapidly growing group of 'postmodern' marketing academics already exists. Nevertheless, it is not an exaggeration to state that marketing remains an essentially positivist or positivistic discipline (in that it seeks, as we shall later discover, the grail of universal laws and objective knowledge). The Kotlerite marketing message of analysis, planning, implementation and control is basically modernist in tenor. All too often at conferences one hears disparaging remarks about 'postmodern' marketing and consumer researchers ('consumer research has gone plumb crazy'; the Odyssey is 'what we did on our holidays', etc.). This essay will endeavour to show that 'postmodern' marketing academics have not gone crazy (well, not completely) and that mainstream 'modern' marketers, even if they choose to resist its blandishments and spurn the invitation, have something to gain from exposure to the precepts of postmodernism.

The Dirty Dozen

At this point in the proceedings, most readers might reasonably expect a pithy definition of postmodernism or, at the very least, a discussion of extant endeavours to encapsulate the postmodern condition. As is so often the case with postmodernism, however, things are a little more complicated than this. Life in a postmodern world is not that simple. Before we stare into the postmodern abyss; prior, as it were, to setting out on our suicide mission, it is necessary to get into training. It is important to outline the genesis, structure and limitations of this particular volume (Chapter 1) and discuss the all-important questions, 'is there anything in it for us?', 'why does marketing need postmodernism?', 'what is there about contemporary marketing that necessitates a postmodern infusion?' (Chapter 2). If, of course, you can't wait to find out, feel free to fast-forward to Chapter 3, which discusses the nature of the postmodern project, Chapter 4, which describes some postmodern marketing practices, Chapter 5, which examines the theoretical implications of postmodernism, or Chapter 6, which attempts to pull the argument together (and apart). Indeed, such a strategy of chapter surfing is very much in keeping with postmodernism – Deleuze and Guattari (1988), for instance, advise the readers of *A Thousand Plateaus* to dip into the text at will – but it might be easier to approach this particular volume in the traditional, linear manner.

In his seminal study *The Condition of Postmodernity*, David Harvey (1989, p.viii) prefaces his enquiry into the origins of cultural change with the words, 'I cannot remember when I first encountered the term postmodernism'. Would that I could say the same. My first exposure to the term is indelibly burnt into my memory, as it occurred under the most trying of circumstances, a job interview. Anxious as I was on entering the room to find myself facing a panel of eleven full professors and one vice-chancellor, my personal stress-o-meter hit record levels when the first post-pleasantries question was posed. 'What are the implications of post-modernism for the wheel of retailing theory?' It may surprise you to hear that the interview was not an unalloyed success, my exemplary performance on the day is not recounted in reverential tones by the Chartered Institute of Interviewees, if there is such an organisation, and, not to put too fine a point on it, I didn't get the job.

After shedding a few bitter tears, kicking the cat and being slightly more obnoxious than usual to my family and friends, I decided to find out about this thing called postmodernism. Needless to say, as an unreconstructed 'modern' marketing academic (though I didn't know it at the time), who worshipped the water Shelby Hunt walked upon, I had no idea of what I was letting myself in for. I had no notion that before too long I would be contemplating Lyotard's interpretation of the Kantian sublime (don't ask), pondering Habermas's theory of communicative action (Chapter 5, but try to restrain yourself) and laughing aloud at Baudrillardian *aperçus* or indeed the jokes in *The Modern Review*. Most fundamentally of all, it never struck me that a few years on, I would be so taken with postmodernism, despite all the depression and frustration it induces, that I – as a sort of undeconstructed 'postmodern' marketing academic – would endeavour to communicate my understanding of the movement, imperfect though it undoubtedly is, to marketing practitioners, marketing students and my academic marketing colleagues.

My interest in and admiration for postmodernism stems from two main stimuli. The first of these is marketing's permeation of the postmodern condition. On reading the copious literature on this intellectual affectation, almost irrespective of discipline or source, one cannot help but be struck by the prevalence of what are essentially marketing phenomena – shopping centres, department stores, advertising campaigns, package designs, new product development and the entire consumption experience. Granted, an academic discipline is not defined by its subject matter alone. Marketing does not 'own' new product development; it does not possess a monopoly on distribution channels or pricing strategies; and, only the most reactionary or recidivist scholar would consider advertising and promotion to be marketing's disciplinary preserve. Nevertheless, the very fact that researchers from other fields are examining and commenting on what, for good or ill, academic marketers consider to be important aspects of their domain makes them worthy of closer examination. More to the point, when these exogenous insights seem to be more meaningful, original and insightful than those typically encountered in the mainstream marketing literature, then very serious attention is warranted. If, as many might conclude on examining Table 1.2, that such, by no means atypical, descriptions of marketing phenomena are both astonishing in their acuity and dazzling in their brilliance, then the marketing community simply cannot afford to ignore the advent of postmodernism.

Table 1.2 Postmodernists on marketing phenomena

Phenomenon	Description	Source
Shopping centres	'The mall offers the previously unexperienced luxury of strolling between stores which freely offer their temptations without so much interference or glare from a display window. The central mall, a combination of rue de la Paix and the Champs-Elysées is adorned by fountains and artificial trees. Kiosks and benches are completely indifferent to seasonal changes and bad weather. . . . Here we are at the heart of consumption as the total organisation of everyday life as a complete homogenization. . . . Work, leisure routine and culture, all previously dispersed, separate and more or less irreducible activities that produced anxiety and complexity in our real life . . . have finally become mixed, massaged, climate controlled and domesticated into the simple activity of perpetual shopping. All these activities have finally become desexed into a single hermaphroditic ambiance of style.'	Baudrillard (1988a, p.34)
Disneyland	'Disneyland is more hyperrealistic than the wax museum, precisely because the latter still tries to make us believe that what we are seeing reproduces reality absolutely, whereas Disneyland makes it clear that within its magic enclosure it is fantasy that is absolutely reproduced. The Palace of Living Arts [the wax museum] presents its Venus de Milo as almost real, whereas Disneyland can permit itself to present its reconstructions as masterpieces of falsification, for what it sells is, indeed, goods, but genuine merchandise not reproductions. What is falsified is our will to buy, which we take as real, and in this sense Disneyland is really the quintessence of consumer ideology.'	Eco (1986, p.43)
Compact discs	'CDs are, in fact, a notable case of preprogrammed cultishness. Who can resist these mercurially silvery little discs with just a hint of credit card iridescence to reinforce the enigma inherent in all records – that, until they are played, their mysterious surface autism offers no clue as to what they might contain? Who can resist that surface value of necessary superfluousness (without futility there can be no real sense of luxury) represented by the random key that allows you to play tracks in any order you like? Why, even the little perspex boxes, snapping open and shut with the chic click of a silver cigarette case, have been designed for maximum tactile *jouissance*.'	Adair (1992, p.27)

The second cause of my fascination with the postmodern movement is the personal affinity I feel for its premises. The films I particularly enjoyed – *Blue Velvet*, *Diva*, *The Terminator*, *Blood Simple*, *Subway*, *True Stories* and, above all, *Streets of Fire*; the books I read with avidity – *The Name of the Rose*, *Leviathan*, *If on a Winter's Night a Traveller*, *American Psycho*, *Neuromancer*; and the television programmes I never missed – *Twin Peaks*, *The Singing Detective*, *Red Dwarf*, *Miami Vice*, *Rock 'n' Roll Years* and, embarrassing though it is to confess, *Telly Addicts*, are all prime examples of postmodernism. Equally postmodern, so it seems, are the idiosyncrasies and stylistic tics of my own, admittedly undistinguished, academic output – a preoccupation with anniversaries (see Johnston 1991) and textual marginalia like acknowledgements, exclamation marks and footnotes[1] (Derrida); the great store I place by book reviewing (Barthes); my weakness for tangential or unconventional introductory paragraphs (Foucault); and, my oft-criticised use of the wheel of retailing as a 'free floating signifier' – i.e. applying it to everything that moves (Baudrillard). Indeed, the more of it I read, the more I realise that I have long been a closet, albeit unwitting and no doubt witless, postmodernist. The crucial difference, however, is that I actually *enjoy* the 'surrounding environment of philistinism, of schlock and kitsch, of TV series and Reader's Digest culture . . . that whole landscape of advertising and motels, of the Las Vegas strip, of the late show and Grade-B Hollywood film' (Jameson 1985, p.112), that many commentators on the postmodern condition find so distasteful.

Bringing Up Baby

Outing aside, perhaps the most important point to be made about postmodernism at this stage in our deliberations, is that it is unlike almost anything else you can imagine. It is essentially intangible; a mood, a moment, a perspective, a state of mind, rather than a body of theory, a conceptual framework, a set of guidelines (though terms such as these will be employed, for the sake of convenience and notwithstanding the danger of reification, in the course of our argument). In many ways, postmodernism reminds me of parenthood. Like parenthood, postmodernism is an existential condition that can never be effectively communicated to the childless, but the nuances of which are instantly recognised by those who have undergone the experience. Like parenthood, it is a parallel, hitherto unexplored universe containing familiar, everyday items viewed from a strangely unfamiliar perspective (everyone knows that nappies, buggies, toys, car seats, etc. *exist*, but actually coping with them is something else again). Like parenthood, it is immensely frustrating yet enormously rewarding; 90 per cent hell yet 10 per cent heaven; and, given the choice of whether to do it all over again or not, the former wins hands down (though please don't ask me after yet another sleepless night). Like parenthood, indeed, postmodernism imposes a whole new set of problems, dilemmas and adjustments, it engenders a seemingly perpetual sense of personal inadequacy and, above all, it is initially alien, confusing and decidedly disconcerting.

The bewilderment that accompanies most people's initial exposure to postmodernism is attributable to several closely related factors, prominent among which is the notorious lack of a clear-cut definition. True, there are any number of pithy resumés and amusing epigrams – 'the Toyota of thought' (Connor 1989, p.19), 'excremental culture' (Kroker and Cook 1986), 'the cartoon-cat of modernism' (Updike 1991, p.694) and the like – but postmodern thinkers' wilful unwillingness to define the concept, for fear of blunting its cutting edge and precipitating absorption into the mainstream, can reduce even the most open-minded commentators to exasperation and despair. Postmodernism, as Gellner (1992, pp.22–3) points out,

> is a contemporary movement. It is strong and fashionable. Over and above this, it is not altogether clear what the devil it is. In fact, clarity is not conspicuous among its marked attributes. It not only generally fails to practise it, but also on occasion actually repudiates it . . . there appear to be no 39 postmodernist Articles of faith, no postmodernist manifesto, which one could consult so as to assure oneself that one has identified its ideas properly.

This initial 'but what on earth is it?' reaction is exacerbated by the fact that postmodernism has come to mean different things in different fields (Connor 1989; Featherstone 1991). Depending upon which authority you consult, the exact same phenomena, ranging from systems analysis and the Pompideau Centre to the novels of James Joyce and Saul Bellow, have been posited as exemplars of both modern and postmodern conditions (Rosenau 1992; Hassard 1993). For the cynical, indeed, the only discernible point of consensus among postmodernists is their lack of consensus on postmodernism. Some regard it as a continuation of modernism (Berman 1983), others consider it to be a complete break with the past (Bell 1976). Some deem postmodernism to be degenerative and destructive (Habermas 1987), others revel in its irreverence and cynicism (Kroker *et al.* 1989). Some draw distinctions between 'postmodernism', 'postmodernity' and 'postmodernisation' (Featherstone 1988), others treat the terms synonymously (Jencks 1989). Some date its commencement to the 1960s–1970s cusp (Harvey 1989), others ascribe its origins to Toynbee's pronouncements on civilisation in the 1950s (Smart 1992), Frederico de Onis's literary criticisms in the early part of this century (Hassan 1985), the avant-garde artistic movements of mid-nineteenth century Paris (Lash 1990) and, *in extremis*, to the Augustinian subversion of disembodied power in the fourth century AD (Kroker and Cook 1986). In these circumstances, therefore, it comes as little surprise to discover that the scholars most closely associated with the movement – Baudrillard, Lyotard, Foucault, Derrida, Jameson – have, almost without exception, distanced themselves from and publicly repudiated postmodernism. As Dick Hebdige (1986, p.78) points out, in a justly celebrated *sentence* (where you can almost hear the initial, deep intake of breath),

> When it becomes possible for people to describe as 'postmodern' the decor of a room, the design of a building, the diegesis of a film, the construction of a record, or a 'scratch' video, a TV commercial, or an arts documentary, or the 'intertextual' relations between them, the layout of a page in a fashion magazine or critical journal, an anti-tele-ological tendency within epistemology, the attack on the 'metaphysics of presence', a general attenuation of feeling, the collective chagrin and morbid projections of a post-War generation of Baby Boomers confronting disillusioned middle age, the 'predicament' of reflexivity, a group of rhetorical tropes, a proliferation of surfaces, a new phase in commodity fetishism, a fascination for 'images', codes and styles, a process of cultural, political or existential fragmentation and/or crisis, the 'de-centring' of the subject, an 'incredulity towards metanarratives', the replacement of unitary power axes by a pluralism of power/discourse formations, the 'implosion of meaning', the collapse of cultural hier-archies, the dread engendered by the threat of nuclear self-destruction, the decline of the University, the functioning and effects of the new miniaturised technologies, broad societal and economic shifts into a 'media', 'consumer' or 'multinational' phase, a sense (depending on whom you read) of 'placelessness' or the abandonment of placelessness ('critical regionalism') or (even) a generalised substitution of spatial for temporal co-ordinates – when it becomes possible to describe all these things as 'postmodern' (or more simply, using a current abbreviation, as 'post' or 'very post') then it's clear we are in the presence of a buzz-word.

Another contributory factor to the puzzle that is postmodernism, is the manner of its introduction into host disciplines. With some noteworthy exceptions, most introductory overviews concentrate on the ideas of post-modernism's leading theorists, even though these can prove to be the most abstract and inaccessible points of entry (e.g. Cooper and Burrell 1988; Burrell 1988, 1994; Cooper 1989). Such expositions also tend to give the impression that the movement is much more systematic and better inte-grated than it actually is. As with most fields of knowledge, postmodernism is a very broad church – exceptionally broad – and riven with internal conflict. Although an impression of coherence is necessary for the purposes of explication, it can serve seriously to mislead, especially with a subject as unabashedly inchoate as postmodernism and when newcomers are being directed to the widely divergent and by no means immutable views of key figures in the field. Postmodern cognoscenti, moreover, are often inclined to adopt a 'production orientation', to coin another phrase, in that they treat the concept as if it is interesting in itself rather than in terms of its relevance to the current concerns of the audience, most of whom are likely to have more important things on their personal research agendas than the latest efflorescence from the intellectual hothouses of the Left Bank and other continental centres of cerebral calisthenics and cosseted contempla-tion. Indeed, cynics are likely to be chary of uncritical endorsements of con-ceptual catholicons and regard them less as problem-solving procedures than as vehicles for the explicant's self-aggrandisement (of course, certain PoMo enthusiasts – mentioning no names – are above such grubby careerism).

Equally commonplace among exponents of postmodernism is a propen-sity to provide inventories of indicative adjectives – fragmentation, ephemerality, heterogeneity, plurality, playfulness, paradox, irony, anarchy, difference, self-referentiality, etc. – or tables of typically modern and post-modern characteristics (e.g. Table 1.3). While such exercises arguably give a feel for the subject area, eclectic lists of decontextualised adjectives can be taken to mean almost anything. Ironically, and as we shall discover in due course, this very indeterminacy lies at the heart of post-structuralist linguistics and literary theory. The contents of the tables, furthermore, not only differ considerably from compiler to compiler and imply that inex-tricably interwoven relationships are clear cut and dichotomous, but they also suggest, again erroneously, that postmodernists prioritise and elevate one set of perspectives over another (in practice, admittedly, they do, but in theory they don't). However, by appropriating an example, such as Table 1.3, it is possible for certain unscrupulous authors to reap the benefits bestowed by such tabular endeavours whilst avoiding the responsibility that accompanies their compilation (and which can be further evaded by an ironic parenthetical explanation).

My Left Foot

Postmodernism's status as a latter-day 'riddle wrapped in a mystery inside an enigma' is not entirely due to definitional difficulties, the inevitable distortions that accompany the interdisciplinary diffusion process and the all-but intractable problems facing prospective explicants. There is also a basic communications problem arising from the sheer impenetrability of the source material and the Marxist tenor of the accompanying debate. As a glance at the works of (say) Lacan, Derrida or Deleuze and Guattari eloquently testifies, the style of writing that prevails among postmodernists

Table 1.3 Relative emphases in modernism and postmodernism

Modern emphasis	Postmodern emphasis
Object	Image, symbol
Cartesian subject	Symbolic subject
Cognitive subject	Semiotic subject
Unified subject	Fragmented subject
Centred subject	Decentred subject
Signified	Signifier
Objectification	Symbolization
Representation	Signification
Truth (objective)	Truth (constructed)
Real	Hyperreal
Universalism	Localism, particularism
Society as a structure	Society as a spectacle
Logocentric reason	Hermeneutic reason
Knowing	Communicating
Economy	Culture
Capitalism	Late capitalism
Economic systems	Symbolic systems
Production	Consumption
Shift from use value to exchange value	Shift from exchange value to sign value
Science/technology	Science/technology (*sic?*)
Mechanical technology	Digital/communicative technology
Sciences	Humanities
Euro-American centrism	Globalism
Phallocentrism	Feminism/genderism
Orientalism, colonialism	Multiculturalism, globalism

Source: Venkatesh *et al.* (1993)

is often allusive, opaque and, for those who believe in the Orwellian (1962) precepts of clarity, economy and precision, all but unreadable. There are, as shall become apparent, very good reasons for this approach – postmodernists emphasise that texts do not have a single, clear-cut meaning and they write accordingly – but an appreciation of the underpinning 'rationale' does not make the reading experience any less painful for the uninitiated. Truth to tell, it is the sheer obscurantism of postmodern writers that drives many critics and commentators into states of refutational apoplexy. For example:

- Camille Paglia (1992), cultural icon and the dominatrix of American academe, variously describes it as 'pedantic jargon, clumsy convolutions and prissy abstractionism' (p.ix), a 'meat grinder of hack-work gibberish' (p.183), and 'garbled, labyrinthine *junk*' (p.273, emphasis in original).

- Robert Hughes (1993, pp.71–2), scourge of both left and right, argues that 'though it has filled the seminar rooms for the last decade and given us a mound of largely unreadable cultural criticism . . . [it has had] . . . little lasting effect on the way people in general write, think or act.'
- David Lodge (1990, p.14) remarks that 'this discourse is so opaque and technical in its language that the first glance – baffled, angry or derisive – is likely to be the last one.'
- Allan Bloom (1987, pp.379–80), in his devastating critique of American higher education, states, 'it is the last, predictable stage in the supression of reason and the denial of the possibility of truth in the name of philosophy. . . . This fad will pass, as it already has in Paris. But it appeals to our worst instincts and shows where our temptations lie. . . . Fancy German philosophic talk fascinates us and takes the place of the really serious things.'
- And John Updike (1984, pp.577–8), after reading Barthes' *S/Z*, concludes, 'I cannot remember another book ostensibly in the English language which gave me such pains to peruse . . . [and which] . . . produced in this reviewer sensations of forestalment and obstruction so oppressive that relief chronically manifested itself in the form of an irresistible doze and, once, of an absolving dyspepsia.'

This communications problem is compounded by political considerations.[2] Many of postmodernism's leading lights occupy positions on the far left of the political spectrum, though partly as a result of the events of May 1968, when the student revolt in France was betrayed by the Communist Party, most have broken with the movement and formally renounced the tenets of Marxism. This, in turn, has led to their denunciation as right wingers or 'Young Conservatives' by defenders of the Marxian faith, most notably Habermas and his fellow travellers in Critical Theory (on this basis, we can only surmise that most marketing practitioners and academics lie somewhere to the right of Jean-Marie Le Pen or 'mad' Vlad Zhirinovsky). Nevertheless, the fact remains that postmodernists tend to be preoccupied with the traditional Marxian concerns of the internal contradictions of capitalism, the class struggle and the need for revolutionary political change. The literature, therefore, is replete with the left wing lexicon of 'hegemony', 'praxis', 'recuperation', 'transcendence', 'false consciousness', 'commodity fetishism', 'instrumental rationalisation' and so on, which, despite the endeavours of several prominent scholars (e.g. Rogers 1987; Hirschman 1993), is comparatively rarely encountered in mainstream marketing publications. Indeed, one suspects that very few marketing academics would recognise the hostile stereotype of marketing that continues to stalk the pages of the Marxian literature. Stools, so it seems, in the excrement of late capitalism, marketers are

Table 1.4 Contrasting definitions of 'consumer'

'In modern English *consumer* and *consumption* are the predominant descriptive nouns of all kinds of use of goods and services. The predominance is significant in that it relates to a particular version of economic activity, derived from the character of a particular economic system. ... The modern development has been primarily American but has spread very quickly. . . . The development relates primarily to the planning and attempted control of markets which is inherent in large-scale industrial capitalists (and state capitalist) production. . . . *Consumer* as a predominant term was the creation of such manufacturers and their agents. It implies, ironically as in the earliest senses, the using up of what is going to be produced, though once the term was established it was given some appearance of autonomy (as in the curious phrase *consumer choice*) ... the predominance of the capitalist model ensured its widespread and often over-whelming extension to such fields as politics, education and health. In any of these fields, but also in the ordinary field of goods and services, to say *user* rather than *consumer* is still to express a relevant distinction.'

(Williams 1983, pp.78–9)

'Strictly, the ultimate consumer of a product, the ultimate user of a product or service; the person who derives the satisfaction or benefit offered. The consumer is not necessarily the customer, since there are often "customers" in the buying/distribution chain; moreover, the customer is frequently not the person who makes the buying decision; for instance, in the case of many household products, where the housewife may make the purchase but consumption or use is by the whole family. "Consumer" is not normally applied to the purchase of industrial goods and services where the customer is usually a corporate body. Nevertheless, consumable goods are sold to industry for corporate purposes and the consumers of these goods can be identified for marketing practice.'

(Hart and Stapleton 1992, pp.48–9)

---

typically portrayed as cynical, manipulative, unethical and possessed of powerful techniques, such as subliminal advertising, with which to milk the hapless public, whilst expounding hypocritically on the sovereignty of consumer choice. Consider, for example, Raymond Williams' discussion of the etymology of the term 'consumer' and compare it with a definition taken from a typical dictionary of marketing terms (Table 1.4).

Difficult as the 'intellectual dandyism' of postmodern thinkers undoubt-edly is and unhappy as most marketers are likely to be with their portrayal as twenty-first century snake oil salespersons – though there is some evidence that the left is beginning to adopt a better informed and more sophisticated line on the practice of marketing, if not the theory – perhaps the most disconcerting aspect of postmodernism is its counter-intuitive and contradictory characteristics. In their denial of all truth claims, their rejection of rationality, their refusal to countenance cause and effect relationships, their espousal of the 'death of the subject', their contention that history has ended, their belief in the impossibility of meaningful representation, their assumption that authors are not responsible for what they write and their assertion that there is nothing outside the text (in other words, that there is no knowable external reality), postmodernists adopt philosophical positions which are, frankly, alien to many marketing academics and practitioners, and, if taken at face value, are readily dismissed as laughably absurd or, in some cases, morally reprehensible. Jean Baudrillard's famous suggestion, for example, that the Gulf War would not take place, was not taking place and did not take place undoubtedly encapsulated the televisual, arcade game aspects of the conflict, but at a time when 'real' rockets were being fired, air strikes launched and soldiers and civilians killed, such intellectual exercises are both questionable and insensitive, to say the least (Norris 1992; Harvey 1993).

Although the ambiguities surrounding postmodernism are undeniable, they are insufficient in themselves to justify outright rejection of the phenomenon. Definitional difficulties, after all, are not exactly unknown in marketing, whether it be the precise characteristics of 'impulse shopping', 'perceived risk', 'psychic distance', 'branding' or, for that matter, 'marketing' itself. Marketing, moreover, is by no means devoid of jargon, as the necessity for specialised 'dictionaries' bears witness; academic marketers are not exactly renowned for the limpid pellucidity of their mellifluous prose and the language of advanced mathematics that characterises the leading journals is no more impenetrable than the convoluted and elliptical cogitations of prominent postmodern thinkers. Indeed, if it were simply a question of counter-intuitive and contradictory concepts, not only would quantum physics be called into question, but the marketing philosophy itself would also fail to pass muster. Is it not one of our discipline's proudest boasts that the marketing concept ran counter to the once prevalent 'production' and 'sales' orientations? With this in mind, perhaps marketers should not be too quick to pass judgement on a conceptual opportunity which, while undeniably difficult, may have much to offer or, at the very least, may tickle our intellectual fancy (Burrell 1994).

Cinema Paradiso

Obscurantism notwithstanding, an extensive secondary literature on postmodernism now exists and several excellent introductory texts have been published, albeit not for a specialist marketing audience. The books by Featherstone (1991), Harvey (1989), Callinicos (1989), Sarup (1993) and Rosenau (1992), in particular, are required reading, as are the papers by Hassan (1985), Jameson (1985), Huyssen (1984), Hebdige (1986), and Boyne and Rattansi (1990). When the copious literature on postmodernism is examined, two broad but contrasting approaches to the condition can be discerned. The first and, it has to be acknowledged, by far the clearest expositions tend to examine postmodernism from the outside, as it were, in order to explain this intriguing yet incoherent phenomenon or indeed to contest its sometimes questionable premises. Featherstone (1991), for example, argues that the task facing academic sociologists is not to formulate a postmodern sociology, as this parasitical project is doomed to inevitable failure, but to provide a sociology of postmodernism. In other words, to explore the development, production, circulation and consumption of postmodern theories, experiences, cultural practices and so on. Harvey (1989), moreover, maintains that postmodernism is not new; it does not represent a rupture or distinctive break with the past. On the contrary, it represents the latest, and admittedly complex, phase in the organisation of late twentieth century capitalism, but that it can be none the less theorised, comprehended and explained using the traditional tools of Marxian analysis. Callinicos (1989, p.ix), likewise, commences his polemic *Against Postmodernism* with the words,

> This book is an attempt to challenge the strange mixture of cultural and political pessimism and light-minded playfulness with which – in a more than usually farcical reprise of the apocalyptic mood at the end of the last century – much of contemporary Western intelligentsia intends to greet our own *fin de siècle*.

The foregoing texts may be models of lucidity and detailed argument, but their analytical, objective, even-handed and, let's be honest, humourless approach leaves them open to the charge of failing fully to comprehend the postmodern moment, of attempting to bring essentially 'modern' – and hence inappropriate – criteria to bear on the irreverent, ironic, sardonic and playful postmodern project. Granted, the above authors occasionally attempt to indulge in postmodern whimsy – Harvey (1989), for instance, assembles a collage of modern and postmodern terms which he describes as both 'fun' and 'instructive' – but the humour is invariably forced and the outcome considerably less than convincing. The second approach, therefore, usually involves endeavours to enter into the spirit of things and allow the form of the exposition to reflect the perceived content of the postmodern. Indeed, for anyone who is in any way sympathetic towards postmodernism, such an approach is compelling and almost irresistible. After all, it is very difficult to capture the eclecticism, cynicism, subversiveness, energy and self-referentiality of postmodernism in ponderous academic prose.

Unfortunately, however, the outcome of such endeavours can be pretentious at best and excruciatingly embarrassing at worst. Thus, we find ourselves in a noisome netherworld of 'postmodern' poems, prayers, sketches, tropes and textual affectations. Heller (1993) treats her treatise on the postmodern historical consciousness as a paraphrasis of a musical composition, including a finale, you'll be pleased to hear, in *allegro vivace* (encore!). Borgmann (1992) takes us on a journey across the postmodern mountain range, pointing out the distinctive features of the landscape as he goes. The first page of Marshall's (1992) Introduction consists of a list of postmodern terms scattered willy-nilly across the page like a literary I-Ching. Zurbrugg (1993) includes sixteen pages of text, in a sort of pre-credits sequence, *before* the flyleaf, dedication, preface, acknowledgements, contents pages, etc. (unless, perhaps, I have purchased a defective copy of his book). And Burrell (1993) describes, in toe-curling detail, his attempts to make a postmodern video, which he expected and failed to have treated as legitimate academic output, his assault on fellow conference participants with a loaded water pistol and, most mortifyingly of all, his mid-life priapic urges.

As is already apparent from the cover design, chapter headings and section titles, this particular book on postmodernism is premised on a loose cinematic or movie-going analogy. Although such an approach is not without attendant risks – it may serve to distract, irritate, become an end in itself rather than a means to an end, and, as we have seen, can all too easily descend into pretentiousness and indecorum – there are several specific reasons why it has been adopted on this occasion.

In the first instance, it is compatible with postmodernism's ironic, iconoclastic, irreverent and playful emphasis on non-traditional approaches to explication and, for Lyotard (1988) at least, its elevation of the figural (image) over discourse (the written word). Indeed, in many respects it is more appropriate than the usual poems, prayers, orchestral conceits and so on. Postmodernism, after all, treats low or degraded cultural forms (comic books, football, hairstyles, rock music) with the seriousness traditionally accorded to high culture, yet expositional tropes invariably rely on the latter in preference to the former. Utilising an explanatory format based on popular culture is not only long overdue but, more to the point, it also develops and projects a cinematic preoccupation already apparent among the postmodern intelligentsia in general and the 'postmodern marketing' community in particular. Baudrillard (1990a), Jameson (1991), Harvey (1989), Lash (1990) and Lyotard (1989), for instance, have all devoted considerable space to discussions of cinematic representations in postmodernity. Holbrook and Hirschman (1993) have analysed the portrayal of consumption behaviour, myth, materialism and the marketing concept in films such as *Out of Africa*, *Beverly Hills Cop*, *Tin Men*, *Gremlins* and *Star Wars*. And Belk (1989) has performed a similar service in his comprehensive investigation of materialism and the modern American Christmas (see also O'Guinn *et al.* 1986; Belk and Bryce 1993).

Second, the proposed approach is unashamedly metaphorical. Whereas the positivistic research tradition considers the use of figurative language to be 'deviant and parasitic' (Ortony 1979, p.2), most postmodern philosophers and post-structuralist literary theorists maintain that knowledge claims are inherently metaphorical (Sarup 1993). Tropes lie at the very heart of our understanding of the world and figurative thinking is central to the process of theory articulation (Norris 1991). Physicists, for example, inform us that light behaves *like* a wave. Organisation theorists tell us that bureaucracies operate *as if* they are machines. Psychologists maintain that our brains function *like* computers. And marketing educators and consultants instruct practitioners to act *as if* they are preparing a meal from the ingredients of the marketing mix. Moreover, a moment's reflection (in a figurative mirror) reveals that marketing is replete with metaphorical reasoning – the product life cycle, the wheel of retailing, marketing myopia, channels of distribution, relationship marketing, involvement, marketing warfare and, not least, the metaphor that marketing is not metaphorical.

Third, the analogy reflects the close but often overlooked parallels between marketing and the movie industry. Both phenomena date (officially) from the turn of the present century and are totally dominated by American output, much to the chagrin of many Europeans, who actually led the way in both fields (Norman 1989; Jones and Monieson 1990). As Table 1.5 indicates, marketing institutions are frequently depicted in films, movies are occasionally set in marketing milieux, the cinema provides the basis of marketing phenomena, and marketing artefacts the inspiration for movies. All manner of products – beer, cigarettes, cars, computers, clothes, etc. – are regularly 'placed' in films, for a suitable fee, thereby adding to the 'authenticity' of the experience and, apparently, to overall audience appreciation. Equally, the tie-in merchandise from a major movie – toys, T-shirts, books, baseball caps, soundtracks, computer games and suchlike – is widely distributed as a rule and aggressively advertised. So much so, that the marketing budget of a blockbuster film often exceeds its production costs and the merchandising revenue its ticket receipts. Occasionally, indeed, product placement and tie-in merchandising are ingeniously combined, as for example in *Jurassic Park* which contains a scene featuring a display of the fictional theme park's associated merchandise. Not only is this identical to the film's tie-in merchandise but, in a wonderful self-referential flourish, the book of the making of the film features prominently in the display. Thus, at this point in the film the audience is viewing the film of the book of the film of the film of the book. What is more, as the book of the making of the film also refers to this scene (Shay and Duncan 1993), we are actually dealing with the book of the film of the film of the book of the film of the film of the book. Now, *that's* postmodernism!

Fourth, and if truth be told, the *real* reason for the cinematic metaphor is that it represents my only 'original' contribution to the postmodern debate. When asked, some time ago, to describe postmodernism in a

Table 1.5 Marketing and the cinema: some examples

Films set in marketing contexts	Film derived marketing phenomena (and vice-versa)	Products developed by film stars/ directors	Marketing institutions in films (example)
Big	Disney Retail Stores	Cher (perfume: *Uninhibited*)	Restaurants (*When Harry Met Sally*)
Tin Men	Universal Studios Theme Park	Francis Ford Coppola (wine)	Bars (*48 Hours*)
How to get Ahead in Advertising	Planet Hollywood Restaurants	Paul Newman (sauces, salad dressings)	Department stores (*Miracle on 34th Street*)
The Coca-Cola Kid	Alien War ('total reality' experience)	Spike Lee (retail stores, *Spike's Joint*)	Shopping centres (*The Blues Brothers*)
Glengarry Glen Ross	Jurassic Park Computer Games (etc.)	Robert Redford (mail order catalogue)	Motels (*Psycho*)
Crazy People	*The Baby of Macon**	Gerard Depardieu (wine)	Banks (*Three Fugitives*)
Mannequin	*Super Mario Brothers*	Elizabeth Taylor (perfumes: *Passion*)	Speciality stores (*Manhattan*)
Pret à Porter			Fast food outlets (*Falling Down*)
Will Success Spoil Rock Hunter?			Supermarkets (*Married to the Mob*)
			Nightclubs (*Casablanca*)
			Casinos (*One From the Heart*)
			Theme Parks (*National Lampoon's Vacation*)

* Peter Greenaway's film *The Baby of Macon* was inspired by a Benetton advertisement.

nutshell, I replied that it was the *Jurassic Park* of scholarship. At the time, I was not thinking of the postmodern aspects of the film itself – set in a theme park devoted to extinct animals, the 'realism' of the special effects, the self-referential merchandising, the self-conscious stylistic evocation of Spielberg's earlier films (thus making it a 'nostalgia' movie in the Jamesonian (1985) sense, except that we are nostalgic not for an era (*Chinatown*) or a viewing experience (*Star Wars*) but for classic Spielberg films like *Jaws, Close Encounters* or *ET*). Nor, for that matter, was I referring to the fact that *Jurassic Park*, like postmodernism, has proved enormously popular despite decidedly mixed reviews. Nor, indeed, was I alluding to the remarkable temporal coincidence between the release of *Jurassic Park* in the summer of 1993 and postmodernism's dramatic arrival on the mainstream marketing scene (see Brown 1994b). Nor, finally, was I trying to reflect the fact that film is *the* archetypal postmodern medium (it is a simulacrum, in that it is a copy of a non-existent original). I was thinking simply of the scene where the cloned, computer-generated and virtual *Tyrannosaurus rex* escapes from its enclosure and descends with devastating results upon the hapless visitors to the theme park. The parallels with the effects of postmodernism on stricken academic disciplines almost go without saying.

Ironically, and as might be expected from a phenomenon that has been defined as 'never having to say you're sorry for not having an original idea in your head' (Beaumont 1993, p.43), I have since discovered that my metaphorical postmodern attempt to meld marketing and the cinema is not entirely new. There are several instances in the media studies literature, most notably the book *Window Shopping* by Anne Friedberg (1993), where researchers have identified similarities between cinema going and the 'gaze' that characterises shopping behaviour, or have drawn parallels between cinematic representations and the nature of postmodernity (Denzin 1991; Žižek 1992). My 'original' insight, therefore, turns out – entirely appropriately, as we shall discover – to be a case of what postmodern literary theorists term the 'always already said'.

The Mission

Be that as it may, this book represents an attempt to screen postmodernism for the marketing community; that is, marketing academics, marketing students and (academically minded) marketing practitioners. It has been written in the belief that postmodernism is too important to be left to postmodernists, with all their obscurantism, obfuscation and impenetrability, and that the movement has much to contribute to marketing discourse. Postmodernism provides an insight into the dramatic changes that are taking place in the marketing arena and conceptualising the growing crisis of representation in the discipline. Equally, this book is premised on a conviction that the current enthusiastic promulgation of postmodernism by a small but influential group of marketing scholars is somewhat misplaced. Postmodernism is not a solution to all of marketing's apparent ills, it brings costs as well as benefits. Indeed, it is arguable that uncritical advocation of postmodernism will only serve to alienate or raise the suspicions of the mainstream marketing community. Many postmodern marketers, admittedly, may prefer to abandon the mainstream to its fate and endeavour to forge links with like-minded individuals in cognate subject areas (e.g. Hetrick 1993). It is my belief that such crying in the wilderness, such marginalisation, represents a renunciation of our responsibilities. Even if they choose not to receive and act upon the postmodern marketing message, every student, academic or practitioner of marketing is likely to benefit from their exposure to the principles of postmodernism. The widest possible audience, therefore, should be sought.

In its search for the widest possible audience, and given the increasingly blurred boundaries between academic disciplines, it is highly probable that this volume will be picked up by non-marketers – sociologists, communication theorists, cultural studies students, etc. Inevitably, they are going to be disappointed as the book is not for them, though if they have paid hard cash before they discover this fact, I really couldn't care less. (What do you mean you're reading this in a bookshop? Either buy the thing or put it back, preferably the former!) Indeed, having perused a fair proportion of the sociological and cultural studies literature in this area, and cognisant as I am of both their rapidly diminishing enthusiasm for postmodernism and long-standing antipathy towards marketing, many sociologists or cultural studies specialists might conclude that the appearance of an introduction to postmodernism for marketers is proof positive that the postmodern moment is over, that the movement has finally hit the buffers of the academy. Although such an attitude is guaranteed to anger many mainstream marketers, who deeply and rightly resent the caricature of rapacious capitalists and second-rate scholarship that still regrettably prevails in the sociological literature, it has to be acknowledged that such sentiments are not entirely misplaced. After gaining access to the information superhighway of postmodern pluralism, it is difficult not to conclude that much (but by no means all) of academic marketing research is still depressingly reliant on old-fashioned, albeit tried and tested, single axial cable.

Disappointing as it may prove to any passing sociologists or cultural studies students, this book is not about postmodernism *in* marketing – marketing practices, in other words, that are recognisably postmodern – though these issues are of course examined. It is rather a simple and basic diagnosis of the postmodern condition for a marketing audience, a sort of 'rough guide' to postmodernism's dark continent (yes, I know I'm mixing my metaphors, make that a sort of rough film guide). Such an aspiration, whether it is successfully or unsuccessfully realised, invariably invites charges of misrepresentation and oversimplification. The former arises from any attempt to tame the untamable, to recuperate, in a Marcusean sense, the postmodern moment, to wash, launder and hang the project out to dry. Postmodernism, like the soap bubbles blown by children, cannot be grasped except with extreme care and then only for an instant, but the ephemeral cascade can be enjoyed, admired and is glorious to behold.

Just as postmodernism is all too easily misrepresented – how can it be otherwise when it means so many different things in so many different fields? – so too a text of less than 250 pages can hardly do justice to such an intricate, inchoate subject. Nor, for that matter, can it expect to say all that needs to be said about marketing, which is not exactly short of publications and commentary. Both these charges are true, but this book does not aim to be encyclopedic, the equivalent of a Halliwell's guide. Again at the risk of mixing my metaphors, it is a sample, a signpost, an *hors-d'œuvre*, a prelude, a stepping stone, a prologue, an advertisement, an overture, a trailer, if you will, for the main feature, the manifold excellent texts on postmodernism and, no doubt, the more comprehensive volumes to come on postmodern marketing. Indeed, when I reflect on the next-to-impossible task that this essay is undertaking, I draw comfort from the words of proto-postmodernist, Friedrich Nietzsche (1977, p.18). 'Profound problems', he states in *The Gay Science*, 'are best treated like cold baths – quick in, quick out.'

In its desire, therefore, to screen postmodernism for a mainstream marketing audience this book does not pretend to be a director's cut or aspire to be the last word on the genre. It is merely a selection of edited highlights from the vast and tangled academic footage that has accumulated on the postmodern condition. It attempts to freeze and frame a flickering, fast-moving and often blurred image which, despite its undeniable complexities, has much to contribute to marketing understanding. This endeavour, what *Variety* would no doubt describe as 'oh no, slo-mo po-mo promo', is accomplished through a personal selection of films (plus derivations of film titles and snatches of dialogue), some aspects of which are deemed relevant to the point being made. However, in keeping with postmodernism's propensity for tongue-in-cheek allusions and espousal of multiple interpretations, the nature of the relationship between film and accompanying text is not specified in detail, but left for the audience to decide. The essay, in short, is 'double coded' (a phenomenon which many commentators consider to be *the* distinguishing feature of postmodernism), in that it can be read with or without the overarching cinematic metaphor, depending on your personal preference. Thus, by employing the movement's own tools of irony, irreverence, cynicism, playfulness and, occasionally, polemic, the text seeks to capture the essence of the postmodern moment for a mainstream marketing audience, examine the nature of postmodernism in contemporary marketing theory and practice, clarify some of the misunderstandings that surround the postmodern concept at present and temper some of the over-inflated claims of its proponents. Most importantly of all, it aims to leave the plot sufficiently unresolved to ensure the possibility of a money-spinning sequel. . . .

2 I coulda been a contender!

There is something extremely odd about the geography of supermarkets.
I may not have studied it deeply, nor experienced it widely, nor even consid-
ered it generally: but I know one most peculiar aspect of it rather well,
and I have experienced it in every one of the dozen or so countries in
whose supermarkets I have stood, disorientated and uncertain, while the
hurtling trolleys of orientated and certain foreigners have ricocheted off
mine as their drivers glowered and babbled at the obstructive stranger that
was within their gates.

The peculiar aspect is that whenever one is in a new and therefore
uncharted supermarket, whether in Dundee or Stuttgart or Cairo, not
knowing which way to turn for some simple staple, one invariably ends
up in the pet food section. . . .

Quite why this should be so is a very great mystery indeed . . . [though]
. . . it is just possible that it is a mystery no longer. I have this noontide
returned from the huge Leclerc in Vence, where it was, a mere hour ago,
dawning on me that this . . . was a trick of marketing strategy so bril-
liantly cunning as to administer the antidote with the poison − irritation
at the cunning by which one was being seduced was instantly mitigated
by the recognition of the brilliance with which it had been done.

I had fetched up, after the statutory 20 minutes, staring at a display (I
swear) of TV dinners for cats. . . . And, immediately a French shopper
beside me began talking about her cat, inquiring after mine and so forth.
And it suddenly struck me that this selfsame thing had happened several
times before in other foreign supermarkets. . . . Within seconds, I had
explained my shopping needs to this lady, within nanoseconds thereafter
she had begun not only dragging me around the place but recommending
all sorts of goodies, special deals, own-brand bargains and so forth, which
I could never have sussed for myself. I thus ended up spending three times
as much as I should have done unassisted.

(Coren 1990, pp.50–3)

The Greatest Story Ever Sold

As an *aficionado* of mainstream marketing textbooks, or at least of the introductory sections where the authors attempt to capture the magic of the marketing concept, it seems to me that there are at least four basic approaches to this next-to-impossible encapsulatory task (Table 2.1). The first involves some sort of quasi-evangelical homily, a mini-case study of a deeply troubled organisation that is unfamiliar with or has strayed from the path of marketing righteousness. By embracing the marketing philosophy and giving the customers what they want, however, the organisation is replaced, or set, on the straight and narrow, the one true path to business salvation.

The second approach comprises a lightning sketch of hundreds, occasionally thousands, of years of economic history – western economic history – which culminates, fortuitously, with the emergence of the modern marketing concept in the early 1950s. Thus, from the primordial soup of the 'production era', and the neanderthal practices of the 'sales era', we have evolved into the homo sapiens and higher life forms of the current 'marketing era'.

The third perspective adopts an 'attack is the best form of defence' policy by directly addressing and endeavouring to refute popular misconceptions about marketing, the regrettably widespread view that it is manipulative, devious, unethical and inherently distasteful. Although unsavoury and unprincipled practices undoubtedly occur in the name of marketing – just as there are negligent doctors, unprofessional lawyers and dishonest politicians, so too some marketers are deeply suspect – such activities, so the argument goes, are *not* representative of marketing as it is understood and performed by the vast majority of practitioners and academics.

The fourth and, as Kotler employs it, the introductory approach to which most marketing neophytes are exposed involves an imaginative flight of fancy, an attempt to capture the sheer ubiquity, extent and importance of modern marketing. After all, it pertains to the food we eat, the clothes we wear, the entertainments we enjoy, the sports we play, the cars we drive, the presents we buy, the services we procure, the jobs we do and so on *ad infinitum*. Indeed, as brand names are often cited in these explications, we can probably conclude that, in what must be the outer limit of marketing's pervasiveness, the space in the textbooks concerned has been sold to participating marketing organisations.[1]

(There is, of course, a fifth strategy, the strategy of outlining the introductory strategies employed by marketing textbook writers. Such a meta-strategy, however, is just too juvenile for words and it is never employed, except by dilettantes, charlatans and the academically challenged. Under no circumstances whatsoever believe a single word of a book that utilises this particular approach to the marketing condition. . . .)

Table 2.1 The magic of modern marketing: textbook approaches

Approach	Indicative texts	Authors/ Publisher (year)
Case study	*Marketing: An Introduction*	M. Christopher and M. McDonald/ Pan (1991)
	Fundamentals of Marketing	W.J. Staunton/ McGraw-Hill (1984)
	Marketing Strategy and Management	R. Markin/ Wiley (1982)
	Marketing Concepts and Strategies	S. Dibb, L. Simkin, W.M. Pride and O.C. Ferrell/ Houghton Mifflin (1994)
Western history	*Modern Marketing*	F. Jefkins/ Pitman (1993)
	Marketing Today	G. Oliver/ Prentice-Hall (1980)
	Marketing Made Simple	B.H. Elvy/ Heinemann (1984)
	Introduction to Marketing	J. Frain/ McDonald and Evans (1983)
Misconceptions	*Principles of Marketing*	G. Randall/ Routledge (1993)
	Marketing	M. Cameron, A. Rushton and D. Carson/ Penguin (1988)
	The Essence of Marketing	S. Majaro/ Prentice-Hall (1993)
	The Basic Arts of Marketing	R. Willsmer/ Business Books (1984)
Ubiquity	*Marketing Management*	P. Kotler/ Prentice-Hall (1988)
	Managing Marketing	J. Murray and A. O'Driscoll/ Gill and Macmillan (1993)
	Marketing	W. Zikmund and M. D'Amico/ Wiley (1986)
	Marketing: An Introduction	P. Kotler and G. Armstrong/ Prentice-Hall (1993)

Although, as the Kotlerite wannabes constantly remind us, the marketing system is all but ubiquitous at present, it is by no means a new arrival on the socio-economic scene (academically, admittedly, it can be considered something of an *arriviste* among the social sciences). On the contrary, marketing practices have been around since the dawn of civilisation or, depending on which definition of 'civilisation' you subscribe to, even earlier still (Cotterell 1988). For example, flint and obsidian axe heads, in both finished and semi-finished form, were traded over literally thousands of miles in late palaeolithic times (Clark and Piggott 1990). Precious metals and minerals, such as gold, tin, copper and lapis lazuli, were widely exchanged throughout ancient Mesopotamia prior to the advent of the Sumerian civilisation (Gurney 1990). The economy of pre-dynastic Egypt, given the locality's complete lack of natural resources, was heavily reliant on trading relationships (Walters 1988). And amber, pottery, bone figurines and personal adornments fashioned from the marine shell *Spondylus gaederopus* were being exchanged in Europe before 4500 BC (Renfrew 1978). Along with the domestication of plants and animals, fixed settlements, monumental architecture and the advent of literacy, long-distance trade is widely considered to be one of the mainsprings of civilisation (Renfrew 1988).

Activities analogous to marketing, as we now understand it, undoubtedly occurred before the 'marketing revolution' of the 1950s, but it is common knowledge, among marketing textbook writers at least, that these activities were basic, naive, rudimentary and primitive. At best, they can be described as proto-marketing practices rather than marketing practices *per se*. They refer to marketing as a *function*, which has to be performed in all exchange situations, rather than in the modern sense of a marketing-orientated management *philosophy* (Baker 1991). As is so often the case, however, this common knowledge is more than a little suspect. Notwithstanding the dangers associated with a Whig view of history – interpreting the past by the standards of the present – pre-marketing era marketing activities, so to speak, were often highly complex and astonishingly sophisticated, more sophisticated on occasion than today. For example:

- a customer focus was evident among the traders of classical and pre-Hellenic Greece, whose lines of merchandise (textiles, pottery and food, for example) were adapted to allow for differences in taste between markets, modified to meet changes in demand through time and presented in ways, such as stamped and shaped amphorae, which enabled customers to identify their place of origin (Nevett and Nevett 1987);
- the marketing strategies of participants in the medieval book trade involved, according to Rassuli (1988), tailoring the product to the needs

of the target market, selective distribution, celebrity endorsement, sponsorship, test marketing, market development and the choice of appropriate store locations;

- international marketing, as practised by the textile guilds of northern Europe, was supremely well organised in the Middle Ages, with stalls in foreign fairs and markets being rented *en bloc* often years in advance of the gathering, tax burdens being shared, most notably the imperiously imposed Royal 'prize', and strict control exercised over the quality of goods sold in the organisation's (brand) name (Moore 1985);
- the periodic markets of eighteenth century Ethiopia, as decreed by the great king Adrianampoinimerina, comprised a complex, carefully coordinated 'ring' (days on which the markets assembled) and the internal layout of these marketplaces was minutely controlled, more so even than the tenant placement policies of modern shopping centres (Brown 1992);
- youth-based market segmentation long predated the 'Pepsi generation' of 1940, having previously been employed by nineteenth century newspaper publishers, retail stores, financial institutions, automobile dealers, office equipment manufacturers, entertainment facilities, non-profit-making organisations and many more (Hollander and Germain 1992);
- and, as Fullerton (1988) describes in some detail, many 'modern' marketing practices like branding, segmentation, advertising, market analysis, credit provision, vertical marketing systems and market-plus pricing were in widespread use in Britain, Germany and the United States by the late nineteenth century.

Just as marketing practices long predated the putative marketing revolution of the 1950s, so too marketing theory and thought is by no means a post-war phenomenon. As noted in the previous chapter, marketing scholarship 'officially' dates from the early 1900s when the first university-level courses, textbooks and academic publications emerged in the United States. Particularly important in this respect were the pioneering contributions of Edward D. Jones, Simon Litman, George M. Fisk and James E. Hegarty at the universities of Michigan, California, Illinois and Ohio respectively (Bartels 1951). Important though they were, these US developments were based in turn on the German historical school of economics, which advocated inductive, comparative and literal approaches to business study. Many of the pioneers of US marketing education and thought were actually educated in Germany and, as Jones and Monieson (1990, p.111) speculate, 'marketing courses may actually have been offered in Germany before those offered in American institutions at the turn of the century'. In Britain, moreover, the first bachelor's degree, faculty and professorship in Commerce were established by the University of Birmingham in 1901 (the professorship incidently was held by Sir William

Ashley, who was also heavily indebted to the German historical school of economics) and the Chartered Institute of Marketing, the principal professional body in the UK, was also established (as the Institute of Sales and Commerce) before the First World War. Indeed, if a fairly liberal interpretation of marketing 'thought' is adopted, then its lineage can be traced back through the early sales training programmes (see Fullerton 1988), *The Retailer's Manual* (Terry 1869), Adam Smith's (1776) *The Wealth of Nations*, Daniel Defoe's (1745) *The Compleat English Tradesman*, Martin Luther's (1524) treatise on *Trade and Usury* and suchlike, to a starting point that is almost as indeterminate as marketing 'practice' itself.

Peter's Friends

Although marketing practices and thought have been around for a very long time, even the sternest critics of the marketing discipline's depressingly presentist perspective are prepared to acknowledge that an appreciable intensification of marketing activity, a new phase in the development of marketing thought, has taken place in the last half century (see Fullerton 1988). Apart from the environmental factors that underpinned this process, primarily the post-war economic miracle, growing consumer affluence, high levels of intra-sectoral competition, and a situation where supply often exceeded demand (Baker 1991), the 'trigger' of this transmutation is traditionally held to have taken place in 1954, when Peter Drucker stated that,

> The customer is the foundation of a business and keeps it in existence. He alone gives employment. And it is to supply the customer that society entrusts wealth-producing resources to the business enterprise. . . . Because it is its purpose to create a customer, any business enterprise has two – and only these two – basic functions: marketing and innovation. . . . Marketing is the distinguishing, the unique function of the business. . . . Actually marketing is so basic that it is not just enough to have a strong sales department and to entrust marketing to it. Marketing is not only much broader than selling, it is not a specialised activity at all. It is the whole business seen from the point of view of its final result, that is, from the customer's point of view. Concern and responsibility for marketing must therefore permeate all areas of the enterprise.
>
> (Drucker 1954, pp.35–6)

While this assertion merely repackaged a long-held principle of business success, that customers are the be-all and end-all of organisational well-being, Drucker's elevation of marketing to a position of paramount importance, and his spellbinding rhetoric, represented a forceful articulation of what has come to be known as a marketing orientation – viewing the business from the customer's standpoint and placing the customer at the very centre of an organisation's endeavours.

Drucker's seminal, albeit brief, exhortation was subsequently expanded upon and codified in perhaps the two most frequently anthologised papers in the marketing literature, 'The marketing revolution' by Keith (1960) and 'Marketing myopia' by Levitt (1960). The former described the experiences of the Pillsbury Company, contending that the organisation (like many other American businesses, according to Keith) was in the throes of a marketing equivalent of the Copernican revolution. From the late nineteenth century to the 1930s, the company was 'production orientated', in that it was preoccupied with the manufacturing process, with new products being launched to dispose of manufacturing by-products rather than serve a market need. From the 1930s to the 1950s, Pillsbury was characterised by a 'sales orientation', where a sophisticated sales organisation, backed up with advertising and market analysis, was assembled to dispose of the company's product lines. The subsequent era, however, was 'marketing orientated', in that the purpose of Pillsbury was no longer to mill flour, nor to manufacture and sell a wide range of products, but to satisfy the needs and desires of its customers.[2] This tripartite periodising schema, though deeply flawed as a general model, has since become a mainstay of marketing ideology (its belief system in other words). As the content analyses conducted by Hollander (1986) and Fullerton (1988) have shown, variants of the production era, sales era, marketing era schema are indiscriminately recycled in almost every introductory text-book – even today.

Alongside Keith's so-called marketing revolution, Levitt (1960) high-lighted the dangers of 'marketing myopia': companies' failure to respond to the changing requirements of consumers; their preoccupation with the products they produce rather than the markets they serve; a tendency to define their purpose and customer needs too narrowly (railroads rather than transportation, movies as opposed to entertainment, etc.); and an inability to recognise that all industries, even the then rapidly growing chemicals and electronics industries, would one day decline like the corner grocery stores, dry cleaners and buggy whip manufacturers before them. He emphasised, in addition, that businesses must develop 'backwards', commencing with the customer's needs, through the delivery of customer satisfaction, and the creation of new products, to finding the raw materials from which these needs are ultimately satisfied. The whole purpose of the exercise, in effect, was not to produce goods and services but to buy customers. Although Levitt's polemic has since been dismissed as contra-dictory, ambiguous and misleading (e.g. Kaldor 1971; Marion 1993), his paper undoubtedly encapsulated the essence of modern marketing, succeeded in setting the agenda for a generation of marketing academics and practitioners and, over thirty years later, it has lost little of its extraordinary resonance and rhetorical power.

The criticisms of Keith and Levitt should not disguise the fact that, along with several other enthusiasts, most notably McKitterick (1957), they were responsible for the propagation of the modern marketing concept. Albeit expressed in a variety of colourful apophthegms – 'customer satisfaction engineering' (Kotler and Levy 1969, p.10), 'creating and keeping profitable customers' (Brown 1987, p.30), 'selling goods that don't come back to people that do' (Baker 1991, p.4) etc. – and albeit predated, as Powers and Martin (1987) have shown, by the writings of Charles W. Hoyt, Ralph Star Butler and Percival White in the early part of this century, the marketing concept is generally considered to comprise three elements: an awareness of customer wants, which are regarded as the point of departure for a marketing-led organisation; the integration and co-ordination of all the activities of the firm around this basic customer orientation; and regarding profit rather than sales volume as the measure of success of the organisation's marketing activities (Hollander 1986). As we shall presently discover, not everyone subscribes to this particular definition and distinctions are sometimes drawn between the associated family of terms (e.g. marketing concept, marketing philosophy, marketing orientation, market orientation and customer orientation), but the nuances of these categorisations, though a boon to academics in pursuit of publications, are unimportant for the purposes of our discussion. The essential point is that marketing in general and the marketing concept in particular are widely regarded, by academics and practitioners alike, respectively to comprise the single most important management function and the key to success in business (Baker and Hart 1989; Kheir-El-Din 1991).

Indeed, there is considerable empirical evidence to support this contention. To cite but a few examples:

- Barksdale and Darden's (1971) early survey of business executives and marketing educators in the US revealed a widespread belief in the efficacy of the marketing concept. Interestingly, however, top managers were more favourably disposed toward marketing than marketing managers, who in turn were more positive about the concept than marketing educators.
- Hooley and Lynch's (1985) detailed analysis of 1504 British companies found that 'high flyers' exhibited a significantly greater market orientation, as measured by their use of market research in all its forms, strategic sensibility and concern with product quality and design than the 'also rans'.
- Narver and Slater (1990) examined the marketing orientation of the top managers of 140 strategic business units (SBUs) in the USA, using a comprehensive, multiple-item scale, and discovered not only a clear

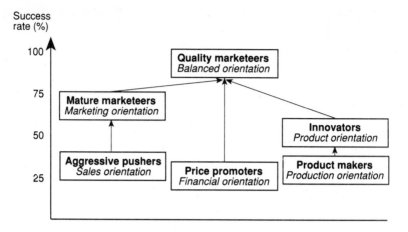

Figure 2.1 Business orientation and success rates
Source: Wong and Saunders (1993)

relationship between marketing orientation and profitability but also that the *highest* degree of marketing orientation was exhibited by managers of the *most* profitable companies.

- Kohli and Jaworski (1990) reported, on the basis of 62 semi-structured interviews with marketing practitioners in four US cities, a high degree of familiarity with the three component parts of the marketing concept – customer orientation, co-ordination and profitability, though the last of these was seen as a consequence of the marketing concept not an integral part of it – and that the perceived benefits of the marketing philosophy included better overall performance, benefits for employees and more positive customer attitudes.
- Wong and Saunders' (1993) multivariate study of matched Japanese, American and British companies demonstrated that organisations. classified as 'innovators', 'quality marketeers' and 'mature marketeers' were significantly more successful in terms of profits, sales and market share than those classified as 'price promoters', 'product makers' and 'aggressive pushers' (Figure 2.1).

Many other ringing endorsements of the marketing philosophy could be paraded but suffice it to say that the relationship between marketing and business 'success' appears to hold regardless of company size, sector or geographical context (see Kheir-El-Din's (1991) detailed review of the literature). Conversely, some of the principal reasons for failure in business are weaknesses in marketing performance – inability to develop a distinctive image, a lack of understanding of company strengths and weaknesses and unwillingness to adjust to changing times and consumer needs. Doyle (1985), for instance, contends that inept marketing is the primary cause of British industry's continuing lack of international competitiveness and rather than seeking macro-economic solutions to the country's commercial ills, much greater attention should be paid to improving the marketing competence of individual companies.

Phil and Ted's Excellent Adventure

If, thanks to the endeavours of Levitt and his fellow evangelists, the late 1950s–early 1960s witnessed the efflorescence of modern marketing,[3] the subsequent decades have been characterised by periodic, occasionally intemperate and undeniably stimulating debate. These debates have ranged from the efficacy of individual marketing constructs or principles (attitude–behaviour consistency, the product life cycle, hierarchy of advertising effects, for example) and the periodic attempts to develop an all-encompassing 'general' theory of marketing, to the old 'art versus science' chestnut alluded to in the previous chapter. Clearly, it is impossible to do justice to these controversies in an essay such as this. However, three issues have proved to be of particular importance: (1) marketing's domain, the area over which it extends; (2) marketing's core, its unique distinguishing feature; and (3) the precise character of the marketing concept itself.

The debate over marketing's proper domain was initiated by Kotler and Levy (1969) when they contended that marketing was an all-pervasive activity which applied as much to the selling of politicians, universities and charities as it did to toothpaste, soap and steel.[4] As a consequence of dramatic, post-war social changes and the emergence of large, complex, professionally managed non-business organisations, such as museums, police departments and trade unions, it had become necessary to broaden the concept of marketing. Traditional notions of the 'product', the 'consumer' and the marketing 'toolkit' had to be redefined in non-business terms and attempts made to transfer the principles of effective marketing management – generic product definition, target groups identification, customer behaviour analysis, integrated marketing planning, continuous feedback and so on – to the marketing of services, persons and ideas. In effect, 'the choice facing those who manage non-business organisations is not whether to market or not to market, for no organisation can avoid marketing. The choice is whether to do it well or poorly' (Kotler and Levy 1969, p.15).

Developing this theme, Kotler (1972) went on to argue that it was necessary to extend the concept even further. There were, he maintained, three stages of marketing consciousness. The first represented the traditional view of marketing that it was essentially a business-oriented philosophy involving market transactions, the economic exchange of goods and services. Consciousness two held that marketing was applicable to all

Table 2.2 Kotler's typology of publics, products and organisations

Publics	Products	Organisations
General public	Goods marketing	Business organisations
Special publics	Services marketing	Political organisations
Competitor publics	Organisation marketing	Social organisations
Government publics	Person marketing	Religious organisations
Support publics	Place marketing	Cultural organisations
Employee publics	Idea marketing	Knowledge organisations
Supplier publics		
Agent publics		
Consumer publics		

Source: Adapted from Kotler (1972)

organisations that had customers or clients, even though payment in the normal sense may not take place. However, the third level of conscious-ness, deemed the 'generic' concept, contended that marketing was not only relevant to *all* organisations, be they churches, political parties or govern-ment departments, but to the relations between an organisation and *all* of its publics, not just the consuming public. To this end, Kotler developed a typology of nine distinct publics, six types of products and six types of organisation (Table 2.2). In fact, he went even further still, extending the concept beyond organisations to transactions between any two parties or 'social units' (e.g. watching television) and, in what can only be described as a rush of blood to the head, he concluded that 'marketing can be viewed as a *category of human action*, distinguishable from other categories of human action such as voting, loving, consuming and fighting' (emphasis in original).

Needless to say, not everyone shared Kotler's marketing megalomania and several critics warned of the dangers of over-extending the concept. Luck (1969) believed that marketing should be confined to considerations of market transactions and decried the 'semantic jungle' that broadening entailed. Laczniak and Michie (1979) held that it was becoming all but impossible to distinguish between marketing and non-marketing transac-tions. And, in a particularly prescient paper, Bartels (1974) predicted that broadening would only serve to direct attention away from important but neglected areas of marketing activity, like physical distribution, lead to an emphasis on methodology rather than issues of substance, and give rise to an increasingly esoteric and abstract marketing literature. Set against this, however, Kotler's (1972) denunciation of his critics as 'myopic' (which, thanks to Levitt, remains the most damning indictment in marketing's lexicon), his declaration that failure to rethink marketing at a time of great social change ran the risk of marginalisation and irrelevance (which dovetailed neatly with contemporaneous concern about the nature of the relationship between marketing and society) and, not least, the simple fact that the marketing message was deemed relevant to, and hence enthusiastically embraced by, individuals and organisations outwith the traditional marketing arena, rapidly rendered the 'broadening' debate irrelevant. Only five years later, Hunt (1976) could declare the battle won by the broadeners and all that remained was the need to (a) go forth and multiply by 'marketing marketing to non-marketers' and (b) develop a framework which did justice to the enormous scope of marketing. Fortunately, Hunt had one to hand, a typology made up of three dimensions – normative/positive, micro/macro and profit/non-profit – which when combined produced eight cells of contrasting marketing foci (Table 2.3). Although this 'three dichotomies' model has been severely criticised in turn – a cynic once described it as 'the three calamities model' (Brown 1995, p.37) – it has not yet been superseded and remains, arguably, the definitive statement on marketing's vast domain (see for example Robin 1977; Arndt 1981; Hyman *et al.* 1991; Hunt 1991a).

If marketing is as ubiquitous as Kotlerites maintain, then the question must be asked, what is the common denominator, what makes marketing different from other areas of intellectual endeavour? When watching television, religious experiences, human relationships, self-image and the trading practices of neolithic man are considered legitimate topics of marketing inquiry, what distinguishes the subject from media studies, theology, sociology, psychology and history? Clearly, it is not the phenomena under investigation. As noted in Chapter 1, just as marketers claim dominion over non-business arenas, so too sociologists, psychologists, theologians and historians are happy to explore the nooks and crannies of the marketing edifice. Nor is marketing distinguished by a distinctive methodology. Not only are most of our procedures employed by other academic specialisms, but, as Bagozzi (1975) points out, defining a discipline by its tools and techniques is both reductive and circular (in that marketing is defined by its tools and its tools are defined by marketing). Nor, for that matter, is the discipline distinguished by a particular scale of analysis. Marketing is concerned with everything from the workings of the human brain (in the study of memory effects, for example) to globalisation tendencies in the world economy (courtesy, once again, of Levitt), and if attempts to communicate with alien life forms are included (interstellar 'messages' often include advertisements as examples of human culture), then the entire universe falls within marketing's ambitious orbit.

Although marketing is characterised by attempts boldly to go where other disciplines have gone before (yes, I know I've unsplit the infinitive, but, this is supposed to be a work of scholarship, remember!), it has often been argued that marketers adopt a particular perspective, that the specialism has a distinctive focus, that the core concept of marketing is

Table 2.3 The three dichotomies model

	Positive	Normative
	PROFIT SECTOR	
Micro	Problems, issues, theories and research concerning: individual consumer behaviour; firms' determination of prices, products, promotions, channels of distribution; and, case studies	Problems, issues and research concerning how firms *should*: determine the marketing mix; implement the marketing concept; and, make pricing, product, promotion, packaging, purchasing and international marketing decisions
Macro	Problems, issues, theories and research concerning: aggregate consumption patterns; legal and comparative aspects of marketing; and the relationship between marketing and economic development	Problems, issues and reseach concerning: how marketing can be made more efficient; whether distrubution costs too much; and whether marketing should have special social responsibilities
	NON-PROFIT SECTOR	
Micro	Problems, issues, theories and research concerning: consumers' purchasing of public goods; non-profit organisations' determination of prices, products, promotion and channels of distribution; and case studies	Problems, issues and research concerning how non-profit organisations *should*: determine the marketing mix; implement the marketing concept; and, make pricing, product, promotion, packaging, purchasing and international marketing decisions
Macro	Problems, issues, theories and research concerning: the institutional framework for public goods; whether television or public service advertising affects behaviour; and, the efficiency of distribution systems for public goods	Problems, issues and research concerning: whether society should permit the 'selling' of politicians; and, whether the demand for public goods should be stimulated

Source: Adapted from Hunt (1976)

exchange. Admittedly, many other academic subject areas, such as economics, anthropology and geography, have demonstrated an interest in exchange relationships, but many academic authorities consider 'exchange' to be the very essence of the marketing condition (Baker 1987, 1992; Houston and Gassenheimer 1987; Dwyer *et al.* 1987). Bagozzi (1975, 1979), in particular, has gone to great lengths to propagate the 'marketing as exchange' paradigm, arguing that three types of exchange – restricted, generalised and complex – can be identified and that exchange relationships carry three types of meaning for the parties involved, utilitarian, symbolic and mixed. Indeed, Bagozzi (1975) went so far as to assert that not only is marketing a general function of universal applicability but that it is the discipline of exchange behaviour, no less.

As was the case with the debate over marketing's domain, not everyone subscribes to the marketing = exchange analogy. On the contrary, the concept has been examined in detail and found wanting. After examining Bagozzi's typology of exchange, for example, Foxall (1984a, p.36) concluded 'it is difficult to imagine how this line of marketing thought can be reconciled with the fundamental principle, namely consumer sovereignty'. Martin (1985, p.21), moreover, maintained that the notion was 'nebulous and ambiguous', and even Houston and Gassenheimer (1987, p.17), who have provided one of the most detailed and sympathetic explications of the exchange paradigm, concede that, 'it has yet to fulfil it promise of providing a coherent structure for the discipline' (see also Firat 1984; Hirschman 1986; Belk and Coon 1993). Inevitably, a host of alternative disciplinary foci have been proposed – 'matching', 'transactions', 'potency', 'market behaviour' and so on – but it is fair to say that none of these have managed to unseat 'exchange'. As with the equally debatable three dichotomies model, marketing = exchange is very deeply entrenched in the disciplinary psyche and, although the question of marketing's core concept periodically surfaces in the literature, it is generally considered to be a dead or irresolvable issue.

Marketing, like many academic disciplines, may lack a universally agreed core, its boundaries may be ragged and ill-defined, and aspirant explicants may be reduced to such neologisms as 'marketing is what marketers do', but at least we can rest assured in the belief that the marketing concept itself is unassailable. Unfortunately not. Even the marketing concept, with its tripartite emphasis on customer orientation, overall integration and profit maximisation, has been the subject of extensive debate and periodic modification (see Houston 1986). Apart from intractable, albeit comparatively minor, issues like the operationalisation of the measure of profit or the relationship between profit and market share, the all-important stress placed upon meeting customer needs has been criticised, firstly, for its failure to take the offerings of competitors into account. Success in marketing, so the argument goes, is gained not by meeting customer needs *per se*, but by meeting them better than the competition (Sachs and Benson 1978). Secondly, the emphasis on customer orientation has been condemned for diverting attention away from the product and its manufacture. By focusing attention on the consumer's perceived needs, the marketing concept has served to stifle innovation as, in many situations, consumers are incapable of articulating latent needs and talk in terms of the familiar. This gives rise to the proliferation of minor twist, 'me too' products and the eventual loss of technological leadership (Tauber 1974; Bennett and Cooper 1981). Third, and most importantly, it has often been contended that the marketing concept should transcend mere customer orientation and deal instead with broader societal concerns (Bell and Emory 1971; Kotler and Zaltman 1971). The key question, in other words, is not whether products or services *can* be developed to meet consumer needs, but whether they *should* be developed in light of the attendant social consequences (environmental pollution, depletion of natural resources, global warming, neo-colonialism etc.).

Marketers, not unnaturally, have responded vigorously to the attacks on and controversies surrounding the marketing concept. Interestingly, however, the defenders of the faith did not react to the challenge by arguing, in line with Drucker's original exposition, that marketing's domain did *not* extend to innovation and that the concept was being criticised unfairly. Such a stance was clearly impossible given marketing's less than modest post-Kotler claims to universality. Instead, the response has been to extend the marketing concept to incorporate the competitive context, technological innovation and societal concerns. For example, most latter-day definitions of the marketing concept in mainstream textbooks specifically mention the need to meet customer needs more efficiently and effectively than competitors, and great store is placed on strategic considerations generally (Kotler 1988; O'Shaughnessy 1992a). Many theorists also include 'technological push' as well as 'market pull' in their conceptualisations, even though the former places marketers in the paradoxical position of appearing to advocate the once-reviled 'product orientation' (Samli *et al.* 1987). Similarly, societal concerns have been embraced with some vigour, especially by the macromarketing fraternity and notwithstanding the fact that to non-marketers this altruism smacks of 'poacher turned gamekeeper' at best and breathtaking cynicism at worst (Sheth *et al.* 1988).

Although often bitter and polemical, and although they remain resolutely unresolved and hence subject to periodic exhumation, the above debates concerning the concept's domain, core and composition should not disguise the fact that marketing has made remarkable strides in the post-war era. As Figure 2.2 demonstrates, this process of development can be described in terms of Ansoff's celebrated and much-cited product–market matrix. The first cell, *penetration*, comprises the early attempts to demonstrate the

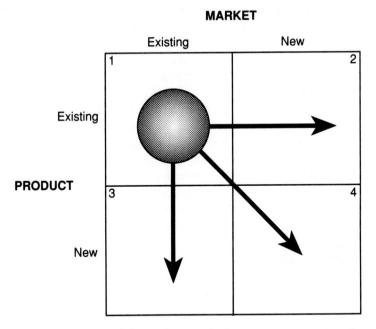

Figure 2.2 The evolution of the modern marketing concept
Source: Adapted from Ansoff (1957)

veracity of the modern marketing concept, to highlight its superiority over the sales and product orientations that once prevailed, and to promote its acceptance throughout the business community. The second cell, *market development*, refers to the revolution, initiated by Kotler and Levy, involving the application of the marketing concept to all manner of non-business organisations, from charities to high schools, and to all of an organisation's constituents. *Product development*, the third cell, pertains to the subsequent modifications of the original marketing concept, which was expanded to embrace the competitive environment, strategic concerns, technological push and suchlike. The final cell, *diversification*, alludes to the societal concept of marketing, in so far as this involved a reformulation of both the product/concept itself (the key issue is not consumer needs or profit but societal concerns) and the market/domain to which it pertains – public policy, consumerism, resource exploitation, the deficiencies of the marketing system etc.

Phil and Ted's Bogus Journey

In their recent book, *Competitive Positioning*, Hooley and Saunders (1993, p.3) argue that the marketing concept has come of age. Whereas a decade or two ago marketing was misunderstood by most senior managers and typically considered to be a new name for old-fashioned selling, marketing is now 'on everyone's lips'. Certainly, there is much to support this contention. As we have noted already, there is considerable empirical evidence that a marketing orientation is the key to long-term business profitability and survival (Baker and Hart 1989). Innumerable surveys of senior management attest to its continuing importance (Wong 1993). The marketing concept has been deemed applicable to fields as diverse as healthcare, public administration, the not-for-profit sector, aesthetic accomplishments, individual people and religious experiences (Hirschman 1983, 1987; Doyle 1993; Walsh 1993; Jennings and Saunders 1993). It is rapidly colonising the erstwhile command economies of Eastern Europe where the market is supplanting Marxism as the societal touchstone, albeit not without privation (see Hooley 1993). The proliferation of publications, professorships, degree programmes and autonomous university departments testifies to the fact that marketing is in the ascendant as an academic discipline. And, as Huczynski (1993, p.35) has shown, the diverse writings of the new generation of management gurus – Tom Peters, Michael Porter, Kenneth Blanchard, etc. – concur on one point, 'that the central fact of business today [is] the emergence of consumer sovereignty'. In these circumstances, indeed, it is fair to surmise that approximately forty years after Drucker's original exposition, thirty-five years after Levitt's codification and a quarter of a century after Kotler and Levy's endeavours to broaden its base, the modern marketing concept has fully matured.

Yet despite the undeniable achievements of modern marketing, an undercurrent of concern is equally apparent. Many latter-day commentators on the marketing condition have concluded that something is amiss, that the concept is deeply, perhaps irredeemably, flawed, that its seemingly solid theoretical foundations are by no means secure and that the specialism is teetering on the brink of a serious intellectual crisis (Cova and Svanfeldt 1992; Marion 1993). True, people have been declaring that marketing is in some sort of 'crisis' from time immemorial (e.g. Bartels 1962; Bell and Emory 1971; Bennett and Cooper 1981). After all, the identification of spurious crises and the provision of a timely 'solution' is a standard ploy in the game of academic self-aggrandisement and personal fortune-hunting. Nevertheless, such is the pervasiveness of the current unease – the 1993 Academy of Marketing Science (AMS) conference, for example, devoted a special session, featuring some of America's foremost marketing scholars, to the issue and a contemporaneous European conference entitled 'Rethinking Marketing' was also considered necessary – and so prominent are the practitioners, consultants and academics concerned, that even the staunchest defenders of modern marketing might be prepared to concede that the field is facing a crisis of representation (self-aggrandisement, *moi?*).

- Piercy (1992, p.15), for example, maintains that the traditional marketing concept, 'assumes and relies on the existence of a world which is alien and unrecognisable to many of the executives who actually have to manage marketing for real'.
- Gummesson (1987, p.10) states that 'the present marketing concept . . . is unrealistic and needs to be replaced'.
- Nilson (1992, p.4) contends that 'a revision of the marketing concept is necessary'.
- Rapp and Collins (1990, p.3) suggest that 'the traditional methods . . . simply aren't working as well anymore'.
- Brownlie and Saren (1992, p.38) argue that 'it is questionable whether the marketing concept as it has been propagated can provide the basis for successful business at the end of the twentieth century'.
- McKenna (1991, p.67) concludes that 'there is less and less reason to believe that the traditional approach can keep up with real customer wishes and demands or with the rigors of competition'.
- And, Professor Michael Thomas (1993), one of the most respected marketing academics in Britain, has recently made the frank, and frankly astonishing, confession that after thirty years of disseminating the marketing message, he is having serious doubts about its continuing efficacy.

If, as many authorities appear to imply, marketing is facing the onset of a 'mid-life crisis' (Brady and Davis 1993; Wilson and McDonald 1994), there is less consensus on the most suitable means of transcending this unfortunate state of affairs and the future direction that the specialism should take. For the sake of argument, however, the various suggestions can be summarised in the four-cell matrix illustrated in Figure 2.3., which involves the inversion or reversal of our earlier product–market typology. The first position, *realisation*, subscribes to the view that the modern marketing concept is basically sound, but that the problem is one of implementation. In other words, the traditional difficulties of getting the concept accepted by top management, of distinguishing successfully between marketing philosophy and function, trappings and substance, rhetoric and reality etc., have been superseded by a concern with *making marketing work* through a heightened understanding of organisational politics and inter-functional rivalry. To this end, a programme of internal marketing – marketing the marketing concept within organisations – is often advocated. Typically, this involves a series of decisions on organisation, information gathering, planning, budgeting, control procedures and, above all, *action*, ensuring that the transformation process actually takes place (e.g. Piercy 1992).

The second position, *retrenchment*, also regards the marketing concept as reasonably acceptable in itself, but acknowledges that there are certain

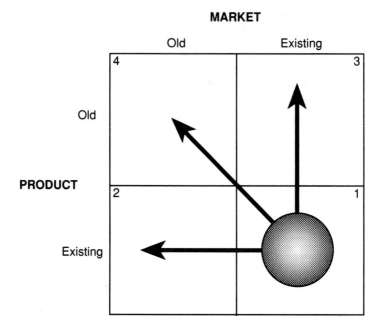

Figure 2.3 Marketing's mid-life crisis
Source: Adapted from Ansoff (1957)

circumstances in which it is either inappropriate or of minor rather than major relevance. For some people, it is irrelevant in hi-tech industries where discontinuous innovation is the norm and traditional marketing research can inhibit rather than enhance the process (Workman 1993). For others, it is unsuitable in basic commodity markets where the opportunities for meaningful differentiation are less clearly marked than is the case elsewhere (Narver and Slater 1990). For yet others, the concept has shortcomings when applied to certain sectors, such as services, public administration and not-for-profit (Wensley 1990); in certain countries, most notably in Eastern Europe (Thomas 1993); for certain companies depending on their specific organisational, competitive and market circumstances (Kohli and Jaworski 1990); and, in certain macro-economic conditions (Foxall 1984a). These uncertainties, it must be emphasised, do not represent a re-run of the old questions 'how does marketing differ in various settings – industrial versus consumer, domestic versus international, goods versus services and so on?' The key point is not that the nature of marketing differs, but that the marketing concept itself is deemed inappropriate when applied in certain contexts.

Rearrangement, the third position, does not so much take issue with the domain of the discipline as the very character of the marketing concept, and how it needs to be modified to meet today's marketing realities. According to Webster (1988), for example, it has become necessary to 'rediscover' marketing, to scrape away the encrustations of strategic management, which have led to an unhealthy and (surprise, surprise) myopic preoccupation with competitor activity and market share, and replace them with a renewed focus on the customer. To get back, in effect, to the basics of the original marketing concept – customer orientation. Baker (1989), by contrast, contends that too much emphasis has been placed on the consumer, consumerism and societal concerns generally. Marketing, he argues is about exchanges which are mutually satisfying for both consumers and providers. More fundamentally perhaps, many scholars maintain that attention should increasingly focus on a very specific aspect of the marketing concept, namely, 'relationships' (Christopher *et al.* 1991). In other words, to the establishment and maintenance of long-term marketing relationships rather than the former preoccupation with one-off transactions. Indeed, it is no exaggeration to state that, at the time of writing, relationship marketing is the single most popular topic on the academic research agenda, though it is noteworthy that most of the studies thus far are concerned with relationships in the profit sector. Broadening the concept of relationship marketing to the not-for-profit and non-business sectors has yet to be meaningfully addressed (Butler and Brown 1994).

Reappraisal, the final and by far the most radical position, comprises an acknowledgement of the simple fact that the marketing concept has not succeeded and is unlikely to prove successful in its present form. Despite the latter-day 'triumph' of marketing, the failure rate of new products is as high as it ever was – possibly higher. Consumerism, the so-called 'shame of marketing', is still rampant, especially in its virulent 'green' mutation. Selling has not, contra the marketing concept, been rendered redundant because few products actually sell themselves. Companies in countries where the marketing message has not been received loud and clear, such as Japan and Germany, continue to outperform their Anglo-American counterparts and, even in the latter milieux, businesses can still succeed without the aid of modern marketing (Piercy (1992) cites The Body Shop, Amstrad, Ratners and Marks and Spencer as prime examples).

In these circumstances, it has been suggested that marketing should revert to pre-marketing era marketing; in other words, to adopt a neo-sales or post-product orientation. Dickinson *et al.* (1986), for instance, stress that marketing is basically manipulative and monopoly seeking, that customers in many instances are totally unaware of their needs, and that marketing's task is to *shape* consumer wants, *determine* their perceptions and *persuade* them of the attractiveness of what the company has on sale. Likewise, Chen *et al.* (1992, p.441) have recently made a case for the pre-eminence of production, concluding with the words 'the conventional wisdom that marketing is expected to play a major role in formulating corporate strategies, with manufacturing simply responding to these strategies, is no longer affordable'. An alternative form of reversion, to an intuitive, creative, flexible, idiographic, essentially 'non-scientific' marketing concept, has also been suggested. This approach recognises that 'each marketing situation should be treated as unique and in its own right, drawing upon all the available knowledge that may help in handling the situation' (Gummesson 1987, p.19). Another, and potentially the most extreme position of all, highlights that marketing-orientated management is an historical artifact which emerged in certain countries under a particular set of socio-economic conditions (Foxall 1984a; Baker 1989). Just as the sales and product orientations were appropriate to their own particular historical eras, so too a marketing orientation is a product of its time. For a growing number of commentators, what is more, that time has passed and we are facing nothing less than the end of marketing (cf. Lynch 1994).

Howard's End

Above and beyond the uncertainty surrounding the continuing relevance of the modern marketing concept, there is evidence of a deepening crisis of representation in several other areas of marketing endeavour. Indeed, this crisis contributes to and is reinforced by the palpable sense of aimlessness and unpredictability that characterises the underpinning marketing concept. For the purposes of our discussion, this predicament can be summarised under four headings: *practice, principles, philosophy* and *prescriptions.* The four Ps in other words. These categories, of course, are not clear cut and, as we shall see, a postmodernist would reject out of hand any such attempt to impose order on what is undeniably a complex, inchoate and tightly interwoven process. But in the interests of convenience – and in pursuit of the postmodernist grail of intertextuality – they can be described as the four Ps.

Whenever one examines the current *practices* of marketing, the process of disintegration looms large. Analyses focus on the massive fragmentation of markets into smaller and smaller, more and more inaccessible segments, and the associated proliferation of offerings in existing product categories – soft drinks, washing powder, yellow fats, etc. (Mueller-Heumann 1992). Consumer researchers note the rise of new individualism, a desire to 'keep away from the Joneses', the sheer unpredictability of buyer behaviour and the difficulties of selling to 'Generation X' (McMurdo 1993; King 1994). The new world order, or rather disorder, that has transpired since the break-up of the communist bloc into a multiplicity of nation states and ethnic enclaves, coupled with the emergence and reorganisation of trading blocks (EC, NAFTA, ASEAN) and the convolutions of the GATT agreement, have served to undermine the basic premises of the globalisation concept and, at the risk of gross understatement, rendered international trade increasingly problematical (Ogilvy 1990). Competition is proliferating in almost every sector of the economy as a consequence of the pace of technological change, the just-in-time revolution, the rapid diffusion of know-how, the shortening of product life cycles, the advent of flexible manufacturing systems and the increased porosity of barriers to entry as economies of scope supersede economies of scale (Imrie and Morris 1992). Marketers, moreover, appear to be going to ever-increasing lengths in order to reach and satisfy customers, even to the extent of customising individual products, promotional material and so on (Pine 1993). This has led Hoyt (1991, p.4) to the inescapable conclusion that practitioners are increasingly dealing with segments of one and, as a consequence, 'we don't do marketing here anymore'.

Likewise, the literature is replete with considerations of the reorganisation of organisations and assessments of the implications for marketing (Gummesson 1991; Achrol 1991). This ranges from the flattening, de-layering and re-engineering of management hierarchies, and the demise of marketing as a separate function, to the increasingly blurred boundaries between companies. The necessity for and benefits of joint ventures, collaborative networks, strategic alliances, dedicated suppliers, multi-layered partnerships, overlapping organisations, hollow corporations, virtual companies and their ilk are being enthusiastically extolled with evangelical fervour, though the extent to which rhetoric and reality coincide is rather less certain (Bucklin and Sengupta 1993). Nevertheless, as Webster (1992, p.14) points out, not only is it not uncommon in today's marketing environment for a producer or supplier to be 'simultaneously customer, competitor, and vendor, as well as partner', but also that 'the clear distinction between firms and markets, between the company and its external environment, has disappeared'.

In these turbulent and seemingly paradoxical circumstances, where the certainties of the past are no longer certain and the era of mass marketing is but a dim and distant memory, it is perhaps not surprising that there are many extant declarations of discontent with long-established marketing *principles*. Whether it be the product life cycle, market segmentation, the hierarchy of advertising effects, the classification of goods, Fishbein's behavioural intentions model, the wheel of retailing, the stages of internationalisation concept, the celebrated Howard–Sheth model of consumer behaviour, the strategic matrices of Porter, Ansoff and the Boston Consulting Group, or, come to think of it, the four Ps itself, the continuing utility of these models and constructs is being increasingly called into question (e.g. Wood 1990; Foxall 1984b, 1990; Sparks 1990; Turnbull 1987). The fact of the matter is that, despite decades of research and replication, the validity, reliability, universality and predictive power of these and many other prominent marketing principles are far from established (though, it goes without saying, my own use of such models as argument-framing devices remains the one island of certainty in a sea of conceptual ambiguity).

Worse, the constructs themselves may have a counterproductive or deleterious effect on marketplace behaviour. It is not unknown, after all, for perfectly sound products to be killed off because of management's belief in the existence of a product life cycle (van Rossum 1984). The codification of the retailing hierarchy concept has contributed to decades of conflict between urban planners and retail organisations and impeded the introduction of innovative retailing formats, as has the classification of goods typology (Brown 1993a). STP (segmentation, targeting, positioning) stands accused of reinforcing managers' preoccupation with existing product and service offerings, or minor variants of existing offerings, rather than developing them anew (Bennett and Cooper 1981); the stages theory of internationalisation provides the basis of government export assistance policies, yet the model itself is far from proven (Bell 1994); and the four Ps framework, according to Gummesson (1991) and Groonos (1990), is a conceptual strait-jacket which has served to misdirect both practitioners and academics. A recent evaluation of the Boston matrix, moreover, found that, 'it is a real worry that the original matrix is seductively simple and the temptations of using it off the shelf are real. . . . Those who now use it may be boxed in terms of restrictive assumptions about both the nature of market and competitive dynamics. . . . It is a badly taught, outmoded and discredited orthodoxy, which is seductive and dangerous for our young managers of tomorrow' (Morrison and Wensley 1991, p.118).

Just as the practices and principles of marketing exhibit crisis-like tendencies, so too the underpinning *philosophy* of science in marketing appears to be in turmoil, though it is debatable whether this represents a true paradigmatic crisis in the Kuhnian sense. As Barnes (1982) has shown, fully-fledged paradigm shifts are rare in the social sciences. Be that as it may, Hunt's (1993) recent paper in the *Journal of Marketing*, and all the previous papers in the (interminable) series 'Shelby Hunt versus the barbarian hordes', specifically mentions the 'crisis' literature (e.g. Hunt 1991b, 1992). The perceived bifurcation, in other words, between the positivist and logical empiricist defenders of the marketing faith, though they are at pains to reject such appellations (thereby effectively deflecting some of the criticism), and the profusion of relativistic philosophical heresies – phenomenology, hermeneutics, semiotics, existentialism, historicism, literary theory, critical theory, ethnomethodology, etc. – propounded by post-positivist, interpretive, constructionist and humanistic marketing researchers (see Sherry 1991). Summarised in Table 2.4, this latter group espouses a methodology (procedures and aims), epistemology (theory of knowledge), ontology (assumptions about existence) and axiology (overriding values) that are markedly different from the marketing research mainstream.

Table 2.4 Positivist and interpretivist paradigms: key features

	Positivist paradigm	*Interpretivist paradigm*
Basic beliefs:	The world is external and objective	The world is socially constructed and subjective
	Observer is independent	Observer is part of what is observed
	Science is value-free	Science is driven by human interests
Researcher should:	Focus on facts	Focus on meanings
	Look for causality and fundamental laws	Try to understand what is happening
	Reduce phenomena to simplest elements	Look at the totality of each situation
	Formulate hypotheses and then test them	Develop ideas through induction from data
Preferred methods include:	Operationalising concepts so that they can be measured	Using multiple methods to establish different views of phenomena
	Taking large samples	Small samples investigated in depth or over time

Source: Adapted from Easterby-Smith *et al.* (1991)

In fairness, it must be emphasised that both the 'positivists' and 'interpretivists' have gone to great lengths to stress their open-mindedness and their support for a multiplicity of epistemological perspectives (e.g. Hunt 1989; Hirschman 1989a). Nevertheless, to the uncommitted, the unedifying sight of prominent marketing scholars indulging in gratuitous mud-slinging and name-calling contests looks very much like a debilitating, demeaning, unnecessary and potentially ruinous civil war (though, let's be honest, most of us secretly revel in their amusing attempts to maintain a modicum of academic decorum whilst slugging it out). At one extreme, Shelby Hunt (1994, p.21) is happy to dismiss all interpretive approaches as unworthy of serious consideration by marketing scholars and asks pointedly, 'how could marketers *trust* the output of such research methods?' At the other extreme, committed interpretivists like Holbrook and Hirschman (1993) are openly advocating the secession of consumer research from the marketing mainstream and an abandonment of the long-standing connection with practising managers. As Gellner (1993, p.215) rightly points out, 'dogmatism is not uncommon among creative intellectuals, even or especially among those who preach liberalism'.

This all-pervasive sense of crisis is exacerbated by the plethora of *prescriptions* pertaining to the marketing condition and the host of conceptual cure-alls that have recently materialised. In a recent overview concerning the state of marketing research, for example, Hodock (1991) concluded that the seductiveness of quantification, rating scales and sophisticated data-gathering technology has led to a situation where researchers are increasingly out of touch with real market needs and the voice of the consumer. Wells (1993) contends that progress in consumer research has been inhibited by the mistaken assumptions that (a) students represent consumers, (b) the laboratory represents the real world, (c) statistical significance confers real significance, (d) correlation equates to causation, and (e) mentioning limitations makes them go away. Strategic marketing stands accused of ceding territory to other academic specialisms, standing idly by while its concepts and methods are appropriated by non-marketers, and of adhering to outmoded characterisations of strategy processes and issues (Day 1992). The editors of prominent marketing journals complain of unoriginal insights, me-too contributions, redundant research and 'mechanical' manuscripts comprising marginal additions to and minor variations of well-worn themes (Peterson 1992; Ingene 1993). Dickinson (1992) lists no less than nineteen frequently recycled 'myths' about marketing ranging from the supposed congruence of marketer and consumer goals, and the presupposition that individuals are motivated by self-interest, to researchers' preoccupation with identifying similarities among marketing phenomena (and hence generalisability) rather than seeking differences. When it comes to marketing education, moreover, the traditional curriculum has come under attack for its functional orientation rather than multifunctional emphasis, its concern with analytical skills instead of action-orientated skills and, in the United States at least, the lack of attention to internationalisation.

Although periodic diagnoses of the marketing condition are prudent and healthy, the very act of examination only serves to undermine confidence, especially when the scrutiny is conducted by established and respected figures in the field (the attacks of outsiders and newcomers can be dismissed as ignorance and self-promotion respectively). This sense of uncertainty is compounded by the current rash of conceptual restoratives, the very existence of which comprise an implicit criticism of mainstream marketing. Apart from the manifold interpretive research perspectives, which will be discussed in detail in Chapter 5, these solutions to marketing's ills come in several forms, though a suitably snappy, dynamic, trendy, virile, evangelical or alliterative title is common to all – maxi-marketing, turbo-marketing, neo-marketing, micro-marketing, after-marketing, value-added

Table 2.5 Marketing panaceas: some examples

Terminology	Definition	Sources
Micro-marketing	'marketing so finely tuned that, if applied properly, it will speak to customers almost individually'	Schlossberg (1992)
Maxi-marketing	'direct contact, dialogue and involvement with the individual prospect or customer leading to increased sales and brand loyalty'	Rapp and Collins (1990)
Database marketing	'direct marketers' (ability) to talk to their audiences as individuals in very large numbers'	Davies (1992)
New marketing	'we are witnessing the emergence of a new marketing paradigm – not a "do more" marketing that simply turns up the volume on the sales spiels of the past but a knowledge- and experience-based marketing that . . . finds a way to integrate the customer into the company, to create and sustain a relationship between the company and the customer'	McKenna (1991)
Wrap-around marketing	'two perennial problems in marketing are getting customers and keeping them. Traditionally, most marketers have spent their time getting customers. But the truth is we ought to start spending more time on the problem of how to retain the customers we have'	Kotler, quoted in Caruso (1992)
Value-added marketing	'improve existing products and concepts rather than launch new ones'	Nilson (1992)
Relationship marketing	'has as its concern the dual forces of getting and keeping customers. Traditionally much of the effort of marketing has been directed towards the getting of the customers rather than the keeping of them. Relationship marketing aims to close the loop'	Christopher *et al.* (1991)
Neo-marketing	'the basic rule is break the old rules'	Cova and Svanfeldt (1992)

marketing, transformational marketing, relationship marketing, interactive marketing, thrust marketing, macho-marketing, testosterone-marketing, take-me-I'm-yours marketing, if-I-can-think-of-a-sexy-metaphor-I-can-make-a-fortune marketing, and so on *ad infinitum* (see Table 2.5). True, the marketing of marketing nostrums has always gone on to some degree – after all, it is only through the identification of extant shortcomings and the provision of an expensive remedy that management gurus and marketing consultants can reap the rich financial rewards that are their due – but this process is arguably more prevalent than before and involves prominent, mainstream marketing scholars (Kotler, Sheth, Christopher, Piercy and their ilk), as opposed to the lunatic fringe. The lunatic fringe, suffice it to say, is writing books on postmodern marketing.

Play it Again Stan

If, to summarise our argument thus far, the conventional wisdom of main-stream textbooks and the rhetoric of its professional and academic devo-tees are to be believed, the nature of modern marketing is as follows: marketing is practised within, and influenced by, a highly complex socio-economic environment characterised by intense competition and rapid change (Figure 2.4). Scientific study of this marketing environment, by means of systematic market research and (ideally) computerised marketing intelligence systems, leads to the development of clear, formally stated marketing strategies designed to serve specific segments in precisely defined markets. These strategies are translated into cogent and carefully planned programmes of marketing action, which involve totally integrated offer-ings tailored to the identified and thoroughly researched needs of the chosen target markets. The offerings involve elements of product and price, a programme of persuasive communications, an effective distribution network, and after-sales service, where necessary (see Piercy 1992).

Apart from its obvious utility as a pedagogic aid, in so far as it implies that a logical, atomistic, step-by-step approach can help organisations match their offerings to perceived or latent customer needs and hence render manageable the unmanageable marketing environment, this conven-tional model of marketing has clear political overtones. It intimates that for an organisation to succeed in a complex, competitive, ever-changing world, marketing must not only take precedence over production, human resources, finance and so on, but that these functional areas are actually part and parcel of marketing. Marketing, if fully embraced, properly imple-mented and relentlessly pursued (and, of course, if we wish hard enough and *really, really* believe in it), is the key to prosperity and long-term busi-ness survival. As we have already noted, some enthusiasts have gone much further, claiming that marketing is a universal verity and one of the fundamentals of the human condition. Unfortunately, this can lead to

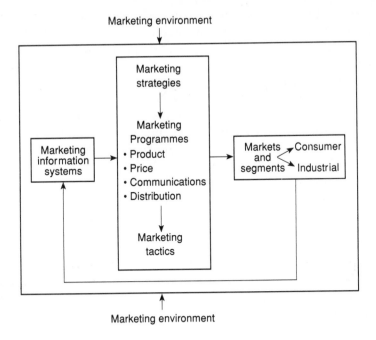

Figure 2.4 The conventional model of marketing
Source: Piercy (1992)

pronouncements which sound entirely plausible to true believers but strike agnostics as somewhat imaginative at best and sheer fantasy at worst. Consider, for example Sheth et al.'s (1988, pp.5–6) by no means atypical declaration that, 'As the population of the world increased dramatically and marketing struggled to continually advance the general standard of living for this growing populace, many members of society began to realize that some critical resources in the environment were being placed in jeopardy. . . . Fortunately, the marketing discipline has responded to society's call'. Quite.

The problem with such overweening pride and self-importance is that the hubristic fall from grace, when it occurs, is all the more precipitous. Admittedly, it may seem churlish to criticise the traditional *normative* model of marketing for its *positive* failings. After all, numerous surveys reveal a substantial discrepancy between what marketing practitioners *should* be doing, according to the conventional model, and what they *are* doing (Greenley 1986; McDonald 1992). Nevertheless, as we have noted, the complexity and flux of today's competitive environment appears to have rendered marketing mutant and unable to adapt. Extant strategic frameworks seem directionless and dangerous. The marketing mix is all mixed up. We suffer from unprincipled principles. Marketing philosophers increasingly indulge in unphilosophical mud-slinging. Tried and trusted research techniques are both untrustworthy and trying. The marketing concept is in the throes of deconceptualisation. And, even marketing intelligence is oxymoronic.

Nor is it true to claim that marketing's intra-organisational hegemonic aspirations have gone unchallenged. On the contrary, surveys of senior management reveal that, although *marketing* is considered to be of paramount importance, *marketers* are often deemed to be unprofessional and lacking in sophistication (Wong 1993). Whittington and Whipp (1992) describe how marketing's failure to develop an effective professional ideology thus far is largely responsible for its inability to overcome deeply entrenched rivals in other functional areas, especially accounting and R & D, though their suggestion that marketing should attempt to wrest the mathematical high ground from the accountants is nothing less than a recipe for professional suicide. Claiming to represent the voice of the consumer is a powerful political weapon, which is often pressed into the service of organisational change and transformation (Morgan 1992), but many accountants, human resource managers and operations researchers remain reluctant, to put it politely, to cede authority to marketing. As Willmott (1993, p.213) points out,

> when marketers advocate a generic concept of marketing, they are likely to find themselves in direct conflict with the efforts of other specialists . . . that do not necessarily fully understand, share or endorse the 'marketing concept', its professed orientation or its alleged understanding of human wants and values or its view of how organisations should be managed.

In these salutary circumstances, which contrast sharply with the bland self-assurance of the generic marketing concept, it is all too easy to dwell on the current conceptual and political shortcomings of marketing. (Indeed, as this sensitises an audience to the imminent appearance of a candidate solution to marketing's ills, such an expositional stratagem possesses considerable rhetorical power – though it is not as powerful as pretending to eschew a powerful rhetorical option.) It is, nevertheless, important to place marketing's post-imperialistic malaise in some kind of perspective. Although our specialism seems to have curbed its megalomaniac tendencies, and although the supreme self-belief of a few years back now strikes us as decidedly optimistic or slightly absurd, marketing's self-aggrandising endeavours are common to most emerging academic disciplines. When we read, for example, that 'English was not just one discipline among many but the most central subject of all, immeasurably superior to law, science, politics, philosophy or history' (Eagleton 1983, p.32); or that 'Geography provides the acid test of the adequacy of social or economic theorising' (O'Brien and Harris 1991, p.3); or indeed that, 'in the early days of

American sociology, some transatlantic disciples of Compte seriously suggested in a memorandum to the president of Brown University that all the departments of the latter should be reorganised under the department of sociology' (Berger 1963, p.17), then marketing not only seems to have conducted itself with comparative decorum, but it could also be accused of being insufficiently brash, of failing to market itself properly. More to the point, the above-mentioned 'crisis of representation' is by no means confined to ourselves. Many social sciences, most of which are longer established and more respected than marketing, are expressing uncertainty about their certitudes, suffering from unprincipled principles, floundering in conceptual quandries and experiencing existential angst. Imagine, for a moment, the self-doubt that the collapse of Marxism has precipitated among radical sociologists, economists and political scientists (e.g. Bennett 1993). Consider also the implications of latter-day challenges to the interpretive authority of social anthropologists or legal precedent for jurisprudence (Rosenau 1992). By comparison, the travails of marketing seem fairly trivial and potentially surmountable (though perhaps we have not yet given it sufficient thought).

Above and beyond the crumbs of comfort that marketers can derive from the problems that afflict other areas of academic endeavour and the realisation that our earlier imperialistic ambitions are neither unique nor unduly immodest, it is worthwhile reminding ourselves of the enormous strides that marketing has made in the post-war era. Apart from its adoption, nominally at least, by innumerable business and non-business organisations, its recognition as a reputable professional body (blessed since 1989, in the UK, with a Royal Charter) and its emergence as a legitimate, if not exactly Nobel Prize garlanded, social science with specialised degree programmes, university departments and the accompanying academic paraphernalia, the all-round standards of marketing scholarship have improved markedly in the forty years since Drucker's timeless contribution. You only have to glance through the back issues of major marketing journals to appreciate the technical, methodological and philosophical upgrading that has taken place. Technically, a host of sophisticated statistical procedures and mathematical models, such as MDS, Conjoint Analysis, LISREL and NBD Dirichlet, are regularly deployed. Methodologically, the issues of internal and external validity, reliability, generalisability, split-run testing, experimental designs and suchlike are routinely discussed. And, philosophically, the appropriateness or otherwise of various positions – realism versus relativism, empiricism versus subjectivism, positivism versus instrumentalism, etc. – are frequently debated. We have indeed come a long way baby!

If, however, you do choose to peruse the back issues of marketing's premier academic journals, you will probably be struck by at least three other closely related facts. The first of these is that many marketing 'classics', as they are referred to in the anthologies, would simply be unpublishable today. Although the quality of latter-day academic arguments may be no better – possibly worse – than a generation ago, the standards of marketing scholarship have increased so much in the interim that the *Journal of Marketing* no longer appears to have room for papers, like Kotler and Levy's (1969) prizewinner, of six pages and four references. Second, the early 'classics' are almost uniformly optimistic in their outlook, almost embarrassingly so. Their tone is redolent of having discovered the philosopher's stone, the ultimate secret of success in business and that there are no meaningful limits to marketing's applicability. Such exuberance contrasts starkly with contemporary comments on the state of marketing, where an air of pessimism, uncertainty and boundedness seems to prevail (though the boosterism of introductory textbooks remains gratifyingly undiminished). Third, some of the most enthusiastic contributors to the academic journals of the 1950s and 1960s were marketing practitioners (e.g. Keith, McKitterick, Lavidge and Steiner). Today, it is almost inconceivable that an article by a marketing practitioner would appear in the *Journal of Marketing,* the *Journal of Marketing Research,* the *Journal of Consumer Research* or the *Journal of the Academy of Marketing Science* and sightings of practitioners are becoming increasingly rare in British and European journals, which have long prided themselves on horny-handed empiricism, relevance and applicability. On the contrary, the complaint is frequently heard that marketing's premier journals contain little that is of relevance to practitioners. Many papers, admittedly, contain token 'managerial implications' sections, but cynics might conclude that these are included more to appease potentially hostile reviewers than to guide the behaviour of practising marketers. They are little more than nostalgic textual reminders of the early days of the discipline, vestigial appendages long since bypassed by the academic evolutionary process.

In light of the foregoing discussion, it is arguable that the trajectory of marketing thought in the post-war era can be described in terms of a modified wheel of retailing theory (yes, I know it's imperfect and that I've applied it to everything under the sun, but why break the habit of a lifetime?). Illustrated in Figure 2.5, this states that four stages in the evolution of retailing innovations can be discerned. At the outset, the institution is characterised by the sale of a narrow range of cut-price merchandise. This is followed by the broadening of the range of goods on offer and, subsequently, by all-round improvements in the standards, quality and sophistication of the operation. The fourth phase, however, is typified by retrenchment, contraction, intense competition, fragmentation of the offer and the emergence of a new generation of narrowly focused, price-oriented specialists.

Interpreted in these terms, the modern marketing concept emerged in the 1950s as a simple, radical and (at that time) seemingly counterintu-

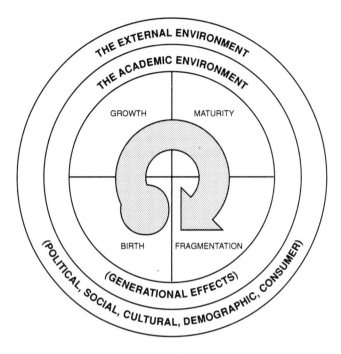

Figure 2.5 The wheel of marketing thought

itive approach to doing business, which proved to be enormously appealing, highly successful and relevant to the needs of practising managers. Through time, and thanks largely to the endeavours of Kotler and Levy, marketing progressively broadened its domain to include all manner of non-commercial fields from health care and politics to education and organised religion. This expansion was accompanied by growing technical, methodological and philosophical sophistication which, as predicted by Bartels (1974), led inevitably to academic esotericism, the pre-eminence of technique over applications and delusions of scholarship, universality and scientific status. Most importantly perhaps, this process of progressive trading-up was characterised by a failure to keep in touch with marketing's principal constituents, practising managers and prospective managers, who faced a business environment which bore little or no relation to that encountered by their predecessors of forty years beforehand. Marketing scholarship, in short, became increasingly divorced from 'reality' and this has been followed by the fragmentation of the discipline into a multiplicity of hostile factions, retrenchment and a search for a new guiding paradigm. In short, a crisis of representation.

Interestingly, however, this process of fragmentation also appears to have been accompanied by another turn of the wheel with the recent emergence of back-to-basics reformulations most notably relationship marketing. It remains to be seen whether RM will stand the test of time, but, in keeping with the first stage of the wheel model, the relationship marketing paradigm eschews esoterism, is highly focused (on the business sector), is experiencing extraordinarily rapid growth, appears to be relevant to and popular with the current generation of practising marketing managers and, not least, the overwhelming optimism of its proponents contrasts starkly with the pessimism that is evident in so many other areas of marketing endeavour – strategy, consumer research, retailing and services marketing, to name but a few. Marketing, in effect, is dead. Long live marketing.

3 What have they got in there, King Kong?

'I want to buy a spider for my godson,' I heard a far voice croak.

'Certainly,' said the assistant. 'We have a wide range of tarantulas, right up to the big bird-eaters.'

He indicated these in the showcase below. You would not want to be a bird. These were not spiders you stepped on. These were spiders who stepped on you. They looked like crabs in toupees.

'He tells me,' I said, squeaking hardly at all, 'that he'd like a Mexican red-knee.'

'Wouldn't we all?' said the assistant, a touch less accurately than he knew. 'A lovely spider, the red-knee, but you try getting them. They are the flavour of the month.'

I felt my mouth purse to a dot. You'll understand.

'What I'd suggest,' he went on, 'is a Chilean rose tarantula. Ideal. Only £35, quite docile, a very nice spider.' He pointed to a glass box. There was a ball of hair in it, the size of a fist. Very nice. Then it moved. Even nicer. Who can say why I stepped back? Doubtless, some silly atavistic twitch. I may have had a Chilean ancestor who made the stupid mistake of going out one night without his blunderbuss. . . .

'I'll take it,' I said. He reached below. 'BUT HE'LL COLLECT IT!'

Only a few customers looked round. A parrot squawked.

I paid cash. I would have given a cheque, but the bank might have queried the writing. Unsteady? Of course not! Just a bit spidery.

(Coren 1993, pp.56–7)

The Little Shop of Horrors

Variously described as 'the new perspective on life and the human condition that is sweeping across the globe' (Firat and Venkatesh 1993, p.227), 'ubiquitous, overused and probably meaningless in the global scheme of things' (Beaumont 1993, p.43), and, not least, 'the most intellectually demanding challenge facing consumer researchers' (Foxall 1992, p.403), postmodernism has attracted an enormous amount of academic and lay discussion in recent years. It is regularly profiled in quality newspapers and magazines (Fielding 1992; *Financial Times* 1992); it is the mainstay of cultural commentators and critics of the contemporary artistic scene (Adair 1992; Thorne 1993); it is part of the lexicon of management gurus and futurologists (Popcorn 1992; Drucker 1993); it has entered popular parlance as a fashionable euphemism for subversive, ironic or chaotic (Andrews 1993; Bradshaw 1993); it is evident in almost every arena of artistic endeavour – music, fashion, film, drama, architecture, photography, literature, television etc. – and, as Table 3.1 illustrates, it has infiltrated the A to Z of academic disciplines, albeit with varying degrees of success.

Given the ubiquity of postmodern discourse in today's intellectual environment, it is not surprising that the movement has been subject to all manner of diverse and mutually incompatible interpretations. As Featherstone (1991) points out, the term 'postmodern' is often employed for essentially political purposes, as a weapon in hegemonic and internecine struggles for control of individual subject areas. Postmodernism, admittedly, is not the first such conceptual weapon to be wielded in this way. The proponents of most innovative academic constructs indulge in a form of avant-garde strategy, which involves coining a term to legitimise a break within a particular field and promote a new mode of analysis ('relationship marketing' is a contemporary case in point). With postmodernism, however, this tendency is complicated by the movement's sheer ubiquity, its apparent ability to intrude into most artistic, cultural and academic walks of life, and the multiplicity of interpretations that this process inevitably spawns. In these circumstances, it is easy to see why the postmodern project has acquired such a reputation for incoherence and ambiguity. Postmodernists, of course, are quite comfortable with a state of ambiguity and incoherence, but this also provides its opponents with an almost limitless supply of ammunition with which to attack the postmodern redoubt.

The sense of uncertainty that surrounds postmodernism is not solely due to its battle-scarred physiognomy, its propensity to be pressed into all sorts of political and epistemological service. It is no less attributable to basic terminological inexactitudes and, as noted in Chapter 1, the irritating issue of indefinite definitions. A moment's reflection on the term 'postmodern', or any of the associated family of terms, reveals that it is ostensibly meaningless. If 'modern' is that which is current, up-to-date or progressive, and 'post' is that which lies beyond, comes after or exceeds, how is it possible, outside perhaps of the pages of science fiction, to be beyond the present, to be later than latest, to exceed the extant – to be postmodern? And, accepting, for a moment, the existence of this incongruous futuristic milieu, the question has to be asked, does the prefix 'post' mean that we have broken with the present – in either a positive (freedom, renewal, innovation) or negative (diminution, decay, entropy) sense – or

Table 3.1 Postmodernism's pervasiveness: some academic instances

Academic discipline	Illustrative text	Author(s) (year)
Architecture	*Post-modernism*	C. Jencks (1987)
Art history	*The End of Art Theory*	V. Burgin (1986)
Anthropology	*Constructing Knowledge*	L. Nencel and P. Pels (1991)
Civil engineering	'Postmodern engineering'	D. Platten (1986)
Cultural studies	*Postmodernism and Popular Culture*	A. McRobbie (1994)
Economics	*The Rhetoric of Economics*	D. McCloskey (1985)
Education	*Postmodern Education*	S. Aronowitz and H. Giroux (1991)
Geography	*Postmodern Geographies*	E. Soja (1989)
History	*Re-thinking History*	K. Jenkins (1991)
Law	*Postmodern Jurisprudence*	C. Douzinas *et al.* (1991)
Literature	*Postmodernism and Contemporary Fiction*	E. Smyth (1991)
Management	'Postmodern culture and management development'	S. Fox and G. Moult (1990)
Media studies	*Imagologies*	M. Taylor and E. Saarinen (1994)
Organisation studies	*Modern Organisations*	S. Clegg (1990)
Philosophy	*What is Philosophy?*	G. Deleuze and F. Guattari (1994)
Political science	*Reading the Postmodern Polity*	M. Shapiro (1992)
Psychology	*Psychology and Postmodernism*	S. Kvale (1992)
Sociology	*Sociology of Postmodernism*	S. Lash (1990)
Theology	*Shadow of Spirit*	P. Berry and A. Wernick (1992)
Women's studies	*Feminism/Postmodernism*	L. Nicholson (1990)
Zoology	*Zoology on (Post)Modern Animals*	B. Verschaffel and M. Verminck (1993)

are we attached by an umbilicus, and, if so, what is the precise nature of the connection?

These questions, needless to say, have divided commentators on the postmodern condition, as indeed have such seemingly arcane issues as the use of a hyphen (i.e. is it postmodern or post-modern?). A succinct definition of postmodernism would immediately dispel these difficulties, but once again we find ourselves in a Goldwynesque dystopia of definite maybes, verbal agreements not being worth the paper they're written on, and every Tom, Dick and Harry being called John. Contrary to what is sometimes suggested, however, there is no shortage of 'definitions' of postmodernism. As the selection in Table 3.2 indicates, these range from the humorous to the incomprehensible. Perhaps the best known exposition, and certainly the most frequently cited, is that proffered by Umberto Eco (1985, pp.67–8) in his *Reflections on The Name of the Rose*,

> I think of the postmodern attitude as that of a man who loves a very cultivated woman and knows he cannot say to her, 'I love you madly,' because he knows that she knows (and that she knows that he knows) that these words have already been written by Barbara Cartland. Still, there is a solution. He can say, 'As Barbara Cartland would put it, I love you madly.' At this point, having avoided false innocence, having said clearly that it is no longer possible to speak innocently, he will nevertheless have said what he wanted to say to the woman: that he loves her, but he loves her in an age of lost innocence. If the woman goes along with this she will have received a declaration of love all the same. Neither of the two speakers will feel innocent, both will have accepted the challenge of the past, of the already said, which cannot be eliminated; both will consciously and with pleasure play the game of irony . . . but both will have succeeded, once again, in speaking of love.

Exquisite though Eco's encapsulation of the postmodern moment undoubtedly is, and apt though an attempt to characterise postmodernism by quoting a much-quoted quotation about quotations seems to be, the overwhelming effect of the above 'definitions' is decidedly underwhelming. For many readers, I suspect, things are not much clearer than before and although such a reaction is perfectly in keeping with the postmodern *Zeitgeist*, most people's patience is probably beginning to wear thin (in the name of goodness, I hear you mutter, we are now 62 pages into this text and he *still* hasn't defined what he's talking about). If, of course, I were a died-in-the-wool postmodernist, I would play you along, especially now that I have momentarily raised your expectations of imminent elucidation, and continue to post-pone our definition until the very last sentence of this book – and then undermine *that* with a throw-away remark.

Table 3.2 Postmodernism is . . .

(i)   ' . . . a con' (Hattenstone 1992, p.7)

(ii)   'something that seems to entail buildings which have been constructed of Lego from designs commissioned by the Mayor of Toytown and novels about novelists experiencing difficulty writing novels' (Watkins 1991, p.21)

(iii)   'the Toyota of thought, produced and assembled in several different places and then sold everywhere' (Connor 1989, p.19)

(iv)   'never having to say you're sorry for not having an original idea in your head' (Beaumont 1993, p.43)

(v)   'the kiss of death to any art form, high or low' (Burchill 1994, p.4)

(vi)   'not a gesture of the cut, a permanent refusal, nor (most of all) a division of existence into polarised opposites. The postmodern scene begins and ends with transgression as the "lightning flash" which illuminates the sky for an instant only to reveal the immensity of the darkness within: absence as the disappearing sign of the limitlessness of the void within and without: Nietzsche's "throw of the dice" across a spider's web of existence' (Kroker and Cook 1986, pp.8–9)

(vii)   'the philosophy of inverted commas' (Scruton 1994, p.504)

(viii) 'an attempt to think the present historically in an age that has forgotten how to think historically in the first place' (Jameson 1991, p.viii)

(ix)   'a kind of cartoon-cat version of modernism – the cat keeps running even though he has only air beneath him' (Updike 1991, p.694)

(x)   'something that gets everywhere but no one can quite explain what it is' (Fielding 1992, p.21)

(xi)   'a chaos of competing styles and cross-references transmitted by a free-market consumerist system that creates its own reality for its own ends' (Thorne 1993, p.199)

(xii)   'finding the places of difference within texts and institutions, examining the inscriptions of indecidability, noting the dispersal of significance, identity and centred unity across a plurivalent texture of epistemological and metaphysical knowledge production' (Silverman 1990, p.1)

Although such a strategy has its attractions – it is guaranteed to drive traditional, modernist marketers into a hair-tearing frenzy and condemnation by the hair-tearers is the best advertisement that this volume could conceivably have – I shall resist the temptation on this occasion, albeit with considerable reluctance. Instead, we shall commence with very brief digression on modern times.

Before we digress, however, it is necessary to digress with a public health warning (I'm seriously tempted to digress again on digressions, but a digression on a digression on a digression is probably too much for most readers – sorry, I digress). Some of the concepts presented in this chapter, especially those pertaining to post-structuralism, are very complex, completely counterintuitive and, on first reading, may strike you as obscure or incomprehensible. Don't worry about this, as things will become clearer as the remainder of the monograph unfolds. Indeed, if you find that these ideas make you feel angry, baffled, elated, frustrated or a panic-stricken combination of all four, just remember that that's the way you're meant to feel – it's a perfectly postmodern reaction. Panic is the archetypal postmodern state of mind (see Kroker *et al.* 1989). So, when things get particularly rough – as they do – please bear in mind that it could have been a lot worse. The first draft of this chapter was half as long again, but test marketing indicated that it was proving problematical for non-specialists. Innocent creatures, in other words, have suffered on your behalf, and while you may not approve of academic vivisection, consider yourselves very lucky!

Modern Times

If, as the terminology implies, postmodernism is related in some way to modernism, it is apparent that a full understanding of the former is only possible through examination of the latter. Saussurean linguistics, after all, teaches us that constructs derive their meaning not so much from their intrinsic characteristics as their differences from other related phenomena – night-time only becomes meaningful in terms of daytime, protestantism in terms of catholicism, male in terms of female, dead in terms of alive, fact in terms of fiction, right in terms of wrong, sacred in terms of profane, and so on. When the analytic spotlight is turned on modernism, however, the irritating problem of determining the indeterminable arises once again. For some people, modern times began in 1436, with Gutenberg's adoption of movable type. For others, it commenced in 1520 when Luther rebelled against the authority of the church. Yet others argue that the American and French Revolutions of 1776 and 1789 respectively, represent crucial turning points in the history of the western world. And, a few maintain that the start of the modern dates from 1900 and Freud's *Interpretation of Dreams* (Toulmin 1990; Giddens 1990; Johnson 1991; Wagner 1994).

Although our endeavours to date the indeterminate, whether it be the beginnings of modernism or postmodernism, seem doomed to inevitable failure, attempts to do so are useful if only because they demonstrate that there is no such thing as a clear-cut starting point for an historical event. Antecedents, however amorphous, can always be identified and this inevitably gives rise to the problem of infinite regress. Habermas's (1985) belief that the onset of modernity began in the fifth century AD and Smart's (1992) assertion that its origins are inscribed in the doctrines of classical antiquity are examples of this line of reasoning. Regardless of the ultimate roots of modernism, there is nevertheless a degree of agreement that the modern world emerged from a series of profound political, economic, societal and cultural transformations which commenced with the Age of Discovery in the fifteenth century and culminated in the Agricultural and Industrial Revolutions of the nineteenth. Five developments are considered to be of particular importance: the emergence of the nation state; the advent of science; economic and technological progress; the rise of the west; and the secularisation and democratisation of society (Hall and Gieben 1992; Allen *et al.* 1992; Bocock and Thompson 1992).

Before the mid-sixteenth century, the foundations of political life in Europe rested on a rigid feudal system of interpenetrating obligations, or vassalage, between the various strata of society. Among other things, this comprised the decentralisation of power among an aristocratic ruling class, a distinctive warrior caste devoted to chivalry and an agrarian economic order in which peasants or serfs worked the land on behalf of the landowners. Although this system survived in certain countries, like Italy and Russia, until the end of the nineteenth century, a combination of religious conflict, the rise of the mercantile classes and the gradual coalescence of independent principalities, stimulated the seventeenth-century appearance of separate sovereign states. As a rule, these were organised around a particular 'nation', with its own language and culture, which was free from outside interference and whose government was regarded as the legitimate expression of national will. Interestingly, this sense of nationhood was achieved through, and reinforced by, the appropriation of past myths, folk traditions, heroes and artistic motifs, which served to generate a sense of national identity, homogeneity and belonging[1] (Gellner 1983).

Alongside the rise of the nation state, the period from the mid-seventeenth century onwards was characterised by a transformation in scientific and philosophical endeavour. From the fifth century AD, knowledge of the western world was premised on religious authority – the Biblical account of the creation, eschaton etc. – which was disseminated and perpetuated through a network of universities, colleges, churches and religious orders. However, developments in printing, the growth of literacy, and the emergence of an educated laity led to the gradual rejection of superstition and tradition, the abandonment of medieval scholasticism and the formulation of new ideas based on first-hand experience. Prefigured by the insights of Galileo, Newton and Keppler in the physical sciences and Bacon, Descartes and Locke in philosophical method, this intellectual revolution came to fruition in the Enlightenment of the eighteenth century. Like most intellectual movements, the Enlightenment exhibited considerable internal diversity, nevertheless it embraced a constellation of concepts including: a belief in the primacy of *reason* and rationality as a means of organising knowledge; *empiricism*, the idea that knowledge of the world is premised on empirical facts which can be apprehended through sense organs; the assumption that *science*, and the experimental method, is the key to isolating truth and expanding human knowledge; *universalism*, the presupposition that reason and science are invariant, apply in all circumstances and that general laws could be derived; *scepticism*, the conviction that no knowledge claims should be accepted at face value but subject to detailed, objective scrutiny; and, not least, *secularism*, a belief that the disinterested pursuit of objective knowledge would lead to the extinction of ignorance, religious dogma, superstition and oppressive clericalism, and hence to a better, more tolerant, free and open society (Porter 1990a).

Political and scientific advances may be central to the emergence of modern society, but many commentators of both Marxist and liberal persuasions have long considered the economic transformation of the eighteenth and nineteenth centuries to be the motor of western modernisation (Coleman 1992). According to the conventional narrative, population increases, rising standards of living, improvements in transportation and communications, advances in agricultural efficiency through husbandry, stockbreeding and the application of 'scientific' farming techniques, the gradual easing of protectionist trading policies and the espousal of *laissez-faire* economics, a series of astonishing mechanical and technological breakthroughs ranging from Kay's flying shuttle to Newcomen's steam engine, and, the emergence of the factory system with its economies of scale, division of labour and methods of mass production, contributed to a period of economic 'take-off' and self-sustaining growth. In short, to the birth of modern industrial society. Recent scholarship, however, indicates that the agricultural and industrial revolutions were not as 'revolutionary' as was once believed (Porter 1990b). Development was piecemeal, the old pre-modern manufacturing system of small-scale, labour-intensive, household-based units of production proved remarkably resilient, and technological innovations were taken up slowly, if at all. Nevertheless, it is undeniable that an economic transformation of some kind did occur in the mid-eighteenth century, accelerated after 1780 and culminated one hundred years later in the 'modern' economy dominated by manufacturing and commerce.

Conventional accounts of the emergence of modern life are also inclined, as Hall (1992) points out, to emphasise *internal* factors, the propitious political, economic and intellectual conditions of Western Europe which precipitated the dynamic, self-perpetuating modernisation process. This trajectory of development, however, was due in no small measure to *external* circumstances, the west's evolving relationship with 'the rest' (Said 1978). As the period of exploration, when Europe 'discovered' many of the 'new worlds', gave way to an era of trading posts, settlement, conquest, colonisation and bitter rivalry among the western powers, which climaxed in the imperialistic 'scramble' for colonies in the nineteenth century, the human and natural resources of these regions were systematically exploited, whether it be American gold, Asian spices or African slaves. The management of such far-flung empires, what is more, necessitated the development of innovative commercial organisations such as joint stock companies and trading houses, and the establishment of a permanent legal, administrative, financial and military infrastructure. Exposure to the ostensibly primitive, brutish, pagan and barbaric customs of the indigenous peoples also contributed to the imperialist belief that western culture was somehow unique, superior, triumphant, the apogee of civilisation to which all societies would eventually aspire, and the mores of which had to be transmitted to the hitherto unenlightened.

The political, scientific, economic and geographical metamorphosis of Western European modernity was accompanied, and in some respects stimulated, by a number of significant societal transformations (Bradley 1992). The political convulsions of the Age of Revolution destroyed the vestiges of feudalism, absolutism and the *ancien régime*, which were gradually replaced with less rigid, more egalitarian, proto-democratic political and judicial structures characterised by equality under the law and wider participation in the electoral process. The anti-clericalism of the *philosophes* and scientific élite contributed to the emergence of a secular society, though religious convictions in the shape of Calvinist asceticism (Weber's (1971) Protestant ethic) played an important part in the advent of the modern market economy and the rise of the middle class. The factory system that slowly replaced household-based units of production was accompanied by massive urbanisation and gross overcrowding, though the former acted as a further stimulus to economic growth and the latter eventually gave rise to programmes of comprehensive urban redevelopment. If, moreover, it were not for the colonisation process, which acted in some respects as a 'relief valve' for the demographic explosion and population migrations of the nineteenth century, the self-sustaining growth of the western world would not have occurred to the extent that it did.

Modernity may be a complex phenomenon, involving a variety of tightly interwoven, often contradictory, processes operating over an extended time-scale, but if it had to be summarised in a single word, that word would probably be *progress*. The modern condition is characterised, above all, by a belief that humanity 'has advanced in the past . . . is now advancing, and will continue to advance through the foreseeable future' (Nisbet 1980, pp.4–5). Although the idea of progress is commonplace today – we naturally expect 'next year's model' to be better than the one being replaced – it remains none the less a comparatively recent worldview (Bowler 1989; Gordon 1991). Prior to the Enlightenment of the eighteenth century, the prevailing perspective was that the past was superior to the present, that human achievements could never hope to match those of ancient civilisations and that life was lived against a backdrop of irredeemable decline (Bury 1987). Indeed, as Williams (1983) demonstrates, the word 'modern' long carried negative connotations, it was considered to be a bad thing, a dangerous idea, something that required justification. However, the seventeenth century 'battle of the books' – won by the 'moderns' – coupled with the Enlightenment-inspired belief that rational, objective, 'scientific' methods could be applied to any arena of intellectual inquiry, led eventually to remarkable advances in medicine, engineering, architecture, technology and the natural sciences. Accordingly, the comforts of modern life – washing machines, refrigerators, televisions, telephones, airplanes, computers, motor cars, microwave ovens *et alia* – have been made available to almost every stratum of western society, thereby relieving us of the existential drudgery endured by our great-grandparents. As Toulmin (1990) emphasises, compared to the bestiality, squalor and degradation of earlier times, it is our good fortune to be born into the modern world. We are better fed and educated, more affluent and live longer than our ancestors, we are free to think and say what we like, and live in the reasonable expectation that things will continue to improve, diseases will be conquered, technological breakthroughs achieved and, periodic economic crises notwithstanding, our material well-being maintained.

Not everyone, however, shares the modernist vision of cosmopolis, a society which, thanks to the application of scientific knowledge, is as rationally ordered as the Newtonian view of nature. On the contrary, critics have argued from the very outset of the Enlightenment project that the material benefits of modernity and promise of perpetual plenitude do not come without cost. The mass of society may be better off than before but, as the homeless and destitute daily remind us, the division of wealth is as unequal, arguably more unequal, as ever. Technological and industrial innovations may have produced the wonders of modern medicine, motorised transport, household appliances, the Sony Walkman and Nintendo Gameboy, but they have also spawned weapons of mass destruction, raised the spectre of genetic engineering and contributed to resource depletion, environmental despoliation and the threat of ecological catastrophe (cf. Chernobyl, *Exxon Valdez*, etc.). As Auschwitz, the Gulag, Tiananmen Square, continuing ethnic conflict and the very existence of Amnesty International indicate, the modernist dream of emancipation, freedom, equality and political tolerance has not been achieved, nor is it likely to be achieved. The rise of the west has been at the expense of the subjugation, exploitation, usurpation and Coca-colonisation of 'the rest', and left a legacy of political instability, famine, desertification, ethnic conflict, racial strife and economic dependency. Indeed, as Weber, Marx, Freud and many other prominent thinkers have argued, the modernisation of western society, for all its industrialisation, bureaucratisation and secularisation, has contributed not only to a gradual decline in morality, charity, spirituality, humanity and the sense of community but to an inexorable increase in crime, delinquency, deviance, drug abuse, mental illness, neuroses, waste, hedonism, materialism, anomie and alienation.

At the risk, therefore, of resorting to gross oversimplification or descending to crass insensitivity, the project of modernity has proved to be something of a mixed blessing. It has provided unimaginable material well-being, incalculable knowledge accumulation, astonishing aesthetic accomplishment and incredible technological innovation. But these have been achieved at a heavy social, political and environmental price. The experience of modernity is inherently paradoxical, unambiguously ambiguous, consistently inconsistent and characterised, above all, by a headlong rush into an uncertain future of ephemerality, contingency and transience, seemingly irrespective of the consequences. To be modern, Marshall Berman (1983, p.15) opines on the opening page of his magisterial text,

> is to find ourselves in an environment that promises us adventure, power, joy, growth, transformation of ourselves and our world – and, at the same time that threatens to destroy everything we are . . . modernity can be said to unite all mankind. But it is a paradoxical unity, a unity of disunity: it pours us all into a maelstrom of perpetual disintegration and renewal, of struggle and contradiction, of ambiguity and anguish. To be modern is to be part of a universe in which, Marx said, 'all that is solid melts into air'.

Back to the Future

Lest any confusion arises from the foregoing, necessarily oversimplified, narrative, it must be emphasised that the emergence of the modern world, characterised by secular political power, a monetary exchange economy and the pursuit of technological innovation and objective knowledge, was a highly complex process. It took place over an extended time-scale, it was punctuated by reversals and periodic crises, the various political, intellectual, social, economic and cultural strands were deeply interwoven – sometimes working together, sometimes cancelling out – and, contrary to the 'one path' model of modernisation that prevailed in the 1950s (see

Rostow 1990), the trajectory of development differed in contrasting social and cultural settings (USA compared to Japan or Italy, for example).

Just as the project of modernity was distinguished by the complex inter-penetration of contrasting aesthetic, technological, economic and philo-sophical components, so too the postmodern moment is made up of a multiplicity of highly diverse, often antithetical, elements. Indeed, in our endeavours to comprehend this fascinating yet frustrating phenomenon, perhaps the single most important point to note about 'postmodernism' is that it is a portmanteau or umbrella term, comprising a number of sepa-rate but interdependent strands. The first, and for most people, probably the most clearly identifiable component of the postmodern condition is a very distinctive post-war artistic and cultural movement (Boyne and Rattansi 1990). In essence, postmodernism in the arts comprises a latter-day reaction against the once radical and challenging but subsequently tamed and canonised, 'modern' movement of the first half of the present century, and a tongue-in-cheek return to pre-modern notions of represen-tation.

In architecture, for example, where the break between modernism and postmodernism is most complete, the modern movement was exemplified by the utopian Bauhaus project of Walter Gropius, Le Corbusier's cele-brated precept that 'less is more' and the functionalist, reductive, unadorned and ubiquitous 'glass box' International Style of Mies van der Rohe and his innumerable imitators. Postmodern architecture, by contrast, represents a repudiation of the modern movement's high-minded determi-nation to revolutionise, rationalise, purify and, through the use of innov-ative materials and construction techniques, transform the existing urban environment – and society as a whole – by creating it anew (Jencks 1987; Klotz 1988). Instead, postmodernists argue, architecture should be sensi-tive to its surrounding context, utilise vernacular forms and established styles, recognise the symbolic and referential qualities of buildings, endeavour to entertain rather than educate and acknowledge that its modernist aspirations to transform and elevate society are arrogant, over-bearing, authoritarian and doomed to inevitable failure. As demonstrated by Farrell's TV-am studios, Moore's Piazza d'Italia, Johnson's AT&T building, Bofill's Palace of Abraxas and Stirling's Neue Staatsgalerie, post-modern buildings are ornamental, playful, allusive, eclectic, prone to self-conscious quotation of past architectural styles and, invariably, much more popular with the general public than the concrete blocks, steel slabs, glass towers and 'machines for living in' that characterised high modernism (Jencks 1989; Caygill 1990).

Although postmodern architecture is often caricatured as candy-striped, pastel-shaded, over-ornamented neo-classicism, and condemned as 'ruth-less kitsch . . . Nazi populism . . . Heppelwhite and Chippendale in drag' (quoted in Jencks 1989, pp.12–13), the essential point is that it is predicated on pluralism, a belief that there is no architectural orthodoxy or single, overarching style. On the contrary, postmodern architects assume that all traditions have some merit; that there is a smorgasbord of architectural choice; and, that the challenge is to combine elements of extant traditions selectively in a double-coded, eclectic, hybrid and, as often as not, ironic fashion.

If the International Style and New Brutalism represent the high-water mark – or, for many people, the nadir – of architectural modernism, Pollock, Rothko and de Kooning's Abstract Expressionism and the Minimalism of Reinhardt, Ryman or Joseph occupy a broadly similar position in the visual arts (Sporre 1989; Hughes 1991; Britt 1989). They represent the culmination of modern art's anti-representational trajectory, its increasingly ostentatious repudiation of figuration, mimesis and 'life-like' pictorial representations of natural objects (impressionism, post-impressionism, expressionism, fauvism, cubism, abstraction, etc.), and, above all, its growing concern with artistic endeavour itself. In other words, art's self-absorbed desire to withdraw from the real world, purge the influence of other media, such as literature and the theatre, and focus instead on the nature, materials and limits of artistic representation – 'art for art's sake'.

Postmodern art, on the other hand, has seen a return to figuration, albeit in an ironic, parodic, eclectic, stylistically promiscuous form; a concern with the history of art rather than the creative process (e.g. the work of Mariani, Fischl and Kiefer); and, as Crowther (1990) points out, a belief that as innovation is dead the only way forward is to adopt, appropriate or allude to pre-existing styles. Thus, the 'shock of the old' has replaced the 'shock of the new'; a profusion of ephemeral styles, schools and movements has transpired; and, the demands of the market have superseded the auratic modernist vision of artist-as-hero, with a mission to shock and alienate bourgeois society (Hughes 1991). Postmodern art is also characterised by an anti-élitist focus on the artefacts of everyday life (Warhol's soup cans, Lichtenstein's comic strips, Morley's postcards), an equally ostentatious eschewal of the institutionalisation of art in museums and academies (for example, body art, street art, land art, process art, the 'wrappings' of Christo) and attempts to subvert the modernist cult of authenticity and authorship (Judd's use of mass-produced industrial objects, Levine's photographs of famous modernist photographs, Kostabi's sub-contraction of everything except his signature, etc.).

Postmodern literature, likewise, is typified by the repudiation of the austere, forbidding and anti-narrative style of modern novelists like Joyce and Proust, which, as Connor (1989, p.105) wryly notes, 'denies readers the pleasure of immediate comprehension'. Accordingly, avant-garde obscurantism, experimentation, élitism, canonisation and concern with form rather than content, have given way to realism, reader-friendly narratives, everyday language, an emphasis on the contributions of marginalised groups (women, ethnic minorities, gays, third world authors) and, not least, the revival, melding and playful exploitation of popular genres such as thriller, romance, detective story or science fiction (McHale 1987, 1993; Ruland and Bradbury 1991). Above all, however, postmodern literature is characterised by the deliberate, self-conscious foregrounding of authorship and the task of writing (McHale 1987). Known as 'parodic metafiction' and exemplified by the work of Auster, Calvino and Rushdie, this involves the intrusion of the 'author' or an author figure into the narrative, though as this author is a construct in itself, the voice of the 'genuine' author, so to speak, is effectively de-centred, hidden among the manifold folds of the narrative, lost in a bottomless pit of potential authors (for example, you didn't actually *believe* all that stuff in Chapter 1 about my researching the shoe market, job interviews and liking *Telly Addicts* or the *Reader's Digest*, did you? Give me a break!).

Besides the intrusion of author figures, postmodern literary endeavours are distinguished by the elevation, indeed canonisation, of the critic. The dominant–subordinate relationship between creator and commentator has been effectively reversed and instead of their traditional roles as 'brushers of noblemen's clothes' (Bacon), 'blood sucking insects' (Nietzsche) or 'despicable rats gnawing away at the fringes of literature' (Burgess), critics are now considered to perform a creative function in their own right (see Brown 1993b). As Ulmer (1985) emphasises, the task of post-criticism is not to tell the 'truth' about the texts under examination, but to improvise on their content, to use them as literary springboards, as means of generating new texts. A celebrated, if next to incomprehensible, example of this procedure is *Glas* by Jacques Derrida (1986). The book consists of two continuous columns of text, one comprising a discussion of Hegel and the other a discourse on Genet, both of which are interspersed by parallel themes, breaks in the typeface and puns across the columns. Or, as Derrida (1986, p.1) expresses it himself, 'two unequal columns, they say distyle, each of which – envelop(e)(s) or sheath(es), incalculably reverses, turns inside out, replaces, remarks, overlaps the other'. Thus by blurring the boundary between literature and criticism, Derrida has succeeded in giving rise to a literary form which, according to Eagleton (1983, p.139), is reminiscent of the experimental, enigmatic and ambiguous achievements of high *modernism*.

Important though literature, the visual arts and architecture undoubtedly are, they do not exhaust the aesthetic possibilities of postmodernism. Almost every cultural practice – dance, theatre, music, design and so on[2] – has been affected by the postmodern movement. Perhaps the most striking development, however, has been the effacement of the boundary between élite and popular cultural pursuits (Lash 1990). Just as popular preoccupations have been appropriated by 'high' culture

Table 3.3 Postmodern popular culture: some examples

Trait	Examples
Juxtaposition	Grunge/punk fashions
	Folk-rock, jazz rock, world music
	TV docudramas/living soaps/*Twin Peaks*
	Films that mix times, places, looks, genres (*Blue Velvet*, *True Romance*)
Plurivalence	'There is no fashion only fashions'
	'There are no rules only choices'
	'Anything goes'
	'Do your own thing'
Retrospection	Spoof rock groups (Bjorn Again, Dread Zeppelin), television programmes (*KYTV*, *The Day Today*), radio stations (Steve Wright)
	Golden-oldie television and radio stations (UK Gold, Capital Gold)
	'Nostalgia' movies (*American Graffiti*, *Raiders of the Lost Ark*)
	Recycling fashions (the mini, antique perfumes, one-piece swimming costumes)
Interactive	TV audience participation (*Crimewatch*, *Challenge Anneka*)
	Films within films (*Last Action Hero*, *The Purple Rose of Cairo*)
	Deconstruction in fashion
	Sampling, rap music
Self-referentiality	Television programmes about television programmes (*Gary Shandling*)
	Television programmes about fashion/the media (*The Look*, *Absolutely Fabulous*)
	Films about making films (*The Player*), rock bands (*This is Spinal Tap*), television series (*The Flintstones*, *Maverick*, *The Fugitive*) and the television industry (*Broadcast News*)
	Newspaper analyses of TV soaps, supermodels, newspaper sales, etc.

(vernacular architecture, pop-art, literary genres) so too serious treatment is now accorded to what were once dismissed as 'low' or degraded cultural forms – film, television, popular music, fashion and so on. Indeed, the latter are often cited as clearest manifestations of postmodernism in the arts (Wyver 1989; Wilson 1990; Denzin 1991; Beadle 1993). Summarised in Table 3.3, they all exhibit the following distinctively postmodern tendencies: first, a propensity for bizarre juxtapositions, genre combinations and general mixing of codes; second, they are plurivalent in that there is no single, dominant or overarching style; third, a retrospective inclination to appropriate and recycle past styles often in an ironic or parodic manner; fourth, the distinction between audience and performer is dissolved or foregrounded, through the deliberate cultivation of an interactive, 'seams showing' quality; and, fifth, they are narcissistic, especially prone to self-referentiality and seem preoccupied with what Cook (1992, p.190) describes as 'intra-discoursal' (films about films, fashions about fashion – cf. Moschino) and 'inter-discoursal' voices (television programmes on the cinema, popular music columns in newspapers, etc.).

The blurring of the boundaries between high art and low is manifest in all manner of cultural spheres (opera stars topping the hit parade, classical music performed by 'punks', the video art of Nam Jum Paik, the 'cells' of Walt Disney sold at auction) but the seriousness with which popular culture is now treated is nowhere better illustrated than in the changes that have recently been wrought in museums (Crimp 1985; Walsh 1992). Long regarded as the codifier, protector and repository of aesthetic accomplishment, artistic genius and national pride, museums have not only burgeoned in number but are increasingly devoted to the vernacular, the regional and the quotidian. As Urry (1990, p.130) points out, 'there has been a quite stunning fascination with the popular and a tendency to treat all kinds of object, whether it is the Mona Lisa or the old cake tin of a Lancashire cotton worker, as almost equally interesting'. Examples include industrial museums, folk museums, open-air museums and museums of photography, design, television, fashion, toys, teddy bears, motor cars, perfume, pencils and many more. Postmodern museums, moreover, are characterised by the abandonment of traditional display cases, silent contemplation and the aura of priceless authenticity, and their replacement with an anti-élitist emphasis on participation, involvement, sound and lighting effects, performance, and the creation of spectacular multimedia 'experiences'. This tendency is epitomised by heritage centres, such as the Jorvick Centre in York, which comprise a curious mixture of museum and theatre. Everything is meant to be authentic but, like the perfect simulacra that they are, nothing actually is, not even the smells.

Henry: Portrait of a Serial Killer

If the first element of postmodernism derives from the realms of aesthetic and cultural accomplishment, the second strand, which is often accorded the term 'postmodernity', rests upon social and economic circumstances (Smart 1993). Indeed, if prioritisation were not proscribed by postmodern thinkers, many would maintain that the dramatic economic changes of recent years represent the single most important influence on the postmodern condition. This is especially true of those on the far left of the political spectrum. After all, one of the root metaphors of Marxism ('base–superstructure') implies that changes in economic circumstances affect events in the artistic, social, intellectual and cultural spheres. Few Marxists, admittedly, now subscribe to the view that the superstructure, made up of legal, political, religious, aesthetic and philosophical phenomena, is *determined* by the base (or substructure) of productive forces and the relations of production. Indeed, both Marx and Engels noted that, as a consequence of their relative 'distance' from the mode of production, developments in artistic or cultural milieux may lag or fail to correspond to events in the material base. Likewise Lukács (1971), Williams (1977) and the critical theorists of the Frankfurt School, especially Adorno and Benjamin, emphasise the dialectical nature of base–superstructure relations and the issue of 'overdetermination', the multiplicity of interacting factors that influence economic and aesthetic change (Held 1980). Nevertheless, it is widely accepted by Marxist thinkers that alterations in economic conditions provide the motor of cultural and intellectual development, albeit in the final instance (Adams 1991).

It almost goes without saying that the profound economic transformations which have taken place since the Second World War have been christened with a plethora of 'posts' – post-capitalist, post-Marxist, post-maturity and post-economic, to name but a few. However, perhaps the most important and certainly the most widely discussed of these are 'post-industrialism' and 'post-Fordism'. The former, as Rose (1991) has shown, dates from Arthur J. Plenty's futuristic speculations in the early years of the present century, but it is conventionally associated with the work of American sociologist Daniel Bell. In his seminal text, *The Coming of Post-industrial Society*, Bell (1973) argued that theimpending post-industrial era would be characterised by five main components:

- an 'axial principle', or driving force, concerning the centrality of theoretical knowledge as the source of innovation and policy formation;
- the reorganisation of occupational structures characterised by the decline of predominantly blue-collar workforces and the rise of the professional and technical class;

- a 'future orientation', especially in terms of the control of technology and technological assessment;
- the creation of a new 'intellectual technology' for decision making; and,
- a shift in the economic domain from the energy-driven production of goods to the information-driven production of services.

Although Bell was not alone in his anticipation of the emerging post-industrial order (see for example Touraine 1971), the emphasis placed on knowledge, information and new technology is central to most analyses. As Figure 3.1 illustrates, post-industrialisation is associated with a constellation of socio-economic changes, but the central idea pertains to a relative decline of heavy manufacturing, smoke-stack factories, large unionised workforces, etc. and the rise of knowledge-based industries organised around the clean technologies of information, computerisation and microelectronics, and accompanied by the emergence of service-based economy where an ever-increasing proportion of employment and wealth creation is accounted for by the tertiary (retailing, transportation), quaternary (trade, finance) and quinary (health, education) sectors. In short, Silicon Glen rather than Clyde shipbuilding, science parks rather than steel works, building societies rather than bricks and mortar, radios and televisions rather than lathes and widgets, and mining museums rather than working pits (Lash and Urry 1987; Allen 1992).

Alongside the knowledge-, information- and services-driven transformations of economic life generally, manufacturing industry has witnessed a series of sweeping changes – stimulated in part by developments in information technology – which together constitute a significant post-war shift from the traditional 'Fordist' regime (Murray 1989; Harvey 1989). Although Henry Ford did not invent the system of industrial mass production that bears his name, Ford's River Rouge plant (opened in 1920) exemplified many of the features which are commonly associated with this approach to manufacturing:

- economies of scale achieved through mass production of standardised products for protected national markets;
- dedicated, task-specific machinery, standardised parts and a moving assembly line;
- a semi-skilled, albeit highly paid, labour force performing specific, routinised tasks according to Taylor's principles of scientific management;
- hierarchical, bureaucratic forms of organisation characterised by functional specialist, divisional structures and centralised decision taking; and,
- the use of mass marketing techniques to stimulate mass consumption, thereby maintaining and perpetuating the whole process.

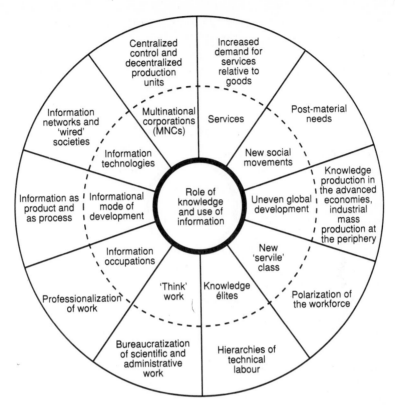

Figure 3.1 Post-industrialism: dynamics and trends

Source: Allen (1992)

This Fordist emphasis on mass markets, with its correlates of large-scale worker deskilling, trades unionism and Keynesian policies of national economic management, has since been superseded by the post-Fordist model of 'flexible specialisation' (Allen 1992; Kenney and Florida 1992). Summarised in Figure 3.2, this regime involves: firstly, the extensive use of computer-controlled and integrated flexible manufacturing systems which, by dint of their ability to fabricate a diverse array of semi-bespoke products in short but profitable production runs, generate economies of scope as well as economies of scale. Secondly, new forms of work organisation involving smaller but more adaptable, multi-skilled workforces committed to teamwork, total quality, mutual support and monitoring, and the eschewal of traditional job demarcation lines, coupled with the increased casualisation of labour through the use of short-term contracts and part-time working at both shop floor and managerial levels. Thirdly, changes in management structure comprising flat or matrix organisational forms, fewer layers, less hierarchy, rigidity and bureaucracy, greater autonomy among – and competition between – divisions or subsidiaries

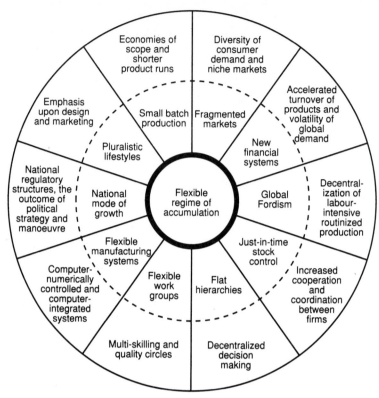

Figure 3.2 Post-Fordism: dynamics and trends
Source: Allen (1992)

and, in theory at least, a more egalitarian managerial ethos. Fourthly, alterations in external relations consisting, on the one hand, of strategic
alliances, joint ventures or consortia with organisations of a comparable
size and, on the other hand, a process of vertical disintegration whereby
production processes are subcontracted to networks of small, specialist
suppliers linked to the core company by just-in-time materials handling
and computerised stock control procedures. Finally, the transition from
Fordism to post-Fordism is marked by a geographical paradox where
routine, labour-intensive production is decentralised, on a global scale,
often to low-cost third world countries, but counterbalanced by the emergence of new 'industrial districts', distinctive clusters of small, highly interdependent, family-owned companies specialising in a particular category
of products – garments, metal goods, electronics, etc. As Cooke (1990,
p.163) points out, this harks back in certain respects to *pre*-modern times;
it is 'a revival of an early-modern, neo-paternalist method of incorporating
the worker into something approaching an industrial "community" with
its own distinctive character'.

This post-war revolution in economic life has been paralleled by a series of profound but paradoxical societal transformations (Turner 1990; Bocock and Thompson 1992; Hall *et al*. 1992). The emergence of an increasingly global ethos, characterised by the rise of transnational organisations from IBM to Greenpeace, and the higher profile of supra-national institutions such as the EC, UN and G7, are counterpointed by the proliferation of putative nation states from the ruins of Eastern Europe and a growing sense of regional identity in countries which are comparatively long-established (e.g. Scotland, Quebec, Catalonia, Pied-mont). Traditional party politics, trades unionism and class-based political activism have been eclipsed by the advent of 'micro-politics', small-group-orientated, single-issue-driven political groupings – nuclear weapons proliferation, gay rights, anti-abortion campaigns, the poll tax revolt, pit closure and transport policy protests, environmental concerns, animal rights, education provision and so on.[3] Albeit lacking in overall cohesion and hence accused of political impotence, 'minority' issues like gender, ethnicity and sexual proclivity now comprise the foci of post-modern social movements and, in so doing, serve to rekindle the sense of community erased by the imposed uniformity of post-war urban redevel-opment programmes. As Maffesoli (1988) observes, however, this renewed sense of solidarity is ephemeral and invariably predicated on a temporary coming together of an emotional community – a postmodern 'tribe' – in which short-lived but extremely intense feelings of empathy and cama-raderie are experienced.

Alongside the creation of these 'communities of affect', which are often organised around issues of moral concern and united by television and the mass media (e.g. Live Aid, Free Mandela, AIDS Awareness), religious observance, orthodoxy and ecumenism have beat a retreat in the face of new age and charismatic dogma, self-actualization doctrine, radical funda-mentalism, religious intolerance, tele-evangelism and, as the paradoxical sight of prominent physicists expounding on 'the mind of God' bears witness, scientific intrusions (Hawking 1988; Küng 1991). The nuclear family and 'traditional' family values have collapsed into a tangle of single parenthood, serial monogamy, disfunctionalism, delinquency and narcis-sistic self-absorption combined with the emergence of the so-called post-modern family, which at first glance resembles the traditional extended family unit but on closer examination reveals a complex mixture of friends and relatives (Stacey 1990). Likewise, the luxury of 'finding oneself' has been undermined by assertions that the unified personality, or even the 'split subject' identified by Freud, is little more than a *mélange* of roles or personae which are adopted, employed and abandoned in rapid succession. The 'wife and mother' of the breakfast table, may give way to the 'career woman' during the working day, the 'sports enthusiast' of the evening or the 'fashion victim', 'DIY enthusiast' or 'culture vulture' of the weekend. The 'empty self' is thus refilled, decanted and replenished with whatever persona the occasion demands (Cushman 1990).

For many, this inexorable fragmentation of modern life, the widespread belief that 'anything goes' and the apparent loss of a fixed point of societal reference cannot be divorced from latter-day advances in telecommunications, information technology, cybernetic networks, expert systems and the mass media generally (Baudrillard 1988a). Such is the ubiquity and instantaneity of satellite communications, for example, that world events are not only brought within easy and immediate reach, but they are increasingly pre-empted or indeed created by the media themselves (consider the cable television crews who were already in place, waiting on the beaches to record the US Marines' recent 'invasion' of Somalia, to the evident astonishment of the soldiers concerned). It is arguable, however, that in an era where news increasingly *makes* the news, television's ceaseless parade of extraordinarily vivid images has denuded people's ability to discriminate between important and trivial, past and present, global and local, fact and fiction, today and tomorrow, and cause and effect, other than in terms of the nature, drama and intensity of the images themselves. Telecommunications has created, in Debord's (1994) celebrated phrase, a 'society of the spectacle'; a three-minute soundbite culture of bored, channel-hopping, MTV-watching couch potatoes; a congeries of restless, cynical, world-weary, self-obsessed hedonists demanding instant gratification and ever-escalating doses of stimulation; a 'moronic inferno of narcissists cretinised by television' for whom literacy and mathematical acumen is less important than an ability to set the video recorder and familiarity with the intricacies of the latest soap opera or computer game (Lasch 1979; Bloom 1987; Callinicos 1989).

According to Jean Baudrillard (1983, 1988a), the much-vaunted high priest of postmodernism, the condition of postmodernity is perhaps best portrayed as a milieu in which there is more and more information but less and less meaning, where everything is commodified and subject to the demands of the market, and in which the production, distribution and manipulation of *image* – the 'political economy of the sign' – is all-important. Postmodernity is a depthless world of simulation, where images bear no discernible relationship to external reality and where artifice, in the words of the postmodern rock group U2, is 'even better than the real thing'. Nowhere is this tendency better illustrated than in Disneyland, which in many respects is more authentic in its inauthenticity than the surrounding environment because Disneyland at least acknowledges its artificiality. For Baudrillard (1983, 1988b), indeed, Disneyland has been created as imaginary in order to make us believe that the rest is real, to disguise the fact that the rest of Los Angeles and America is no longer real but a simulation. In postmodernity, therefore, the 'real' world has imploded into a state of hyperreality, a hallucinogenic simulation of the non-existent, a place where boundaries collapse, opposites coalesce, fact and fiction are fused, and theory and practice metamorphose.

Ironically, however, this demise of the real spawns a nostalgic search for authenticity, though as nostalgia and authenticity are easily reproduced or created, this tendency is also sucked inexorably into Baudrillard's black hole of hyperreality, as are any attempts at subversion or critique. In these circumstances, the only forms of resistance are either the 'fatal strategies' of pushing the logic of the system to its absolute limits (incessant consumption, for example), or silence, apathy, death and a refusal to take things seriously (Baudrillard 1990b, 1993a). For Baudrillard, then, postmodernity is characterised by a culture of exhaustion, where every possibility in art, life, theory, politics and society has already been tried and the only option is to recycle the forms that already exist. Originality is impossible, history has ended, the future has already happened and all that remains is to play with the pieces among the anorexic ruins (Baudrillard 1988c, 1989).

Baudrillard's undeniably brilliant but profoundly pessimistic vision of postmodern times is paralleled in certain respects by the views of two other leading left-wing commentators on postmodernity, Frederick Jameson (1985, 1991) and David Harvey (1989), both of whom have spawned an extensive secondary literature (e.g. Kellner 1989; Morris 1992, 1993a). Although careful to avoid the determinism of a crude base–superstructure model, Jameson maintains that postmodernism in the arts (characterised by 'pastiche' and 'schizophrenia'[4]) comprises 'the cultural logic of Late Capitalism'. Contrary, however, to the traditional Marxian model, television, music, art, literature, film and so on no longer represent epiphenomena of economic relations; they now constitute the central focus of economic activity. They are no longer evaluated against oppositional standards – the ability to shock or alienate – but judged in terms of how much money they make. Culture, in short, has been commodified and commodities have become cultural. Harvey (1989), likewise, notes the close relationship between postmodern cultural phenomena and the rise of post-industrialism-cum-post-Fordism, though he rejects Jameson's assertion that there has been a distinct break between modernity and postmodernity. The present era, rather, has seen an acceleration of pre-existing trends, a new and particularly intense round of 'time–space compression' – the speeding up of transportation, communications, capital circulation, etc. and the effective shrinking of distance that this process entails – which has accompanied the development of capitalism since the eighteenth century and which is reflected, refracted and re-transmitted in the cultural sphere.

The French Connection

The third and for most people the most convoluted and impenetrable aspect of the postmodern condition derives from the work of several prominent, widely cited and much-vaunted post-structuralist thinkers, principally Jacques Derrida, Roland Barthes, Michel Foucault, Jacques Lacan and, perhaps the most celebrated postmodern commentator of all, Jean-François Lyotard (others include Kristeva, Cixous, and Deleuze and Guattari). Although the contributions of these post-structuralists are many and varied, ranging across fields as diverse as linguistics, literary theory, philosophy, history and psychoanalysis, they all exhibit – like the 'structuralists' before them – a concern with textuality, narrative, discourse and *language* (Sturrock 1979a, 1993; Young 1981; Harland 1987).

Language, according to structuralist orthodoxy, does not *reflect* reality but actively *produces* it.[5] The world, in other words, is not composed of meaningful entities to which language attaches names in a neutral, transparent fashion. Language, rather, is involved in the construction of reality, the understandings that are derived from it and the sense that is made of it. (In Japanese, for instance, the term 'blue' is usually translated as *aoi*, but there is no equivalence of meaning as Japanese speakers also use *aoi* to refer to objects that would be described as 'green' in English. Equally, when an English speaker looks at an Arctic landscape, he or she sees 'snow', whereas an Eskimo, with over fifty words for 'snow', sees much more when looking at the exact same landscape.) Indeed, as individuals, we are not free to deploy language as we see fit every time we write or speak. On the contrary, language precedes and exceeds us, it is something we are initiated into, our every utterance is governed or (unconsciously) shaped by deep, pre-existing structures of language. Thus, the free-thinking, self-knowing, autonomous human 'subject' of Cartesian discourse – the intentional being whose desires, motives and beliefs are the source of all meaning and a principle of explanation for thinkers of the humanist tradition – turns out to be less a *producer* of language than the *product* of it. The human subject, as Culler (1979, p.174) points out, is 'something constituted by or resulting from the play of systems rather than a controlling consciousness which is the master and ultimate origin of systems'.

Although most post-structuralists subscribe to this 'death of the subject' thesis and maintain that meaning derives from differences internal to the sign system itself (rather than the common-sense belief that meaning involves some sort of relationship between the linguistic sign and external reality), they reject the idea of a single, deep, determining structure and, in Jacques Derrida's (1991, 1992) case especially, emphasise the inherent instability of the linguistic sign (Hoy 1985; Boyne 1990; Wood 1992). According to Saussure, the linguistic sign is made up of two parts, like two sides of a coin or a sheet of paper: the *signifier*, the word or sound; and the *signified*, the mental concept that is evoked when the sound is heard or word encountered (thus, the word 'coke' brings to mind the idea of a soft drink). The relationship between signifier and signified is completely arbitrary but it is fixed by convention (the word 'coke' does not have any inherent coke-like qualities). A moment's reflection, however, reveals that this relationship is by no means stable. If we look up the signifier 'coke' in a dictionary, several potential meanings (signifieds) are available – the soft drink, cocaine, coal from which gas has been extracted, the core of an apple, etc. – and if any of these signifiers, such as 'drink', are looked up in turn we encounter yet more signifieds (to swallow, the sea, to absorb, intemperance) and so the process continues indefinitely. Meaning, in short, turns out to be very difficult to tie down. It is contingent, unstable, temporary, suspended, postponed and very much dependent on the specific use context. Contra Saussure, the signifier and signified are not like two sides of a coin or sheet of paper, but two constantly moving layers fused together temporarily in the act of reading or listening. For Derrida, then, meaning is not simply a question of differences between individual linguistic signs, as Saussure would have it, but a relentless process of deferral, which he terms *différance* (meaning to differ and to defer), where meaning is constantly flickering, simultaneously present and absent (Derrida 1978a, 1987a). Indeed, this tendency is compounded by the very act of reading (or listening) where the meaning of a sentence is suspended and modified as the process unfolds (Eagleton 1983). In effect, each linguistic sign in a chain of signs contains 'traces' of the signs that precede it, inscribes itself on the signs still to come and, even when read in context, the chain may contain echoes of meaning from other, entirely different texts and contexts (yea, I hate when that happens).

This inherent instability of language is central to deconstruction, the analytical technique for which Jacques Derrida is best known (in the USA, for example, post-structuralist literary theory is generally subsumed under the term 'deconstruction') and which he has applied to the philosophical and literary canon, thereby denuding the traditional boundary between the two (Culler 1983a; Ellis 1989; Broadbent 1991; C. Johnson 1993). Although it has entered popular parlance as a chic synonym for 'criticism', 'subversion', 'investigation' or 'analysis', and although it is a methodology that eschews its methodological status, deconstruction is a procedure for interrogating texts, which, by means of careful and detailed reading, seeks to expose their inconsistencies, contradictions, unrecognised assumptions and implicit conceptual hierarchies. To show, as Norris (1991, p.35) aptly puts it, that a text 'cannot mean what it says . . . or say what it means'. The objective of the deconstructive exercise, however, is not to resolve textual inadequacies, elucidate inherent ambiguities, acknowledge the unacknowledged and reverse pre-existing conceptual rankings, as this merely substitutes one subjective reading for another. The purpose rather is to demonstrate that there are no hidden truths within a text, that there is no fixed, correct or privileged interpretation and, not least, that the desire for a 'centre', or focal point of transcendent meaning, which has characterised the entire project of western philosophy since Plato, is itself meaningless. Meaning is contingent, unstable, dispersed, deferred, absent, disseminated across all manner of other texts and, as often as not, reliant on sublimated metaphor. This is true even in philosophical texts which purport to have identified pure, self-authenticating, eternal truths. Indeed, just as Baudrillard contends that Disneyland is more real than reality, so too it is arguable that literature is *less* deluded than philosophy because it at least acknowledges its reliance on linguistic tropes and rhetorical devices.

Multiplicity of meaning is equally important to the work of celebrated literary critic and cultural commentator, Roland Barthes (Sturrock 1979b; Culler 1983b). Best known in the marketing community for his early semiological studies of advertising, fashion and the detritus of popular culture (see Chapter 5), the later Barthes emphasised the inherent plurality of texts. In his seminal essay 'The death of the author', Barthes rejected the established humanist view that the author is the origin or creator of a text, the source of its meaning and the only authentic voice of interpretation. Like the users of language whose every speech act is essentially pre-formed, authors merely reassemble existing texts – the 'always already written' – and all works of literature are therefore, 'a multi-dimensional space in which a variety of writings, none of them original, blend and clash' (Barthes 1977a, p.146). Literary texts are inherently intertextual. They are woven out of the fragments of pre-existing writings, contain all manner of allusions to and echoes from other sources, and, in Barthes' (1977b, p.160) striking phrase, 'they are quotations without inverted commas'. Only readers can bring temporary meaning to a text as unity lies not in its origin but in its destination.

For Barthes, in fact, readers are free to enter a text at will, undermine or reject the author's intentions, take 'pleasure in the text' (Barthes 1990a) and generate as many meanings as they like, none of which are privileged. In this respect, Barthes (1990b) distinguishes between 'writerly' and 'readerly' texts. The former, of which *Finnegan's Wake* is a prime example, are so written as to encourage the reader to participate in the process, to spawn additional meanings and interpretations, to 'rewrite' the material as he or she goes along. The latter, such as standard realist novels or scientific papers, are comparatively closed, in that they attempt to control meaning, and are designed to be read rather than rewritten. Even self-evidently realist texts, however, can evoke a multiplicity of interpretations. In what is often regarded as one of the crowning achievements of post-structuralist literary criticism, Barthes (1990b) conducted an enormously detailed analysis of *Sarrasine*, a short story by Balzac, and demonstrated how a virtually infinite number of different, but equally legitimate, interpretations is possible. Thus there is no 'true' meaning, no 'right' meaning, no 'determinate' meaning, no 'intentional' meaning, no 'single' meaning, no 'final' meaning, even in works which are conventionally regarded as models of transparency (see Johnson 1981).

French Connection II

Although Derrida's deconstruction and Barthes' espousal of writerly texts are overtly democratic, in that no approach or interpretation is deemed superior to any other, it would be wrong to assume that their work is politically neutral. On the contrary, both Derrida and Barthes considered their analytical practices to be politically motivated, attempts to undermine conventional systems of thought and the associated apparatus of bourgeois social institutions and structures of power (Eagleton 1983). Power, and the all-pervasive operation of power, also lies at the heart of the intellectual project of Michel Foucault, the prolific, supremely gifted, post-structuralist philosopher-cum-historian (Smart 1985; Shumway 1989; Macey 1993). Rejecting the Enlightenment-inspired belief in reason, emancipation and progress, Foucault argued that modern forms of knowledge and social institutions may seem natural, impartial and liberal, but they actually comprise new regimes of power and domination, which are transmitted by the human sciences through their specification of behavioural 'norms' and sanctioned by prevailing but imperceptible forms of *discourse* (Foucault 1967, 1972, 1974, 1977).

Discourses are particularly important to Foucault's project. They are ways of knowing, preconditions of knowledge, sets of linguistic rules which permit some modes of thought and deny others. Discourses determine what can be written, thought, acted upon and, indeed, counts as knowledge in any given field (what is 'madness', 'truth', sexual 'perversion'?; who decides?). Although by no means immutable or universal, discursive formations exert enormous power over human behaviour, they shape our desires, identity, body and soul, and constitute our very being, our sense of ourselves. Thus, the conscious, free-thinking, intentional human subject is neither absolute nor autonomous, but a *construct*, an effect of language, desire and the unconscious, an epiphenomenon of the prevailing discourse in a multiplicity of individual sites and loci of power. Contrary, therefore, to the conventional notion that power is repressive, located within the state or the ruling classes and imposed from above, Foucault maintains that power can be productive, it is ubiquitous, heterogeneous, de-centred, pervasive, inscribed in the practices of everyday life – schools, hospitals, families, the body – and only subsequently taken up by larger structures such as class or the state. State power is the end point of the process, a consolidation of innumerable, individual exercises of power and, as such, cannot be grasped through grand, systematic, overarching conceptual schemata. In these circumstances, the task of the historian is not to formulate universal theories of progressive development and human subjectivity, but to focus on singular events and local contexts, to identify ruptures and discontinuities in the historical record, to adopt a plural, fragmentary, differentiated, spatially specific mode of analysis, to draw attention to the voices of excluded, forgotten, marginalised groups, and to seek to resist domination through 'technologies of the self', the endeavours of individuals to define and re-create their own identities through personal ethical standards and self-denial (Foucault 1990).

If Michel Foucault is generally regarded as the most adroit post-structuralist thinker, even by those who have little time for this particular line of thought (Paglia 1992), Jacques Lacan is widely considered to be the most abstruse (Sarup 1992; Žižek 1992). Surrealist poet turned psychoanalyst, Lacan's published works are a paradigm of post-structuralist impenetrability, having been variously described as 'bafflingly opaque' (Eagleton 1983, p.164), 'exceptionally difficult' (Bowie 1991, p.2) and 'prose of such flamboyance and syntactic oddity, that few can follow it with ease and many cannot follow it at all' (Sturrock 1993, p.98). As these remarks emanate from individuals who are *sympathetic* to the Lacanian cause, the somewhat less restrained comments of his critics are perhaps best left to your own febrile imaginations. Indeed, as the entire psychoanalytical project is now subject to severe and mounting criticism (e.g. Eysenck 1985; Gellner 1993; Kerr 1994), it is tempting to devote as little time to Lacan as he did to his patients (Lacan's sessions were notoriously idiosyncratic, often only five to ten minutes long) or pass him by in the strict Freudian posture of silence. It is necessary to acknowledge, however, that Lacan's reinterpretation of Freud has had an impact on all manner of fields from feminism and film theory to Marxism and, as we shall note in Chapter 6, marketing.

From a post-structuralist perspective, Lacan's principal contribution was his substitution of Freud's essentially mechanistic model of the unconscious with one that is linguistic. According to Lacan (1977), the unconscious is structured like a language, language *creates* the unconscious and, as is the case with language, the unconscious is never entirely under our control. Adopting Saussure's model of the divided linguistic sign, Lacan, like Derrida, stressed its innate instability, the continual slippage of meaning between signifier and signified. In other words, between what patients say or report about their dreams etc. and what these mental constructs actually refer to or contain. Language, likewise, is an integral part of Lacan's hypothesised three-stage process of personal development. Born into a condition of 'lack', which we spend the rest of our lives trying and failing to overcome, we pass first through the pre-linguistic 'mirror phase', where, as a result of (mis)recognising ourselves in a (metaphorical) mirror, we begin to construct a sense of our own self-identity. The second phase, 'fort-da', comprises our introduction into language, the order of the symbolic, which as most post-structuralists stress pre-dates us, shapes us and differentiates us one from another. Hence, it is within language that we move beyond the vague notion of ourselves as separate individuals and begin to acquire our human subjectivity, though given the intrinsic instability of language this sense of being a unique individual is de-centred and decidedly fragile. The final stage of development is the Oedipus complex, our eventual encounter with sexual difference and desire. Desire is the unending but ultimately doomed pursuit, from signifier to signifier and substitute to substitute, of the 'real', the transcendent fixed signified, the initial moment of plenitude, of pure self-identity that we forever, but can never, hope to attain. As Eagleton (1983, p.185) points out, 'In Lacanian theory, it is an original lost object – the mother's body – which drives forward the narrative of our lives, impelling us to pursue substitutes for this lost paradise in the endless metonymic movement of desire.'

Narrative, story-telling and (Wittgensteinian) language games are also integral to the project of Jean-François Lyotard, perhaps the most celebrated commentator on the postmodern condition (Benjamin 1989; Readings 1993). In a detailed report on the nature of knowledge in developed societies, which brought together elements of post-structuralist philosophy, post-industrial theory and postmodernism in the arts, Lyotard (1984) challenged the underlying assumptions of the western world view. Modern science is characterised by its rejection of superstition, myth, story-telling and narrative-based knowledge of traditional societies, but, for Lyotard, the modernist search for impartial knowledge, valid and verifiable laws, absolute truths and eventual release from slavery and oppression, is itself a myth, legitimised by a high-level storyline, or *meta-narrative*, such as the pursuit of 'progress', 'emancipation', 'reason' or 'profit'. In essence, 'scientific knowledge cannot know or make known that it is true knowledge without resorting to the other, narrative, kind of knowledge, which from its point of view is no knowledge at all' (Lyotard 1984, p.29).

Since the Second World War, however, the myth of the modernist, Enlightenment project has been exposed by a catalogue of political and social catastrophes (the Holocaust, neo-colonialism, ecological crises, social polarisation), and the growing realisation that what passes for reason and understanding is really a form of domination which has led to the erasure of difference, plurality and heterogeneity through its ability to enforce consensus and exclude, marginalise or silence dissent. A degraded culture of 'anything goes', or 'slackening', where taste is irrelevant and the money is the only thing that matters now appears to prevail (Lyotard 1984, p.76). Moreover, the potency of metanarratives has declined as a result of the social changes and technological breakthroughs which have accompanied the emergence of our post-industrial, information-rich, computerised era and which have profoundly affected the ways in which knowledge is acquired, classified, stored and exploited. The upshot of these developments, Lyotard maintains, is that knowledge is fragmenting into more and more specialised sub-fields, each with its own incompatible way of proceeding and separate vocabulary (or self-legitimising language game), and the scientific establishment is becoming increasingly concerned with power and self-perpetuation instead of the search for objective knowledge and universal laws. 'The goal', as Lyotard (1984, p.46) puts it, 'is no longer truth but performativity'. Pragmatism, not the pursuit of abstract knowledge, is the order of the day; and, indeed, it seems that the only way to make a new move in the game of science is to rearrange existing information in a different or unusual way.

The postmodern condition, therefore, is one of 'incredulity towards metanarratives', a refusal to accept that there is one particular way of doing things and one way only. No form of knowledge is privileged, no overarching theory obtains and rather than search for non-existent truths, we should be sensitive to differences and the perspectives of marginalised groups, exercise the art of judgement in the absence of rules, emphasise the importance of pragmatism, provisionality and local forms of knowledge, and revel in the proliferation of incompatible language games. We should endeavour to tolerate the incommensurable; embrace the postmodern ethos of uncertainty, agonistics and fragmented individuality; eschew foundationalist or totalising systems of thought; resist the temptation to seek consensus, since this only suppresses heterogeneity; adopt an investigative aesthetic premised on the 'sublime' (a mode of inquiry that recognises our limitations and inability to draw conclusions in cases that exceed the bounds of rational understanding); and, as para-intellectuals, seek to oppose, subvert and destabilise the language games, hegemonic discourse and 'regimes of phrases' of those in authority (Lyotard 1991, 1992).

The Silence of the Lambs

According to Lyotard, conspicuous examples of attempts to subvert or overthrow the existing orthodoxy can be found in the physical sciences. In particular, he cites postmodern scientists' growing concern with such things as 'undecidables, the limits of precise control, conflicts characterised by incomplete information, "fracta", catastrophes, and pragmatic paradoxes' (Lyotard 1984, p.60). In other words, an emphasis on the unknown rather than the known, with dissent from, rather than consensus around, the prevailing paradigm. Although Lyotard was not the first to employ the term 'postmodern science' (see Griffin 1988a; Best 1991) and although some theorists do not consider such phenomena to be part and parcel of the postmodern moment (Connor 1989), latter-day developments within the physical sciences and, moreover, the history and philosophy of science, undoubtedly parallel the postmodern penchant for discontinuity, instability, indeterminacy and paradox. The fourth and final strand of postmodernism, therefore, is located in the arena of scientific accomplishment.

Postmodern science is predicated on a repudiation of the mechanistic, deterministic, static and particularistic world view of 'modern' science in favour of a new paradigm based on principles of uncertainty, chaos, evolution and holism. For Galileo, Bacon, Descartes, Newton and the other giants of modern science, the universe is akin to a vast mechanism governed by inviolate laws which function in a stable, orderly, predictable manner. The nature of these laws, what is more, could be deciphered – and the cosmos thereby understood and predicted – through scientific observation, rigorous experimentation, precise mathematics and the systematic application of the powers of human reason. This is a world where little is left to chance, indeterminacy plays a small part, truths are eternal and unchanging, and (as a consequence of its 'mirror of nature' epistemology, where an unbiased scientific mind contemplates a neutral universe) knowledge is held to be stable, certain and accurate.

Triumphantly successful though it has been in terms of technological and industrial development, and profoundly influential as it proved to be on the aspirations and ethos of nascent social sciences, the traditional, mechanistic model of modern science has been slowly but inexorably undermined since attaining its apogee in the mid- to late nineteenth century. According to Best (1991), three achievements in particular have contributed to the emergence of postmodern science: thermodynamics, quantum mechanics and chaos theory.[6] With its emphasis on energy loss, entropy and the progressive running down of systems and processes, thermodynamics challenged the established Newtonian paradigm in which change and transformation had no place. Quantum mechanics questioned the certainties of modern science at the subatomic scale, in so far as the most basic units of analysis cannot be isolated, identified or grasped as 'they really are', exact prediction is impossible and relationships between the particles cannot be precisely determined. Indeed, as the process of scientific measurement influences the behaviour of the particles, and hence experimental outcomes, the epistemological distinction between neutral observer and inert observed no longer holds at the quantum level.

Chaos theory, furthermore, maintains that the behaviour of even the simplest systems, be they human, physical, mathematical or whatever, is highly complex and operates in an unpredictable way. Whereas the traditional approach rests on assumptions of linearity, in so far as a small change in initial conditions results in a correspondingly small change in the system as a whole, it has become increasingly apparent that many systems (such as the weather) are non-linear, in that small changes in the initial conditions can make vast and totally unpredictable differences to the overall system (for instance, the legendary – and downright irresponsible! – butterfly flapping its wings in the Amazon Basin, thereby generating thunderstorms and tornadoes in the Mid-West). Contrary to the vernacular usage of the term, however, chaos is not a synonym for *disorder*. On the contrary, chaos theory contends that new forms of order emerge spontaneously out of disorder, that there are regularities in the irregular. Examples include the 'dissipative structures' of Prigogine and Stengers, the fractals of Mandelbrot and Lorenz's notion of the 'strange attractor' (see Gleick 1988; Briggs and Peat 1989; Waldrop 1992).

Besides its emphasis on complexity rather than simplicity, change rather than stasis and a participatory rather than spectatorial epistemological standpoint, postmodern science also stresses spiritual awareness, ecological empathy, ethical sensitivity and a holistic interpretation of the relationship between nature and humankind. Exemplified by the Gaia hypothesis, Lovelock's (1982) theory that the earth is an organic entity, a self-regulating essence which transcends its inhabitants, this contemporary tendency – termed the 're-enchantment of science' by Griffin (1988a) – involves the eschewal of consumerism, the espousal of recycling, an emphasis on balance, the natural order and sustainable development, an abandonment of the supposition that nature is passive and inert, the replacement of the mechanistic paradigm with an ecological one, and, not least, an attempt to reconcile the interests of nature and humanity. The consequence of these developments, and the closely related writings of New Age scientific gurus like Carl Sagan, Peter Medawar, Rupert Sheldrake and Fritjof Capra, is that the boundaries between science and cosmology, science and religion, and science and non-science have become increasingly ill-defined.

Although often derided as vacuous New Age nonsense, irredeemably tainted by its association with tree-sniffing, shamanistic drumming, parapsychology, wicca, meditation, crystal- or pyramid-based therapies and all manner of analogous 'alternative' passtimes, the above picture of postmodern science is some way distant from the conventional portrayal of scientific endeavour as the methodical, impersonal, rational, unbiased and logical pursuit of eternal truth, objective knowledge, replicative findings and new discoveries. It has, of course, long been recognised that science is a social institution and, as such, inevitably shaped by social forces (cf. R.K. Merton's (1938) early work on the sociology of science), but perhaps the single most devastating blow to received wisdom of scientific disinterestedness and rectitude was delivered by T.S. Kuhn in the early 1960s.[7] His seminal work, *The Structure of Scientific Revolutions*, demonstrated that far from being open-minded, co-operative and dispassionate, scientists are dogmatic, secretive and strongly committed to their theoretical constructs (Kuhn 1970a). Instead of trying to test their theories rigorously by endeavouring to disprove or falsify them, as Popper prescribes, scientists defend their concepts from attack and appear prepared to make all manner of *ad hoc* modifications rather than give them up.

This manifestly 'unscientific' behaviour was attributed by Kuhn to the lengthy training and apprenticeship procedure, whereby tyro scientists are socialised into and disciplined by the culture of their chosen scientific community (e.g. through publications, promotions, grants, awards, etc.), which tends to be organised around and held together by a shared 'paradigm'. Although Kuhn has been heavily criticised for his inconsistent use of the term 'paradigm', it refers essentially to a research tradition, a world view, a whole way of thinking and working within an established framework of theories, ideas and exemplars. The paradigm thus provides the context within which the research agenda is set, problems are identified, questions posed and facts made meaningful. For Kuhn, indeed, the vast bulk of scientific endeavour involves routine 'puzzle-solving', the elaboration, clarification, articulation and extension of the prevailing paradigm and the resolution of problems or anomalies that inevitably transpire in the course of its investigation. Eventually, however, the accumulation of anomalies is such that the scientific community becomes increasingly concerned about the utility of the paradigm, 'normal science' can no longer continue, philosophical disputes erupt and unconventional notions are entertained. This sense of crisis deepens when a new paradigm, presenting a very different picture of the world, interpretation of the facts and with major implications for future research activity, appears and proceeds to attract the support of certain members of the community – usually the younger generation who have yet to make their mark and are less committed to the prevailing orthodoxy – and the implacable hostility of the scientific establishment. Kuhn, however, emphasises that the switch from one paradigm to another is not based on logical or rational grounds, as there is no independent, mutually acceptable measure for comparing the merits of the two incommensurable world views, but likens it to a religious conversion or 'gestalt switch' after which things can never be the same as before. As Figure 3.3 illustrates, the triumph of the new paradigm constitutes a scientific revolution, which is complete when the community as a whole converts to the new world view, the old paradigm is abandoned, and the puzzle-solving of 'normal science' resumes – until the next upheaval.

A towering achievement in the history and philosophy of science, and a text that continues to resonate in many arenas of academic activity, Kuhn's model of paradigm shifts seriously undermines the 'rationalist' account of scientific endeavour. It repudiates the power of individual reason, presupposes that social factors affect theoretical judgements, rejects the neutral 'mirror of nature' epistemology, demonstrates the historically and socially *relative* character of scientific truths and effectively subverts the assumption that scientific change is progressive. If, as Kuhn implies, science involves the periodic movement from one incompatible paradigm to another, then it is difficult to argue that scientific knowledge

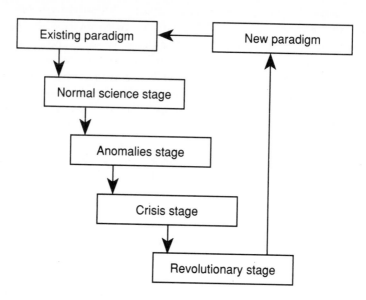

Figure 3.3 The cycle of paradigms
Source: Adapted from Kuhn (1970a)

is cumulative, that it is inexorably (or even fitfully) moving towards perfect correspondence with the 'reality' it describes. Science, in other words, does not grow; it merely changes.

Damaging though this interpretation of scientific endeavour has been, Kuhn's critique is a veritable model of restraint compared to the 'methodological anarchism' of Paul Feyerabend (1987, 1988). Often described as a postmodern philosopher of science (though like many gurus of the postmodern moment, he does not subscribe to such a categorisation), Feyerabend holds that science is just one social institution among many, one world view among many, one ideology among many. Western science does not have a monopoly on truth, it is no more and no less rational than – neither superior nor inferior to – most other, 'non-scientific' forms of knowledge. More to the point, empirical investigation reveals that the practice of science is much 'sloppier' and irrational than the conventional picture would have us believe. According to Feyerabend, there are no methodological standards that can be universally applied, no procedures that guarantee success or pertain to all sciences at all times, no rules that cannot and have not been bent, broken or ignored on occasion, and no single, agreed, uniform scientific method as such. 'There is only one principle that can be defended under all circumstances and in all stages of human development. It is the principle: anything goes' (Feyerabend 1988, p.19).

For Feyerabend, then, scientific progress is not obtained through adherence to the 'proper' procedure, since adherence to the proper procedure *inhibits* progress. It is necessary, rather, to keep our options open when investigating the world, to adopt a pluralistic methodology, to avoid the specification of rules of best practice, to assume that nothing is settled and that no idea, no matter how ancient or absurd, should be abandoned or overlooked. Science, in short, should be an anarchistic endeavour, involving the proliferation of as many incompatible theories as possible, all of which should be tenaciously held, vigorously defended and defiantly promulgated by their proponents, even in light of disconfirming evidence and the disdain of the scientific mainstream. 'Without chaos, no knowledge. Without a frequent dismissal of reason, no progress' (Feyerabend 1988, p.164).

Given the serious implications of Kuhn and Feyerabend's analyses for the conventional, idealised model of scientific endeavour, it comes as no surprise to discover that their conclusions have been subject to vigorous criticism and point-by-point rebuttal. Feyerabend's position in particular has been subject to sustained, often bitter, invective. Although some of these criticisms, such as those concerning Kuhn's (debatable) assumption of paradigm incommensurability, are perfectly legitimate, others involve a complete misrepresentation of the author's original intent. Feyerabend, for instance, does not assert that scientists never follow rules, nor that science is irrational, nor, as he makes perfectly clear, does he subscribe to the view that anything should go (he actually means that any set of methodological rules which goes beyond the non-principle 'anything goes' is likely to inhibit scientific advance and create a distorted image of science as it is actually practised). Indeed, on reading Feyerabend, it is difficult to reconcile his reputation as the 'Hannibal Lecter of the history and philosophy of science' with what can only be described as his ironic, self-deprecating and, yes, level-headed approach to life in general (Weber 1993). Let's be honest, an academic can't be all bad if he concludes his lectures, as Feyerabend was wont to do at University College London, by leaping out of an open window, on to a powerful motorbike and driving off at high speed!

Irrespective of the shortcomings of their philosophical positions (all philosophical positions are imperfect), the pioneering endeavours of Thomas Kuhn and the late, great Paul Feyerabend destroyed for ever the notion that western science is a unique form of objective knowledge unaffected by context or culture. In fact, a host of investigations into scientific controversies (Collins and Pinch 1993), textual representations (Locke 1992) and the minutiae of laboratory life (Latour and Woolgar 1986) have revealed that scientists do not adhere to the Mertonian (1973) norms of universalism, communism, disinterestedness and organised scepticism (though this does not stop them alluding to such norms in the course of their internecine struggles). Science is irredeemably social, inherently 'messy', deeply affected by political, professional and personal interests, and riddled with *ad hoc*, context-dependent decisions concerning experimental procedures, instrumentation, the status of 'observations', what counts as a 'fact', the interpretation of results and so on (Barnes 1985a; Pickering 1992). Specific findings, furthermore, are evaluated on the basis of acceptability, elegance, aesthetic appeal and the prestige, reputation, authority and powers of persuasion of their proponents (Gross 1990). Rhetorical skills, according to Collins and Pinch (1993), are as important as experimental skills in having scientific conclusions accepted; 'the meaning of an experimental result does not, then, depend only upon the care with which it is designed and carried out, it depends upon what people are ready to believe' (Collins and Pinch 1993, p.42).

In scientific discourse, it seems that the real world rarely intrudes (Knorr-Cetina 1981). Reason, logic and methodological rules are merely *post hoc* rationalisations of scientific practice, *not* their guiding light. Scientists, as Woolgar (1988, p.87) describes it, 'are not engaged in the passive description of pre-existing facts in the world, but are actively engaged in formulating or constructing the character of that world'. Contrary to the conventional wisdom of scientific accomplishment, there is no dispassionate search for the truth. Scientific 'truths' and 'falsehoods' are social constructs, agreements to agree, which are culture bound, context dependent and relative rather than absolute. As Pascal is reputed to have said, 'what is truth on one side of the Pyrenees, is false on the other'.

Truth, and the relationship between truth and knowledge, is also integral to the neo-pragmatism of postmodern philosopher, Richard Rorty. According to Rorty (1989, 1991), it is essential to distinguish between the philosophical claim that the world is 'out there' (i.e. external to our senses) from the claim that the 'truth' is out there. Although the external world may well exist independently of our consciousness of it, truth cannot exist independently of the human mind because truth is reliant on language and language is a human construct. Truth, therefore, is made rather than found, a creation rather than a representation of how things really are. It is, admittedly, easy to conclude that our beliefs about the world are true, especially if the world appears to correspond to our descriptions, but 'the fact that Newton's vocabulary helps us predict the world more easily than Aristotle's, does not mean that the world speaks Newtonian' (Rorty 1989, p.6). Our language is not nature's own; reality is indifferent to our descriptions of it; the world does not come in neatly packaged, sentence-shaped chunks called 'facts'. In these circumstances, we should consider our descriptions of the world to be a succession of increasingly useful metaphors rather than an increased understanding of the world as it truly is. Truth, after Nietzsche, is a 'mobile army of metaphors', scientific revolutions comprise 'metaphorical re-descriptions' of nature (Hesse 1980), and philosophy itself consists of a clutch of metaphors masquerading as concepts (Rorty 1989). 'It is pictures rather than propositions, metaphors rather than statements, which determine most of our philosophical convictions' (Rorty 1980, p.12).

In arguing that we should abandon the idea that 'truth' is out there waiting to be discovered, Rorty does not mean that we have at last discovered the awful truth that there is no truth out there. Instead, he maintains that we are wasting our time trying to discover the 'truth' about the world. Hence, we should give up the notion that science is moving toward ever-increasing correspondence with reality and relinquish the assumption that knowledge is an accurate representation of that which is outside the mind. This eschewal of the 'mirror of nature' metaphor and repudiation of old habits of thought does not imply that philosophy has ended, however. On the contrary, it is necessary to generate new metaphors, new language games, new vocabularies and new ways of looking at the world. In this respect, the contributions of poets – as the creators and shapers of new languages – are of paramount importance. For Rorty, the insights of poets, novelists, anthropologists, sculptors or, indeed, television producers, movie makers and journalists have as much to contribute to understanding as the scientist, *if not more* (Tester 1993). Scientific descriptions are not privileged, not a search for objective truth, but simply one discourse among many. As Rorty sees it, there is no 'objective' way of choosing between these vocabularies, other than on rhetorical grounds, because 'the way things are said is more important than the possession of truths' (Rorty 1980, p.359). Truth, therefore, should be re-defined as 'what it is better to believe', as opposed to an accurate representation of reality. It is a label of convenience for ideas that enjoy widespread support and make good sense within a particular language game.

Rorty's replacement for unattainable truth and spurious objectivity thus comprises a pragmatic vision of mutual tolerance, plural language games, continuing search for consensus, solidarity, empathy and edification, and, above all, a recognition that 'conversation' is the ultimate context within which knowledge is to be understood. The role of the philosopher is to keep the conversation going, wisdom represents an ability to sustain the dialogue and knowledge comprises the practical competence that is necessary to participate in the conversation. Philosophy, in sum, needs to drop the long-standing assumption that philosophers know something about knowing which no one else knows so well and, at the same time, attempt to 'decry the very notion of having a view while avoiding having a view about having views' (Rorty 1980, p.371).

It's A Wonderful Life

Although, as the preceding discussion indicates, it is possible to identify four broad strands within the postmodern project – cultural, socio-economic, linguistic and scientific – it is necessary to reiterate the some-what paradoxical but none the less important point that these strands are not entirely separate nor are they directly related to each other. True, a number of prominent theorists, most notably Jameson (1985, 1991) and Harvey (1989) have employed (for want of a better term) a neo-base–superstructure framework, arguing that the dramatic changes in post-war economic life underpin the postmodern convulsions in the artistic, intellectual and political spheres. The task of explication, what is more, invariably involves attempts to separate the strands of postmodernism's tangled skein and the imposition of undue or excessive order on the entire postmodern movement. However, notwithstanding the ruminations of diehard Marxist dinosaurs and the inevitable recuperation process, it must always be borne in mind that the trajectories of postmodernism's cultural, socio-economic, linguistic and scientific components do not run in parallel, there is no one-to-one correspondence between them, and each is driven by markedly different dynamics (see Callinicos 1989, 1990). As Boyne and Rattansi (1990, p.11) rightly point out, 'it can be highly misleading to lump together Cage, Derrida and Lyotard, or Foucault, Rushdie and Rorty as postmodernists and expect to derive collective commonalities which provide collective appropriation or provide a collective critical target'. It is clear, therefore, that just as the project of modernity involved several deeply interwoven strands, sometimes cancelling out, sometimes working together, so too the postmodern movement is a complex, in-coherent phenomenon. Each of its elements exhibits substantial internal contradiction, dissension and mutability, and – a point we shall return to in Chapter 6 – each contains an ineradicable residue of its 'modern' forebears.

The sheer incoherence of the postmodern project is exemplified by what Skinner (1985, p.19) describes as 'clashes between titans', the polemical and often bitter debates between the movement's leading lights. Almost every major figure with 'postmodernist' stamped on their intellectual passport, however reluctantly, has felt it necessary to condemn the con-tributions of one or more of their fellow travellers. Harvey (1989), for instance, has been very critical of Jameson's (1984, 1988) periodising schema of late capitalism and both have lambasted Baudrillard for intim-ating that further resistance to the capitalist system is futile. Baudrillard (1987), by contrast, has dismissed the 'politics of desire' espoused by Lyotard, though the latter responded with the improbable suggestion that Baudrillard remained too much of a rationalist (see Best and Kellner 1991). This paragon of rationality has also denounced, as passé, Foucault's concept of power and exhorted us, in a celebrated essay, to *Forget Foucault* (to which, as Eribon (1991, p.275) reminds us, Foucault famously replied 'I would have more problems remembering Baudrillard'). Foucault was also publicly attacked by his former pupil, Jacques Derrida

(1978b), for failing to scrutinise with sufficient rigour the nature of his own discourse, as indeed were structuralist literary theorists in general (i.e. early Barthes). Lacan, likewise, suffered under the Derridean lash in a celebrated deconstruction of his own deconstruction of Poe's essay, *The Purloined Letter* (Derrida 1987b).[8] Derrida's emphasis on textuality, however, was overturned in turn by Lyotard's elevation of image over language (Bennington 1988), though the latter's interpretation of postmodern science and incommensurable language games has received short shrift from Richard Rorty (1985). Rorty, in addition, has comparatively little time for Feyerabend's methodological anarchism and has been highly critical of Kuhn's (1970a) idealist suggestion that the proponents of different paradigms are, in essence, living and working in different worlds (Rorty 1980). Feyerabend (1970) has also been quick to condemn Kuhn for the ambiguities and ideology implicit in his model of scientific revolutions (Kuhn (1970b), needless to say, has replied in kind), though it is interesting to note that Kuhn's conceptualisation informed Harvey's (1969) early analyses of intellectual change prior to his conversion to Marxism.

Above and beyond the debates between postmodernism's principal theorists and the periodic running battles with authoritative 'outsiders', so to speak (Lyotard and Habermas, Habermas and Rorty, Norris and Baudrillard, Derrida and Miller, etc.), many of the most prominent commentators on the postmodern condition have proved to be decidedly inconsistent in their own thinking (Best and Kellner 1991). The intellectual odyssey of Roland Barthes, in particular, demonstrated numerous marked changes of direction, with almost the only apparent element of consistency being Barthes' inveterate hostility to the prevailing orthodoxy or 'doxa' (Sturrock 1979b). So capricious was he indeed that Culler's (1983b) biographical overview identifies nine contrasting 'Roland Barthes' ranging from hedonist to literary historian. Michel Foucault was no less unwilling to alter his philosophical standpoint and, as often as not, recast his earlier thoughts in light of more mature reflection. Commencing with a series of 'archaeological' analyses of marginal and deviant behaviours, systems of thought and the announcement of the death of the human subject, Foucault shifted in the 1970s to his studies of the 'genealogy' of power/knowledge and, before his untimely death from AIDS in 1984, had reintroduced a form of human subjectivity – technologies of the self – into his work on the history of sexuality. Lyotard, likewise, progressively abandoned his early elevation of image over text and, after indulging briefly in the pleasures of the 'libidinal economy' (an attempt to liberate the flows of desire in art and writing which are oppressed by authoritarian social forces), placed ever-increasing store by language and philosophy. In fact, for a thinker who is irrevocably associated with the dissolution of the grand narratives of the Enlightenment project, much of Lyotard's recent research exhibits a rather incongruous fascination with Kant, a

philosopher traditionally considered to be the embodiment of Enlightenment rationality (Lyotard 1994).

Perhaps the most astonishing series of intellectual somersaults, however,
has been performed by the postmodernist nonpareil, Jean Baudrillard. As
Poster (1988) points out, his initial analyses of consumer society comprised
an innovative fusion of Marxism and semiotics. This was followed by a
sharp break with the Marxian tradition and a 'middle period' devoted to
simulation, implosion, hyperreality and the implications of telecommunications technologies (Baudrillard 1983, 1985). Lately, Baudrillard has
taken something of a metaphysical turn, with a number of aphoristic, often
brilliantly written, meditations on the end of history, society and ideology,
eternal recurrence, America and the ultimate triumph of the object over
the human subject (in other words, we live in a world not where the
subject is dead but where hi-tech objects have taken over and rule in
mysterious ways). Some of the stances espoused by the later Baudrillard
(1988b, c, 1990a, b, 1993b), are so bizarre that they are clearly designed
to infuriate his manifold disciples, with their impeccable left-wing credentials, and to this end his tongue-in-cheek ruminations have proved an
outstanding success. 'Sheer nonsense', says Norris (1992, p.15), 'lacking
sustained, systematic analysis', writes Poster (1988, p.7), 'never afraid to
exaggerate', according to Harvey (1989, p.291), 'cynical beyond belief',
despairs Denzin (1991, p.147), and, for Best and Kellner (1991, p.139),
'Baudrillard's current positions are profoundly superficial and are characterised by sloppy generalisations, extreme abstraction, semiological
idealism and often repeated banalities'. Other supporters, it goes without
saying, are less fulsome in their praise.

So varied, indeed, are the philosophical perspectives sheltering under the
umbrella term 'postmodernism' that a number of attempts have been made
to subdivide the intellectual spectrum of this remarkable cultural colossus.
Foster (1985), for example, distinguishes between a 'postmodernism of
resistance', devoted to the deconstruction of modernism while defying the
inexorable descent into populism, and a 'postmodernism of reaction', which
repudiates modernism completely and celebrates the achievements of popular
culture. Griffin (1988b) contrasts 'deconstructive or eliminative' postmodernism, the nihilistic world-view advanced by Baudrillard and several
analogous French thinkers, and 'constructive or revisionary' postmodernism,
the positive possibilities offered by an amalgam of postmodern science and
religion. In a similar vein, Rose (1991) seeks to separate 'deconstructive'
theories of postmodernism from 'double coded' theories, arguing, after
Jencks, that the former are not postmodernist as such but belong to a
conceptual category which can legitimately be called – wait for it – 'late-
modernist post-modernist'. And, Rosenau (1992) identifies what she terms
'sceptical' and 'affirmative' schools of postmodern thought. Mainly continental European in origin, the sceptics offer a negative, gloomy, despairing

assessment the human condition and see little in the way of comfort for the future (e.g. Baudrillard, Lyotard, Foucault). Affirmative postmodernists, by contrast, are predominantly Anglo-American and posit a more hopeful vision of the postmodern age, one where the dogmatic, ideological strait-jacket of modernism has been cast off and new forms of political activism and personal development obtain (cf. Rorty, Jameson, Harvey).

The sheer heterogeneity of positions within postmodernism goes some way towards explaining the confusion and bewilderment which, as noted in Chapter 1, many people feel on encountering its principles for the first time (the second and third encounters are pretty disorientating too). As Rosenau (1992, pp.14–15) rightly emphasises,

> the cut-and-paste character of postmodernism, its absence of unity is both a strength and a weakness. Everyone can find something about it with which to agree. But because it is not an 'invisible college', an infi-nite number of alternatives allow different and varying ways to put together the elements that constitute postmodernism. No wonder its harmony is disrupted by argument, no wonder it is characterised not by orthodoxy so much as diversity, competing currents and continual schism. . . . There are probably as many forms of postmodernism as there are postmodernists. If it were not so clumsy, we could speak of post-modernisms. . . . Postmodernism is stimulating and fascinating; and at the same time it is always on the brink of collapsing into confusion.

The inherent eclecticism of the postmodern moment might lead many to conclude that it is simply not worth the trouble. However, it is important to re-emphasise that the modern movement itself was far from consistent, by no means systematic and riven with considerable intellectual discord (Bauman 1987). Indeed, just as the project of modernity was characterised, above all, by the notion of *progress*, so too postmodernity is identifiable by its all-pervasive air of *exhaustion*. Whereas modernism was predicated on advance, achievement, amelioration, betterment, breakthrough, exuber-ance, innovation and inexorable forward movement, postmodernism is suffused with stasis, debilitation, dissipation, enfeeblement, entropy, stag-nation and cessation. Irrespective of the affirmatives' belief that a new, postmodern Jerusalem can eventually be built, or the sceptics' contention that nothing remains but to rearrange the deckchairs on the Titanic, post-modernism in many ways represents the terminus, the outer limit, the dead-end of modernism. At the same time, it is also characterised by a strange but remarkably compelling sense of exhilaration in the face of failure, a feeling that there's nothing we can do, so let's have a party. Postmodernism, in sum, is bungee-jumping into the past, free-fall parachuting into the future and idiot dancing on the edge of the abyss. Don't worry, be happy.

4 You can't handle the truth!

These days, who among us can find the time to get to know himself philosophically, when just getting to know himself physically grows more and more difficult with every passing marketing fad? I went into Boots last Saturday at ten o'clock, and when I came out again at half-past, all that I knew about myself was that I now knew less. . . .

I counted 17 sorts of hair, but not only did I not know the categories into which the rest of the family's fell, I did not even know mine. What is dull? What is brittle? How lifeless is lifeless, how unmanageable unmanageable? Is greasy oilier than oily, or vice-versa? Did it need revitilising or merely conditioning? Where did its body lie on the national bodiness scale? I finally grabbed a dozen bottles of something pH balanced with silk protein and enriching moisturisers, which may very well raise barley on my scalp come spring, only because time was pressing and I needed toothpaste.

But did I have sensitive teeth? How could I know? Might my teeth be not merely indifferent, but callous? Brutal even? And how tender does a gum have to be before it requires .05 of an additive bent on sorting it out? How discoloured should discoloured be before special care must be taken when applying something to undiscolour it?

The deodorant shelf needed to know if I had serious perspiration. What is it? Do your boots fill constantly from your upper cataracts? If mine is frivolous perspiration and I spray serious stuff on, will my pores snap shut and my impermeable body slowly swell with incarcerated sweat? As for bath-gel and shaving cream, the choice of both depended on whether the skin was or wasn't delicate. What is mine? If it's crude, will my dirt and bristles refuse to budge? How can I know? What shall I buy? Whom shall I ask?

(Coren 1991, pp.215–17)

Total Recall

Now, I know what you're thinking. You're thinking, what on earth is going on?; you're thinking, is this book some kind of joke?; you're thinking, is that it?; you're thinking, are we seriously expected to give up mathematical modelling, split run testing, SERQVAL and the Edwards Personal Preference Schedule for what can only be described as postmodern poppycock? But most of all, you're thinking, how can I go about getting my money back? Even those of you who are chary about complaining, the 'passives' in Singh's (1990) typology of consumer dissatisfaction, are no doubt reflecting on my earlier extravagant promises that the time spent examining postmodernism would not be time wasted, that postmodernism could provide meaningful insights into the nature of modern marketing, that if we suspended judgement until the end of Chapter 3, everything would become clear, sweetness and light would prevail, joy would be unbounded and, although dancing in the streets might be too much to expect, vigorous toe-tapping remained a very strong possibility. Indeed, at this very moment, some of the more cynical among you, especially those with a working knowledge of the Trade Descriptions Act, may be thumbing through the preceding pages in search of the sentence where I gave a personal guarantee that postmodernists had not gone crazy (you're wasting your time, it won't stand up in court). Conversely, those of you with humanitarian inclinations are probably reflecting on my previous comparison between postmodernism and parenthood, wondering if I am really fit to be a father and whether the social services should be informed.

Setting aside, for a moment, your litigious ambitions or your understandable concern for the well-being of my offspring, I fully appreciate that the pertinence of postmodernism may not be immediately apparent. What, you may well be asking, does the history of architecture have to do with marketing?; or the 'wrappings' of Christo?; or Paul Auster's 'parodic metafiction', come to think of it? Since when did marketing have anything to learn from the rise of religious fundamentalism, pit closure protests, tree-hugging, telekinesis and, now that we've broached the subject, what is shamanistic drumming when it's at home? How, for that matter, can Foucault's analyses of madness in the sixteenth century, medicine in the seventeenth or sexual perversions in ancient Greece possibly inform and illuminate the nature of modern marketing inquiry? Who in their right mind could possibly take Lacan's incantatory ramblings and incessant word play to be anything other than psycho-babble at best or complete clap-trap at worst? When Barthes suggests that we can read whatever we like into a text, without fear of contradiction, does he mean that the Declaration of Independence can be legitimately construed as a shopping list, a scientific treatise, a recipe for pecan pie, the rules of American football? Are we really expected to believe, after Derrida, that books don't mean what they say or say what they mean?; that language controls our every utterance, our sense of ourselves?; that Feyerabend's fondness for high-speed motorbikes somehow legitimises the sheer recklessness of his methodological anarchism?; that Rorty's repudiation of truth should be taken as truthful?; that philosophy is nothing more than metaphors masquerading as concepts?; that language games are irredeemably incommensurable?; and that when it comes to scientific inquiry, rhetorical skills are more important than laboratory skills? After more than four hundred years of scientific and technological progress, how can anyone seriously suggest that science is not scientific? Things may well be bad, but if there is no hope for the future, if atrophy and exhaustion prevail, if, as Baudrillard would have it, the real world no longer exists, why then do we bother to get out of bed in the mornings? Why don't we just give up marketing altogether and devote our time to more rewarding tasks like golf, gardening, good works or – why not – shamanistic drumming?

Marketers, in short, do not need postmodernism. They have better things to do than grapple with incomprehensible texts about topics of little or no relevance to marketing. Fashionable though postmodernism undoubtedly is among disciplines which have lost touch with the real world, marketing can live without such pseudo-intellectual pretensions. Postmodernism is downright absurd, contrary to common sense and to adopt this questionable philosophy would merely invite the ridicule of marketing's principal constituents – students, business people and the policymaking community at large.

Although a hostile reaction to the precepts of postmodernism is eminently understandable, and while many of the foregoing questions are perfectly legitimate, several important points must be taken into account before judgement is finally passed. The first of these concerns the frequently criticised obfuscation, the sheer unintelligibility of many postmodern texts, especially those emanating from continental Europe. Reading Lacan, Derrida or Deleuze and Guattari is undeniably difficult. The rebarbative brilliance of Baudrillard's *bon mots* is accentuated by the often bafflingly enigmatic nature of the surrounding material. Even Michel Foucault, whose empirical analyses contrive to make his writings more accessible than most postmodern thinkers, has had his work described – by an admirer – as something that,

> disturbs the expectations of the reader familiar with social history. There appear to be huge gaps in the narrative, silences that scream at the reader. Topics are annoyingly placed out of normal order, disrupting one's sense of logical sequence. Levels of analysis are mixed together in irritating confusion. . . . The object of investigation is never quite clarified and appears to be neither individuals, nor groups, nor institutions. . . . Worst of all, the author's attitude toward the topic of study never

emerges clearly. He seems to take perverse pleasure in shifting his stance, or simply in adopting provocatively an unorthodox attitude toward a topic.

(Poster 1984, p.72)

The crucial point to bear in mind, however, is that postmodern texts are impenetrable for very good reasons. Lacan's syntax is designed to *exemplify* rather than explicate the linguistic operations of the unconscious. Baudrillard writes postmodernistically, in that the style of his works replicates the superficiality, irreverence, fragmentation, banality and, occasionally, preposterousness of the postmodern moment. The works of Foucault, Derrida and Barthes represent a deliberate repudiation of *la clarté*, the clarity of expression which, in France, has long been considered a national virtue, the mark of a properly educated mind. By offending so egregiously against convention, postmodern intellectuals are demonstrating that there is more to language than lucidity. Lucidity perpetuates the illusion that language is under our control, that it can be made to do our bidding, whereas the reality is that language is difficult to tie down and enjoys a high degree of autonomy. In *Writing Degree Zero*, moreover, Barthes (1970) makes the political point that lucidity is a manifestation of bourgeois sensibility – the bane of the French intelligentsia – and that, by enabling readers to make their own contribution to meaning, ambiguity is more democratic than clarity (incidently, the Declaration of Independence, as a 'readerly' text in Barthes terminology, could not possibly be interpreted as a laundry list, a recipe for mom's apple pie or what have you, though if you insist . . .).

Postmodern texts may well be impenetrable and problematic, but before dismissing them out of hand it is necessary to ask *why* they are presented in the way that they are. More importantly perhaps, it is necessary to examine marketing's intellectual history and inquire whether it is composed solely of penetrable and unproblematic papers, books and monographs. The answer, regrettably, is negative. Notwithstanding the obvious difficulties that many people have with the idiom of inferential statistics, simultaneous equations, matrix algebra and the like, it has to be acknowledged that some of marketing's seminal texts, the 'required reading' of countless undergraduate and postgraduate seminar groups, are just about as convoluted as they come. Harold Barger's (1955) classic volume, *Distribution's Place in the American Economy*, is not exactly a bundle of laughs as I recall. To describe Shelby Hunt's (1991c) much-cited work, *Modern Marketing Theory* as 'arid', 'tiresome' or 'stultifying' is to shower it with extravagant praise (whenever he goes on about the K-K Thesis, I invariably wish that a group of southern rednecks, complete with burning crosses, conical headgear and fashionably capacious white outerwear, would somehow materialise and proceed to put me out of my misery).

And, let's be frank, is there a single marketer anywhere, who has the foggiest idea what Wroe Alderson was trying to say? A giant of marketing scholarship he undoubtedly was, but some of Alderson's writings make wacko-Jacko Derrida read like Jeffrey Archer.

Another, closely related, issue that must be taken into account before judgement is passed on postmodernism, pertains to the patently absurd, seemingly counter-intuitive nature of certain postmodern positions and their failure to accord with what common-sense or everyday experience might lead us to expect. Examined from a matter-of-fact perspective, many postmodern precepts do indeed appear to be irrational, but then again some of the concepts that once enjoyed widespread support within marketing now also look decidedly suspect. The 1950s fetish for motivation research can hardly be considered marketing's finest hour, and are the premises of subliminal, subaudible or 'embedded' advertising any less preposterous than telekinesis or wicca? Aspinwall's (1958) classification of 'red', 'green' and 'orange' goods is premised on an interesting and original metaphor (the spectrum of light) but conceptually it is complete moonshine, as is the venerable and much-vaunted four utilities framework (see Shaw 1991). Surely, moreover, I can't be the only person who finds Kotler's 'Generic concept of marketing', with its paradoxical combination of 'can do', counterculture and conspiracy theory (such as the references to brainwashing, levels of consciousness and the like), as much a manifestation of the late 1960s American *Zeitgeist* as a meaningful guide for today's marketing practitioners. And, to be brutally honest, many of the confident predictions in Levitt's seminal 'Marketing myopia' – rocket-powered cars, ultrasonics, fuel cells, the end of the oil industry by 1985 etc. – turned out to be utterly erroneous. Whatever the article's other merits, its predictions represent a hubristic testimony to Levitt's lack of foresight, to his own marketing myopia. They are, in effect, the buggy-whip manufacturers, the railroad companies, the Hollywood studios of marketing discourse.

Although Levitt's (1960) outlandish predictions make the speculations of Jean Baudrillard seem like a model of circumspection and common sense, it is also worth emphasising that common sense, if not quite 'the collection of prejudices acquired by age eighteen', that Albert Einstein once suggested, is arguably an overvalued attribute. Even allowing for the irredeemably social and political nature of scientific activity and, irrespective of the fact that marketing has traditionally suffered from a severe case of 'physics envy', most of the greatest theoretical and methodological achievements in the natural sciences are completely counter-intuitive and contrary to common sense. According to Wolpert (1992), a prominent apologist for science and the scientific world view, the single most characteristic feature of natural science is its 'unnatural nature'. Whether it be the structure of DNA, the cooling of ice cubes in a soft drink, the Big Bang theory, the burning of a match, the nature of white light, the mathematics of probability, the physics of planetary motion or our taken-for-granted belief that grass is green, rocks are hard and snow is cold, Wolpert's overwhelming conclusion is that the world is predicated on counter-intuitive premises. 'The laws of nature just cannot be inferred from normal day-to-day experience . . . the way in which nature has been put together and the laws that govern its behaviour bear no apparent relation to everyday life' (Wolpert 1992, p.6). In fact, he (1992, p.11) even goes so far as to suggest that, 'if something fits in with commonsense, it almost certainly isn't science'. Granted, Wolpert's definitions of 'science' and 'non-science' are debatable, his stated philosophical position as a 'common-sense realist' (p.106) is somewhat undermined by his evident suspicion of common-sense thinking and he is clearly utilising the tools of rhetoric in an attempt to undermine the charge that science is predominantly rhetor-ical (e.g. Gross 1990). Be that as it may, Wolpert's convincing demon-stration of the counter-intuitive nature of science and Outhwaite's (1985) analogous critique of common-sense reasoning in the social sciences, leads one to question the enormous store that many people place on plausibility, credulity and reasonableness.

In point of fact, some of the best-established findings in marketing's con-ceptual canon are manifestly counter-intuitive. To cite but a single, albeit very clear-cut, example: the manifold studies of 'pre-purchase information seeking' reveal that the typical consumer gathers *very little* information before making a purchase, even for fashionable, expensive, high-involve-ment and infrequently acquired items like furniture, houses and motor cars (Brown 1992). Although completely contrary to what you might expect – after all, it seems eminently sensible to shop around before making a costly or ego-intensive purchase – this finding holds good for each and every potential source of product-related information (e.g. advertising, sales-persons, talking to friends and relatives, store visits, prior experience) and across most socio-economic, demographic, geographic and psychographic categories of consumers. True, the methodologies employed in many of these exercises are questionable, particularly in terms of their inordinate reliance on consumers' notoriously unreliable powers of recall and their tendency to treat each item in isolation rather than as part of a multi-purpose shopping expedition. What is more, the cognitive paradigm may not be the most appropriate conceptual framework for this extensive body of consumer research. Nevertheless, the results of literally hundreds of studies are virtually unanimous – consumers gather very little informa-tion before purchases are made – and, as such, run completely counter to what you might reasonably expect and intuitively anticipate.

Prior, therefore, to casting out the mote of postmodernism, perhaps we should consider marketing's beam of syntactic contortions, conceptual absurdities and arguably undue emphasis on common-sense. Perhaps we should also be prepared to acknowledge that postmodernism may be highly pertinent to marketing, despite its seeming irrelevance. Postmodernism deals with all manner of ostensibly arcane issues like artistic movements, human sexuality and the history of medical science, but as marketing deems itself relevant to almost everything under the sun, it follows that such issues must have some bearing on marketing. In fact, it has often been claimed that the marketing concept is applicable to art and ideology, self-image and sexuality, and, as we shall discuss in more detail in Chapter 5, it has even been suggested that science *is* marketing (Hirschman 1983, 1987; Peter and Olson 1983). More to the point, it is arguable that exposure to outside ideas, especially those from fields far distant from marketing, can only serve to raise the all-round standards of marketing scholarship. Academic creativity, as Holbrook (1984) and Belk (1984) amply demonstrate, comes from reading widely, from a dialectic process involving structure, departure and reconciliation and from the juxtaposition of paradoxical or competing hypotheses. Most of us, admittedly, may disagree with Belk (1984, p.58) when he asserts that 'there is little worth reading in marketing', but it is only by looking around us, by seeing how other people see, interpret and conceptualise the world that we can transcend our current way of thinking about marketing and envision alternative scenarios.

The Postmodernist Always Rings Twice

Postmodernism, of course, comprises more than a congeries of counter-factual concepts, presented in an appropriately unintelligible idiom for autodidactically inclined marketing academics. At the risk of (a) oversimplifying a complex and incoherent phenomenon which, as we have seen, means different things in different fields, (b) applying essentially 'modern' – and therefore inappropriate – criteria to concepts that are resolutely anti-modern and (c) seeking to categorise instantiations that are deeply interwoven and well-nigh inseparable, it can be contended that post-modernism is characterised by seven key features: *fragmentation, de-differentiation, hyperreality, chronology, pastiche, anti-foundationalism* and *pluralism.*

- *Fragmentation* refers to the seemingly inexorable disintegration and demise of political stability, social organisation, mass market economics, the unified self, the nature and grounds of knowledge, and, inevitably, the all-pervasive, disconnected array of vivid images generated by the increasingly hydra-headed media.
- *De-differentiation* involves the erosion, effacement and elision of established hierarchies – high and low culture, education and training, politics and showbusiness – and the blurring of what were formerly

clear-cut entities (philosophy and literature, author and reader, science and religion etc.).

- *Hyperreality*, as exemplified by the fantasy worlds of theme parks, virtual reality and computer games, involves the loss of a sense of authenticity and the becoming 'real' of what was originally a simulation.
- *Chronology* comprises the archetypal postmodern concern for the past (or representations of the past) and the abandonment, in an era when time and space are being increasingly compressed, of the progressive, forward-looking orientation of modernism for an essentially retrospective, backward-looking perspective.
- *Pastiche* consists of a playful, tongue-in-cheek collage or medley of available styles, an ironic, self-referential mixing of existing codes, be they architectural, artistic, cinematic, literary, musical or whatever.
- *Anti-foundationalism* is postmodernism's characteristically deconstructive urge, its antipathy towards orthodoxy, complacency, the establishment and, not least, systematic generalisations, most notably the totalising metanarratives of science, socialism, humanism, etc., which form part of the modern movement's discredited search for universal truths and objective knowledge.
- *Pluralism*, strictly speaking, is not a separate category as such, but a reminder that, in practice, the six preceding 'features' collide, combine and collapse into a paradoxical postmodern melange of incongruous phenomena. It reflects the symptomatic postmodern assumption that anything goes, everything is acceptable and nothing is excluded. There is no right or wrong, the more meanings the merrier, too many cooks won't spoil the broth and, above all, that the four postmodern Ps of paradox, profusion, plurivalence and polysemy prevail.

As marketing, in many respects, reflects developments in the social, economic and cultural spheres generally, it is only to be expected that the characteristic features of postmodernism are apparent – and deeply inscribed – in today's marketing environment. Indeed, if it were not such a blatantly modernist approach to the subject, it would be possible to imagine a matrix with (say) the distinguishing features of postmodernism along one axis and the elements of the marketing mix along the other. Illustrated in Figure 4.1 (purely for pedagogic purposes, you understand), the outcome is an array of neat pigeonholes ready and waiting to be filled in by any passing modernist keen to pin down the infuriatingly elusive nature of postmodern marketing. Such an exercise, of course, is doomed to inevitable failure, not simply because it is totally contrary to the cavalier and insouciant spirit of postmodernism but because it seems much too much like hard work! If, however, we are prepared to suspend temporarily our innate postmodern antipathy to empirical research and prise ourselves

	Product	Promotion	Price	Place	People	Premises	Processes
Fragmentation	?	?	?	?	?	?	?
De-differentiation	?	?	?	?	?	?	?
Hyperreality	?	?	?	?	?	?	?
Chronology	?	?	?	?	?	?	?
Pastiche	?	?	?	?	?	?	?
Anti-foundationalism	?	?	?	?	?	?	?
Pluralism	?	?	?	?	?	?	?

Figure 4.1 Postmodern marketing pigeonholes

momentarily from our admittedly comfortable positions as armchair theorists (in the grand continental manner), it is undeniable that all of the distinguishing features of postmodernism are discernible on the current marketing scene and discernible, moreover, across every facet of marketing from pricing to promotions.

As we noted in Chapter 2, for example, the *fragmentation* of markets into smaller and smaller segments, each with its complement of carefully positioned products, is everywhere apparent. Whether it be the market for computers, coffee, cola, cameras, cigarettes, breakfast cereals, ice-cream, financial services, sports shoes, package holidays, pet foods, disposable nappies, washing powder, recorded music, mineral water, traction batteries, machine tools or, as Alan Coren discovered during his discombobulating visit to Boots the Chemists, the gamut of health and beauty aids, a bewildering array of product and service offers typically obtains (Magrath 1990). Ten years ago, there were seven brands of toothpaste on sale in the UK. Today, there are more than thirty, many of which provide a number of distinct product variations (tartar control, pump action dispensers and so on). In the United States, there are now 240 Weight Watchers products spread across 78 different categories; the number of lagers on sale in Britain has increased by 66 per cent in the last six years; and, such is the prevailing range of credit cards and payment systems that the bygone days of hard cash, personal cheques or, *in extremis*, Access/Barclaycard, seem like a dim and distant memory. Indeed, in the new car market it appears that you can now have any colour, engine size, bodywork variant, trim level, sound system, safety features, optional extras and license plate you like, as long as you're in the black.

Paralleling the proliferation of products – and, in fact, reinforcing the inexorable trend toward micro-segmentation – recent years have witnessed the multiplication of distribution channels and advertising media. The 1980s in particular was an era of niche retailing, characterised by the *fractal* emergence of highly targeted retail outlets selling a very narrow range but in-depth assortment of specific product categories – Tie Rack, Sock Shop, Knickerbox, Benetton, The Body Shop – and the rapid exploitation of retail offers that proved popular with the consuming public (e.g. Next, Next Too, Next for Men, Next to Nothing, Next Interiors). Set against this, average store size increased dramatically, as did the number of products they carried (twenty years ago the average supermarket stocked 2,500 lines, today it is approximately ten times that). Likewise, the number of locational options exploded as the traditional high street shopping experience was supplemented with out-of-town regional centres, retail warehouse parks, festival malls, forecourt retailing, ancillary facilities (in hotels, hospitals, airports and railway stations) and, increasingly, arm-chair or in-home shopping from a plethora of specialogues and dedicated television channels (Parker 1992).

Advertising options have also burgeoned as a result of the proliferation of everything from local free-sheets and company-specific titles (*Marks and Spencer Magazine, McMag*), to glossy 'lifestyle' magazines targeted at specialist audiences. These are further enhanced by the publishers' ability to produce national, regional and, increasingly, local editions of the titles thus enabling advertisers to deliver highly focused messages to specific groups of people. The satellite and cable television revolution, coupled with the deregulation of radio, has contributed to the demise of broad-casting, the rise of narrowcasting, an exponential increase in the avail-ability of advertising space and the emergence of interesting locational or place-specific communications options such as in-store radio stations, satellite television programming for airports, hospitals, health studios and so on (Schlossberg 1991). When combined, moreover, with the much-derided three-minute culture of cocooned channel surfers, and the growing preference among advertisers for shorter commercials (albeit with very high production values), Jameson's (1985) prediction of a 'perpetual present', a world of fleeting, fragmented images of hallucinogenic intensity, seems remarkably prescient.

The collapse of mass marketing is perhaps best illustrated by the recent changes in Coca-Cola Classic's advertising strategy (Edwards 1993). The 'Always' campaign, which comprises twenty-six contrasting ads – for the same product – each targeted at different market segments, is a world away from 1985's unequivocal assertion that Coke is 'it' or the company's earlier McLuhanesque attempts to teach the world to sing in perfect harmony. However, if current predictions are to be believed, the twenty-six alternatives of the 'Always' campaign will seem crude and unsophisticated in the not too distant future. The emergence of 'category management', for instance, enables multiple retail organisations to adapt the range, assortment, stockholding levels and, ultimately, marketing strategy of each individual store in the chain to the unique requirements of its catchment area (Schlossberg 1993). Sales promotion activities, such as money-off coupons, free offers, trial purchase vouchers and loyalty or 'reminder' incentives, can be targeted to individual consumers and dispensed automatically at the checkout. Such is the size and sophistication of existing consumer databases, with all the possibilities they offer for highly focused marketing campaigns, that marketers routinely talk about hyper-targeting, segments of one, the mass customisation of individual products and personalised promotional strategies, delivery systems and pricing policies (Honomichl 1992). The Time Warner database, for example, contains information on 53 million Americans, RJR Nabisco's is not much smaller and, according to Rapp and Collins (1990, 1994), some of the world's most successful mass-marketing organisations – Nestlé, Heinz, Bristol-Myers, Seagram, Ford – have enthusiastically embraced the micro-marketing revolution.

Once Upon A Time in America

This seemingly inexorable process of fragmentation is counterpointed to some extent by a clearly discernible trend towards *de-differentiation*, the blurring of what were once clear-cut marketing boundaries. Marketing, in fact, figures prominently in what is generally considered to be the paradigmatic instance of de-differentiation, the much-debated effacement of the distinction between high and low culture. As Huyssen (1984) points out, the first generation of American postmodern artists and architects drew inspiration from the output of Madison Avenue (Warhol's soup cans) or the billboards, casino culture and commercial kitsch of the Las Vegas strip (Robert Venturi). More recently, displays of advertising 'art' have become a commonplace (the Tate Gallery's exhibits of Bovril labels and shopping bags); some museums have added posters and advertisements to their collections (the Victoria and Albert Museum owns several of the celebrated Benson and Hedges posters and British Airways' 'Manhattan' is displayed in the New York Museum of Modern Art); the British Academy (BAFTA) awards now include a category for artistic achievement in advertising; and, the Guggenheim, no less, is endeavouring to exploit its brand name through a vigorous, and much-criticised, programme of international franchising (Olins 1992; Bell 1993a).

Counterbalancing this 'debasement' of high culture – a world where the theme tune from Cadbury's Flake has been played at the Proms and where

Figure 4.2 De-differentiation in advertising: Harvey Nichols inspired by Rothko

Hovis, Hamlet and Old Spice have done more to popularise Dvořák, Bach and Orff respectively than any number of performances in the Albert Hall – the exponents of degraded cultural forms have elevated themselves in turn by appropriating the motifs and institutional settings of modern art (Figure 4.2). The award-winning Benson and Hedges poster campaign, which ran from 1975 to 1993, was inspired by Magritte (Woodward 1993); Mondrian has been inadvertently responsible for innumerable package designs (e.g. the L'Oréal hair styling programme); the attempt to 'brand' Spain as a holiday destination utilises a logo based on Miro's *Sun*; several major international brands, such as Coca-Cola, Nike, Dunhill and Guinness, have 'museums' devoted to their history and development; 'exhibitions' of fake products have been mounted by Gucci, Rolex and Louis Vuitton among others; and, like the works of art that they undoubtedly are, many advertisements are now blessed with a title and the author-ity of the responsible creative genius is acknowledged (Hugh Hudson's 'Face' for British Airways, Tony Kaye's 'Relax' for British Rail, etc.).

Apart from marketing's active participation in the melding of high and low culture, all manner of other boundaries within or adjacent to marketing are – as the terminology employed often indicates – in the throes of erosion. The borderline between advertising and television, for example, has been dissolved by the recent, rapid advent of 'infomercials', extended length commercials (thirty minutes usually) for individual products presented in talk show or news programme format (Zagor and Mead 1992). The 'advertorial', an amalgam of advertisement and editorial, performs a broadly similar function in magazines and newspapers. 'Edutainment' is a marketing neologism coined by the manufacturers of computer games in an attempt to mollify parents fearful of the addictive power of their products (Miller 1993). And, if the predictions of the so-called 'telecomedia' industry are correct, the barriers between company and customer will soon be completely effaced by the widespread avail-ability of interactive television, interactive shopping, interactive banking and interactive entertainment (Kehoe 1993; Cassidy 1993).

This ethos of dissolution is no less evident in the rise of 'scrambled merchandising', retailers' tendency to extend the ranges of merchandise they sell beyond 'traditional' trade boundaries (e.g. Marks and Spencer's successful foray into financial services, Asda's abortive attempt to distribute motor cars); the growth of vertical marketing systems, where the entire channel of distribution is carefully co-ordinated, operated as a unit and, increasingly, linked by a fully integrated EDI network; and the emergence of innovative retailing hybrids such as shopping centres-cum-theme parks, retail warehouses, combined bookshops and restaurants, factory outlets, warehouse clubs, integrated launderettes and nightclubs or, indeed, restau-rants like TGIF's or the Chicago Pizza Factory where the serving staff burst 'spontaneously' into song-and-dance routines. Virgin Airway's plans to operate a casino on its transcontinental flights to Hong Kong is yet another instance of this de-differentiation tendency (Betts 1993), as are, to cite several contrasting examples:

- the routine appropriation of high street fashion by *haute couture* houses and vice versa (Hirshey 1993);
- Sainsbury's extremely successful advertising campaign predicated on 'recipes' endorsed by high-profile celebrities;
- cigarette advertising which has become so abstract that the compulsory health warning, as the only discernible signifier of 'cigarette', has effec-tively been absorbed into the copy and its purpose hence defeated (Bracewell 1994);

- the Barcode Battler, a computer game where points are scored by reading the barcodes on various products (such is the Battler's popularity in Japan that it has caused shortages on certain high-scoring product lines and marketers are already working on its wider promotional possibilities); and,
- supermarket own-label products, the packaging of which is all but identical to manufacturer's brands; so much so, that certain manufacturers have instituted, or threatened to institute, legal proceedings against the supermarket chains – e.g. Coca-Cola and Sainsbury (Mitchell 1994a).

Undoubtedly the clearest examples of de-differentiation in marketing are found at the interface of advertising and television. As the postmodernist guru Gilbert Adair (1992) adroitly notes, advertising has its own soap operas (the Gold Blend coffee 'couple'), situation comedies (the 'Beattie' series for BT), real-life dramas (the Audi owner's race to the maternity ward), documentaries (public service ads for AIDS etc.), shock-horror specials (the charity 'nasties'), game shows (will the housewife swap two packets of her ordinary washing powder for one packet of Daz?) and makes widespread use of 'in character' actors (Robert Hardy of *All Creatures Great and Small* endorsing agricultural products, for example). However, it is arguable that, from a marketing management perspective, the most important instances of de-differentiation emanate from the recent and much-vaunted rise of strategic alliances, joint ventures, collaborative networks and boundaryless corporations (Lorenz 1993; de Jonquieres 1993). As the partnerships between (say) Nestlé and Coca-Cola, Pepsico and Unilever, Sears and McDonalds, Time Warner and West Inc, and Pearson and the BBC amply illustrate, the traditional barriers between marketing organisations are in the process of elision. There are, admittedly, some concerns about the extent to which such alliances will fulfil the ambitions of the participating companies and, as you might expect, there is no shortage of consultants ready and willing to advise on the management and maintenance of these often delicate relationships, for a suitably modest retainer. Nevertheless, the advent of strategic alliances represents one of the most significant developments on the contemporary business scene with enormous implications for the organisation and practice of marketing (Mitchell 1993, 1994b).

Alongside the blurring of 'horizontal' boundaries between contiguous organisations, recent years have been characterised by the effacement of 'vertical' organisational forms. Complete tiers of middle management have been swept away by post-Fordist companies bent on 're-engineering' or 'de-layering', and flat or matrix structures have increasingly replaced the traditional hierarchical arrangements. This has led some commentators, most notably Gummesson (1991), to predict the end of marketing as a separate department, though he emphasises that the marketing function will still be practised, albeit in a diffuse fashion across the entire organisation. The inevitable result of this combination of vertical and horizontal restructuring is what has sometimes been described as a 'hollow' or 'virtual' company, the non-existent organisation organisation. In effect, Baudrillard's world of *hyperreality* made manifest in business.

Hyperreality, however, is not confined to the discovery of the black holes of organisation theory, it is apparent across the entire marketing spectrum. It totally pervades the 'dream worlds' of advertising and promotion, where the traditional function of information provision ('this product is good, buy it') has long since been superseded by judicious manipulation of consumer desires, tastes, images and motivations. Meanings have become increasingly detached from their referents and all manner of alternative signifiers or connotations are routinely attached to ostensibly mundane products like toothpaste, soap and deodorant. Sex, for example, has been pressed into signifying service for products as diverse as chocolate (Cadbury's Flake), personal pensions (Scottish Widows), ice cream (Häagan Dazs), household detergents (Ajax), throat drops (Hall's Mentholyptus), gardening requisites (Walkover's sprayers), and those hardy annuals, clothes, cosmetics, motor cars and alcoholic beverages (not to mention, if the trade press is any indication, virtually every promotion directed at grocery or DIY retailers). Harvey (1989), in fact, goes so far as to suggest that if advertising were stripped of allusions to sex, money or power, there would be very little left (though I'm not sure if he means that there would be very little advertising left, or if there is very little else for advertising to appropriate).

Hyperreality is equally evident in the fantasy worlds created by theme parks, hotels, restaurants, pubs, airlines and, increasingly, shopping centres. The designers of festival malls regularly exploit the historical resonances of old buildings and, where necessary, these are embellished and exaggerated to create a sanitised simulation of the past. Thus, the Jackson Brewery in New Orleans and the Cannery in Monterey retain their original brewing and canning equipment respectively, but only for show. The South Street Seaport development in New York, which comes complete with 'traditional' wooden wharf, 'authentic' warehouses, moored sailing ships and suchlike, is almost entirely fake, as are the restorations of 'historic' Williamsburg, Charleston and the Vieux Carre in New Orleans.[1] Indeed, just as these historic shopping developments peddle simulacra of the past, so too mega-scale shopping centres peddle simulacra of the present. The West Edmonton Mall boasts a recreation of a Parisian Boulevard, a Park Lane upmarket shopping area, a section comprising restaurants from around the world and a Bourbon Street entertainments district. Metrocentre, meanwhile, has its Mediterranean Village, Roman Forum and so-called Town Square. The crucial point, of course, is that the recreation of Bourbon Street in West Edmonton is a more pleasant environment for many than the decidedly tawdry 'original'. Likewise, lager louts, sunstroke, food poisoning, unsatisfactory accommodation and recalcitrant air-traffic controllers are unlikely to spoil a visit to the Metrocentre's Mediterranean Village, though the unavailability of duty-free goods and suitably ersatz souvenirs may well act as a disincentive for some.[2]

Although the manifestations of hyperreality are most clearly discernible in advertising campaigns and retailing milieux, there is no shortage of simulacra among the other elements of the marketing mix. Reflect for a moment on the 'pretence' of the typical service encounter, where the salesperson's adherence to a pre-ordained script, rote responses to anticipated enquiries and heroic endeavours to fake sincerity, can give the whole experience a not unpleasant but none the less unreal, illusory, slightly phantasmagorical quality – on some occasions. On other occasions, of course, the mouthing of meaningless banalities – 'have a nice day', 'enjoy', 'missing you already' – or the inept personalisation of direct mailshots not only renders worthless the effort expended, but reduces the simulacrum of service to an object of ridicule. Consider, moreover, the emergence of what can legitimately be regarded as hyperreal products. These include the timeless creations of Cellular Phoney, for individuals who wish to give the impression that they are constantly on call; the bespoke elegance of the Dummy Book Company, which produces fake libraries to order (leather bound, gold lettering, artificially aged and priced, naturally, by the metre); and the rapidly developing worlds of virtual reality and computer games, the most recent generations of which have been described as 'just like reality only better' (Guilliatt 1992, p.33). How, moreover, can we forget those supreme monuments to the new product development process – fat-free fat, beefless beef, decaffeinated coffee, alcohol-less alcohol, sugar-free sugar and, as the appropriately hyperreal brand name, *I Can't Believe It's Not Butter!*, constantly reminds us, butterless butter?

Pricing strategies and sales promotions may also exhibit hyperreal tendencies. It has been argued that the UK grocery retailing industry is in the throes of a hyperreal price war, one that is not taking place, according to the principal protagonists (Brown and Quinn 1993). Likewise, the already infamous Hoover 'free-flights' promotion, where airline tickets to American and European destinations were made available for the price of a £100 vacuum cleaner, led to a bizarre situation in which the Hoover factory was working round the clock to satisfy the demand, newspapers were swamped with small ads placed by people eager to dispose of unused, second-hand vacuums, carpet retailers were giving away free Hoovers with every purchase, travel agents were accepting vacuum cleaners as a deposit for summer holiday bookings, and, in the middle of a deep recession, some commentators were predicting a complete economic recovery predicated on Hoover's ill-fated sales promotion!

It Happened One Night

Incredible though it was, the Hoover 'free-flights' farrago is by no means the most extreme example of hyperreality on the contemporary marketing scene. Others include Reebok's decision to buy advertising space on the buildings in a virtual reality arcade game, the Northern Police Authority's attempt to communicate a 'no speeding' message to drivers by placing cardboard cut-outs of patrol cars in motorway lay-bys, and Ratners' celebrated £3.49 cut-glass sherry decanter, silver tray and six crystal glasses, the sales of which *increased* after it was described by the (then) chairman of the company as 'total crap'. Interestingly, however, and as anticipated by Baudrillard, the very ubiquity of hyperreality appears to have stimulated a countervailing desire for authenticity and heightened concern with *chronology*. Thus, we see periodic campaigns for 'real' beer, bread, eggs, meat, fruit, furniture, holidays, cosmetics and wrought iron railings; renewed interest in 'authentic' music, films, books and cooking (played on original instruments, director's cuts, 'restored' first editions and 'traditional' Greek, French, Italian and Chinese cuisine); and, not least, an increased emphasis on 'real' advertising. Apart from the increasing use of reality-based bylines (e.g. Kodak's 'it's so real it's unreal', Miller's 'as real as it gets'), and periodic paeans to the 'good old days' when advertisers actually indulged in the hard sell, instead of seducing audiences with subtle allusion (Table 4.1), there is a growing trend towards the use of 'real' people as opposed to actors or celebrities (Fielding 1994). These range from the utilisation of home videos (Scottish Amicable, Radion washing powder) and foregrounding the participation of the actual employees of the company concerned (cf. Kenwood Electronics, Nationwide Building Society, Covent Garden Soup Company), to subtitled, albeit less than reassuring, assurances that the featured dentist/scientist/housewife/nurse is a genuine dentist/scientist/housewife/nurse (why, I sometimes wonder, is the 'actress' in the beauty soap commercial invariably someone you have never heard of?; no doubt it's an actress acting an actress).

This emphasis on authenticity in advertising is paralleled, to some extent, in the branding arena, where longevity is considered to be all-important, especially at a time when the new product development rate is seemingly exceeded only by the new product failure rate. As the enormous premiums paid for recognised brand names by acquiring companies amply testifies (e.g. Philip Morris's $12.9 billion takeover of Kraft, at four times book value), and the opportunities for judicious brand extension clearly shows (Mars ice-cream, Persil washing-up liquid, etc.), long-established brand names are *extremely* precious commodities. It would appear that in an increasingly uncertain, fragmented, disorientating and fast-changing world, they provide consumers with a point – an oasis – of marketing stability. They are imbued with an evocative patina of the past and redolent of

Table 4.1 On the ads that drive us mad

Was there *ever* a time when advertisements were about selling us things? I dimly remember a period when women got over-excited about detergent, when Nanette Newman would eerily persuade whole gangs of little boys to wash up for her, when a Mars bar could enable you to 'Work, rest, and play'. It's not like that any more though, is it? Now we get Rutger Hauer being gratuitously weird for Guinness, bionic menstruating women in head-to-toe Lycra being pulled along on skateboards by dogs, increasingly bewildering lager ads, and erotic epics that are designed solely to sell us shampoo.

Advertising no longer seems to be about the things it sells. It is not even about things at all. No, it is about ideas, concepts and most of all other ads. Caught in an increasingly self-referential loop, advertising is mostly about advertising. Never mind the stupid soft drink, feel the art direction. 'Look at me, I'm a really interesting ad,' screams the poster which could be for IKEA, a kitchen appliance or a charity. You never can tell. . . .

The 'creatives' behind so many of these obscure campaigns say it's all about brand loyalty, niche marketing and living in a media-saturated culture. If this is the case, then they are failing miserably. A lot of the time one is at a loss as to what the product is, never mind the brand name. Surely I'm not the only one who, instead of thinking, 'I'll rush out and buy that', wonders what she has just seen has to do with ovens, dog food or a half of bitter. You can laugh at the Gold Blend saga, but apart from the fact that these yuppies are drinking instant coffee, it is at least comprehensible. What's more, it has sold lots of coffee, which I believe is what the game is about.

Apart from neglecting to sell us things, all this in-jokiness has a side-effect: good old-fashioned sexism can creep back in. Women lie on cars, caress everything from cats to ice creams and it's all frightfully ironic. Maybe I shouldn't take all this so seriously, but the point is that advertisers take themselves so seriously. They labour under the illusion that we so want to be part of the joke, that we care enough about their hyperactive doodlings to be lured into this insane fantasy. So while they are busy graffiti-proofing their posters and simultaneously pretending that what they're doing is somehow not advertising anyway, there's only one way to get your own back. Laugh at their jokes if you like (they are free, after all); just don't buy any of them.

Source: Moore (1993), p.5

simpler, better, less stressful times when choice was limited but satisfaction guaranteed. In these circumstances, it is little wonder that many major brands, like Kellogg's corn flakes, Heinz beans, Levi's jeans and Golden Wonder crisps, place great promotional emphasis on their illustrious lineage and, indeed, that many products, whose life cycles have long since run their course, have been successfully raised from the dead. Prominent British examples include Spangles, Vimto, Brylcream, Action Man, Pacamac, Parker Duo-fold pen, Gossard Wonderbra, Worthington's White Shield Ale, Russell Hobbs coffee percolators (1952 vintage) and, not least, the tie-in products from re-runs of old television series such as

Thunderbirds, Stingray, Batman, Captain Scarlet and *Joe 90*. A similar trend is evident in the United States where, among others, Morton salt, Jell-O, Ovaltine, Kool Aid, Bazooka bubble gum, Skippy peanut butter, Birkenstocks shoes, PF Flyers sneakers and Raggedy Ann/Raggedy Andy dolls have been re-launched with some success (Miller 1990, 1992).

If, of course, established, original and long-dead products are not available for exhumation, nothing could be easier than the creation or appropriation of an entirely imaginary past. As the recent, rapid rise of the 'retro' product convincingly demonstrates, a combination of the latest technological advances with appropriately nostalgic styling can prove enormously popular. The current marketing scene is awash with art deco Walkmans and ghetto-blasters, 1950s-style freezers, Box Brownie look-alikes (with motor wind and auto-focus, naturally) and motor cars like the Nissan Figaro and Mazda Miata, which to quote the promotional blurb, 'not only gives you a glimpse of the 90s . . . it takes you back, as well'. Retro radios, televisions, hi-fis, coffee makers, motorcycles, airlines, restaurants, rock bands, soft drinks, bar snacks, magazines, sports shoes, perfume, jewellery and underwear are now available; retro communities are being constructed (Poundbury in Dorset); retro radio stations (Capital Gold) and television channels (UK Gold) are attracting substantial audiences; retro packaging is regularly utilised (Ovaltine, Best Health Seltzers); retro sales brochures are not unknown (Oakdale batteries); retro promotions and promotional icons are back in fashion (Green Shield stamps, the Bisto Kids); retro pricing policies are occasionally employed as, admittedly substantial, loss-leaders (my local pub recently celebrated its 25th anniversary with a '1969 prices' promotion); retro locations are being occupied by retail organisations (Tesco Metro, Sainsbury Central) and in-store environments created (Cullens, Co-op Pioneer); and, not least, retro advertisements, in grainy black and white or featuring long-dead celebrities (Humphrey Bogart, James Dean, Marilyn Monroe), have become a commonplace (Tedre 1993). After unsuccessful attempts at diversification, moreover, many companies appear to be resorting to retro marketing strategies. Habitat's back-to-basics retailing strategy, aptly described by the chief executive as 'our future lies in recapturing the past' (Hollinger 1993, p.20), is an excellent case in point, as are Laura Ashley's extraordinary endeavours to recreate its original bucolic image of softness, femininity and quintessential Englishness. However, as the latter organisation traded on nostalgia to begin with, its current strategy could quite legitimately be described as retro-retro (or neo-retro) retailing (Mulvagh 1993).

Marketers growing preparedness to plunder the past, to substitute 'new and improved' with 'as good as always', is partly a reflection of the widespread, *fin de siècle* belief that 'marketing creativity is impossible, that there can only be the exhuming and recycling of the old' (Barsoux 1993, p.12). It is also, as Harvey (1989) and Jameson (1991) emphasise, a predictable reaction against the rapidity of change in the contemporary business environment. We live in a world where time and space are being increasingly compressed, where product life cycles are becoming ever shorter, where speed to market, or 'concurrent engineering', is the *sine qua non* of new product development, where 'order fulfilment' (the turnaround time in servicing customer requests) is increasingly seen as the key to success in undifferentiated markets, where stockholding is reduced to a minimum but out-of-stock situations deemed intolerable, where deliveries must be made within a fifteen-minute window, where fast-selling lines of fashionable clothing are replenished several times per season, where literally hundreds of thousands of prices can be changed by a single keystroke, where revenue is increasingly measured in dollars or pounds per minute and where everything from supermarkets to stockmarkets is open twenty-four hours a day, seven days a week (Fisher 1993). It is a world where just-in-time is just too late and organisations are being exhorted to 'shape time' (Lynch 1992), 'compete against time' (Stalk and Hout 1990) and adjust to the 'nanosecond nineties' (Peters 1992). It is a world where even the past is speeding up. As the special 'revivals' supplement of *The Modern Review* (1993, p.3) sardonically notes,

> since the mid-Eighties, we have seen a Fifties revival, a Sixties revival, a Seventies revival and even glimmerings of an Eighties revival. . . . The pessimistic belief is that we are heading for some kind of apocalyptic implosion, when the accelerating revival cycle will catch up with the present. This will produce a situation in which we revive periods almost as they happen, and eventually go mad as civilised culture collapses.

Such a scenario, where the revival cycle is effectively eating its young, is somewhat unlikely, as there is nothing to prevent another fifties, sixties or seventies revival. It also remains to be seen, whether revivals can be successfully revived (remember the eighties revival of 1994, those were the days!), but given the incorrigible postmodern penchant for *pastiche*, this possibility should not be discounted completely. Indeed, it is arguable that, despite the undeniable importance of de-differentiation, hyperreality and the others, pastiche is *the* defining feature of postmodernism. Call it what you will – irony, parody, imitation, medley, quotation, self-referentiality, double coding, in-jokes, the knowing wink, tongue planted permanently in cheek, a refusal to take things seriously, not even taking things seriously – but all of these are characteristic of the pasticheur and nowhere is the pasticheur more prevalent than in marketing.

British advertising, for example, is replete with parody adverts and wry self-referentiality. As the instances in Table 4.2 illustrate, these range from fairly straightforward lampoons to the ironic appropriation or adaptation

Table 4.2 Parody and self-referentiality in UK television advertising: some examples

Category	Content	Examples
		PARODY
Direct	One advertisement parodies another	Carling Black Label (lager) spoof of Levi's (jeans) celebrated 'launderette' sequence
		Irn Bru (Scottish soft drink) musical take-off of archetypal (Coca-Cola) soda advertisement
		Hotpoint (washing machines) parody of British Airway's 'face' (Britain's favourite washing line)
Indirect	Advert 'appropriates' byline/icon etc. of another	Lemon Fairy (washing-up liquid) exploits AMEX's 'that will do nicely' for penurious couple facing prospect of washing up in expensive restaurant
		Hamlet (cigars) use of Andrex (toilet tissue) Labrador puppy in tale of woe concerning last of toilet roll
		Do It All (DIY superstores) advertised 'the united colors of Do It All' (Benetton)
		SELF-REFERENTIALITY
Direct	Adverts about advertising (set in advertising agency; adverts for forthcoming ads, etc.)	Vauxhall 'every car you'll ever need' campaign features Tom Conti and Nigel Hawthorne as inept advertising executives
		Next 'instalment' of advertising soap operas (Renault 21 family; Gold Blend couple, etc.) advertised beforehand
		Nationwide Building Society: ad about making advertisement designed by and starring employees of the organisation
Indirect	Retransmission of old adverts that have acquired new meanings in the interim, or stylistic evocation of old ads	Repeat showings of 'I'm going well, I'm going Shell' series featuring Bing Crosby etc. Once innovative, now quaint
		Hovis's 'as good today as it's ever been' sells nostalgia through an ad which is itself nostalgic (the golden age of UK advertising; early work of famous film director Ridley Scott)
		Update of 'everyone's a fruit and nut case' for Cadbury's

Figure 4.3 Advertising pastiche for Panasonic shavers

of well-known advertising copylines. They also range from the brilliantly brazen, such as Panasonic's reference to the time-worn slogan for Whiskas catfood (Figure 4.3), to the decidedly subtle (Figure 4.4). The Lexus advertisement is a fine example of double coding, as few people outside the advertising industry are likely to recognise the allusion to David Ogilvy's celebrated 1950s campaign for Rolls-Royce ('At sixty miles an hour the loudest noise in the new Rolls-Royce comes from the electric clock'). The palette of advertising allusions is not confined to other advertisements, however. Whether it be films, television series, books, architecture, politics, current affairs or, come to think of it, the market research and new product development process, almost every item on the

The loudest sound you will hear inside the Lexus *is yourself thinking.*

Not that the Rolls Royce is cathedral quiet. The V8 gushes a mellifluous roar when ordered to accelerate hard. The Lexus engine is, in contrast, near silent, as velvety as the finest malt whisky.

CAR Magazine, October 1995

You'd expect any luxury car to be quiet. But to learn that the Lexus LS400 is even quieter than the car which, to most minds, epitomises luxury, may be rather surprising. Until you then learn that we built the Lexus from scratch. It entailed taking out over 300 patents, but meant that we could tackle all the usual rumbles, whooshes, drones and whistles at source. For example, when we designed the body, our priority was aerodynamics, not the concern that a new shape might upset existing owners. (After all, we didn't have any at the time.)

As a consequence, not only does the LS400 have the lowest drag co-efficient of any luxury car, but it betters many sports cars too. Even the underside is quietly aerodynamic. Elsewhere, we use 'noise sandwiches.' Two slices of steel with a filling of sound-absorbing resin to isolate bonnet and boot noise away from the passenger compartment. Multi-layer composite flooring does a similar job. Meanwhile, under the bonnet, there's a 4.0 litre V8 engine that's whisper quiet, seated on vibration minimising fluid filled mounts.

Again, with peace in mind, we've developed a revolutionary drivetrain for the Lexus. It's in one straight line from the engine crankshaft right through to the two piece driveshaft. It reduces vibration so it too reduces noise. But the Lexus, of course, doesn't just sound luxurious. With deep carpeting, leather upholstery, walnut trim and air conditioning, it feels it too. And, if you'd rather not sit in silence, it's the perfect auditorium for the seven speaker CD system. To find out more or to arrange a test drive, call Freefone Lexus, and discover for yourself the unheard of lengths we've gone to.

THE LUXURY DIVISION OF TOYOTA

Figure 4.4 'Double-coding' in advertising: Lexus out of Rolls Royce

agenda of popular culture is grist to the marketing mill and exploited as and when advertisers deem it necessary. For example:

- recent cinematic pastiches include *Citizen Kane* (Hanson Trust), *Thelma and Louise* (Peugeot 106), *The Fugitive* (Yorkie), *Apocalypse Now* (Dunlop Tyres), *Raiders of the Lost Ark* (Terry's Chocolate Orange) and *The Hudsucker Proxy* (Volkswagen Polo) – nor should we forget the inclusion of actual movie footage for the Carlsberg (*Ice Cold in Alex*) and Holsten Pils (*Dead Men Don't Wear Plaid*-esque compilations of film noir classics) campaigns;
- the flotation of the third tranche of British Telecom shares was achieved with the aid of *Inspector Morose*, a bumbling equivalent of the cerebral television detective, and Aero chocolate bar has adopted the byline 'lovely bubbly', an allusion to one of the catchphrases of the popular comedy series, *Only Fools and Horses*;
- *Time's Arrow* by Martin Amis, a novel about the Holocaust where the narrative unfolds in reverse (and which led one cynic, Gilbert Adair, to comment 'I haven't read the book but I peeked at the first page to see how it turns out!'), inspired several subsequent advertising campaigns premised on the notion of time running backwards (Ariston, Tennent's Pilsner);
- the launch of the Rover Stirling, a top-of-the-range executive vehicle designed to compete with BMW, Mercedes and Audi, included an advertisement set in Germany and featuring Stuttgart's Neue Staatsgalerie by postmodern 'Britischer Architekt', James Stirling;
- when Halley's Comet reappeared in the late 1980s, to considerable media brouhaha, the long-running campaign for the *Financial Times* ('no FT, no comment') was adapted accordingly ('no FT, no comet') and the Threshergate affair, an unseemly episode centring on the (then) Chancellor of the Exchequer's alleged credit card transactions in an insalubriously situated off-licence, formed the basis of an advertisement for a rival credit card (featuring another ex-Chancellor extolling the virtues of the card – outside an off-licence);
- Guinness, furthermore, recently advertised for 'new product testers' to help with the 'development' of their canned draught bitter, outlining the stages of the NPD process and the type of creative 'input' required at each stage (i.e. a free samples promotion), and, as the 'apology' in Table 4.3 demonstrates, the market research/product recall procedure can also provide ripe pickings for advertising's postmodern pasticheurs.

Popular culture, in turn, is not reluctant to mine the rich and fecund seam of advertising. There have been television series on the history of commercials in the post-war period (BBC2's *Washes Whiter*) and tongue-in-cheek programmes devoted to global variations in advertising mores (Clive

Table 4.3 Postmodern marketing pastiche: advertisement for *The Best of Prefab Sprout*

AN APOLOGY

Some months ago, an advertisement appeared in this publication announcing the release by the band Prefab Sprout of their Best-Of compilation 'A Life of Surprises'. The ad was placed due to the assumption that we would be in some way reaching an audience of Prefab Sprout fans. This assumption was based on a strong but simple gut reaction which subsequently proved unreliable.

Since release of the album, rather more sophisticated research techniques have shown us some what surprisingly that our target audience is in fact Mr. Snotty Smith of 22, Red Chestnut Road, Penrith, a 17 year old thrash metal fanatic.

When contacted, Mr. Smith confirmed he had been, and indeed still was, a life-long fan of the band from their debut album 'Swoon' through the seminal 'Steve McQueen' to the present compilation. Snotty had bought 'A Life of Surprises' which he agreed was a perfect compilation of the first ten years of the band and with 16-tracks, was certainly value for money. However, Snotty had heard of the album release by chance and had not seen any ads. The only publications Snotty regularly reads are 'Metal Muthaf . . . er' and 'Mud Wrestling Mommas' neither of which carried the album advertising.

With these 'surprising' results, we are now fully aware that the ad placed in this publication was indeed misplaced.

We are now in close contact with Snotty who will be updating us as to his reading habits and changes thereof. Further ads for Prefab Sprout will only again be placed here if Snotty informs us he has become a regular reader.

We apologise to 'Q' readers if we have inconvenienced you in any way at all. Not!

Thank you for your time.

Source: Q Magazine

James, Chris Tarrant). Certain self-important rock bands, most notably U2, have been prepared to contribute their two-pennyworth on the morality of advertising by incorporating time-worn slogans into their stage shows and albums (ironically, of course), and few contemporary comedy routines appear to be complete without a quip or two at advertising's expense. (In fairness, since Ben Elton's wonderful parodies of the bobbing heads in shampoo commercials and the poses struck by models in mail order catalogues, it has been impossible to take the originals at face value.) As we have seen, furthermore, films are chock-a-block with direct and indirect allusions to advertising and many daily newspapers allocate considerable space to the latest campaigns or have columns devoted to the comings, goings and general trivia of the advertising industry. A fine example of the former is found in Sylvester Stallone's *Demolition Man*, which is set in a far-distant future where the retro radio station plays nothing but the advertising jingles of the late twentieth century. The latter is exemplified by the front page, banner headlines that greeted the Gold

Blend coffee 'couple's' final declaration of undying love in October 1992. The sort of treatment, in short, tabloid newspapers normally reserve for royal weddings, sex scandals and sightings of Elvis Presley.

Interestingly, the Gold Blend couple figured in yet another self-referential twist when a book based on the advertising campaign was published in 1993. Although *Love Over Gold* proved extremely successful – not least because of a heavy promotional spend by the publishers – its reign at the top of the best-sellers list paled by comparison with *Fly Fishing* by J.R. Hartley. This non-existent volume first appeared in a Yellow Pages television advert, the storyline of which comprised an aged author's fruitless search, from musty bookshop to musty bookshop, for the last, remaindered copy of his (presumably) life's work and which he eventually tracked down by telephone thanks to 'good old yellow pages'. Such was the popularity of the ad, that a ghost-written book, containing fishing hints, anecdotes and pseudo-personal reminiscences, was published in 1991 to enormous popular acclaim (as you might expect, the advertisement upon which it was based was re-broadcast at the time of publication and a second, companion volume appeared the following year).

Besides the 'book of the ad' and, indeed, 'the book of the advertising campaign' (such as *You Got an Ology?*, the complete scripts of the 'Beattie' series for BT – including one that was never broadcast!), a veritable industry of advertising spin-offs now seems to exist in Great Britain. These range from T-shirts or car stickers (Texas Tom) and video anthologies of long-running campaigns (Hamlet, PG Tips), to compilation CDs of advertising theme tunes (both classical and rock). Few, however, have captured the public's imagination to the extent of Levi's celebrated 1986 'launderette' commercial. Not only did sales of the jeans increase by 800 per cent, and the backing track, 'I heard it through the grapevine', reach number one in the popular music charts, but, as a consequence of the actor's 'revelation' that he wore boxer shorts under his 501s, the prevailing fashions in men's underwear were totally transformed, virtually overnight.

Close Encounters of the Third Kind

Another instance of postmodern marketing's self-referential vortex illustrates the very short step from pastiche to *anti-foundationalism*. When the Vauxhall Corsa was launched in early 1993, the campaign featured several of the world's most famous supermodels – Linda Evangelista, Naomi Campbell, Christy Turlington, Tatjana Patitz – in what was billed as a parodic reversal of the archetypal motor car advertising schema. Instead of glamorous bimbos draped alluringly over the vehicle, the provocatively dressed supermodels were portrayed as dominating or outsmarting token/supine/besotted male stereotypes, only to find themselves spurned in favour of another supermodel, the Vauxhall Corsa. The campaign, however, was condemned out of hand by various women's groups, which argued that female sexuality was still being exploited to sell cars, despite the promotion's parodic intentions. So vehement were the complaints and so copious was the publicity generated by the controversy, several commentators concluded – in a sort of double, double bluff scenario – that the controversy itself, and the enormous free publicity that came with it, was the original and sole purpose of the entire promotional campaign (Brinkworth 1993).

Appealing though they are, the problem with such conspiracy theories is that there is nothing to stop them being wheeled out to justify all manner of marketing mistakes from the New Coke débâcle and Perrier's unfortunate brush with benzene, to the Hoover 'free-flights' fiasco (in due course, no doubt). Indeed, the 'it's all publicity seeking' explanation has actually been advanced to account for cigarette manufacturer Philip Morris's seismic decision, of 2 April 1993, to slash the price of Marlboro, its premier product and the world's biggest-selling brand. Variously described as 'marketing apocalypse' and 'a mistimed April Fools' joke', the aftershocks of Marlboro's 20 per cent price cut have since reverberated throughout the global marketing landscape as the brand leaders in a host of markets – computers, sports shoes, credit cards, champagne, condoms, electrical goods, newspapers, nappies, air travel and many more – have followed Philip Morris's lead (Smith and Lynn 1993). Granted, this price-cutting ethos has taken hold more quickly in some markets than others, as Superdrug and several other would-be discounters have discovered to their cost in the perfume and cosmetics business (Bell 1992), but leading manufacturers' willingness to risk their carefully nurtured and expensively acquired brand equities is the complete antithesis of the conventional wisdom of marketing (Lorenz and Alexander 1994).

Philip Morris's eschewal of the received wisdom of branding and the unconventional launch of the Vauxhall Corsa are by no means the only examples of anti-foundationalism on the current marketing scene. As you might expect, this anti-establishment ethos is especially apparent in the world of advertising, where anarchistic and subversive campaigns are becoming increasingly common. Wilful attempts to disorientate or induce misunderstanding are much in evidence, as are 'spot the product' puzzles, adverts that have nothing whatsoever to do with the products they sell, and, not least, an apparent preparedness to outrage consumers outside the target market segment (Kellaway 1994). Thus, the anarchistic 'you know when you've been Tango'd' campaign, which involved guerrilla raids by a bright orange anti-superhero, who rained blows upon unsuspecting bystanders, proved enormously popular with schoolchildren – the principal consumers of soft drinks – but enraged parents and teachers concerned by their charges' imitative tendencies. An equally subversive intention underpinned the 'zoo advertising' approach adopted by Sega, the computer games company, for the launch of its Megadrive. This commenced with advertisements for fake products, such as Ecco washing powder and A la Kat gourmet cat food (the ads for the latter featured a glamorous female model, dressed for a formal dinner party, consuming forkfuls of the product direct from the can), which were subsequently 'hi-jacked' by advertising 'pirates' – with skull and crossbones much to the fore – themselves a front for Sega (Bell 1993b).

Anti-foundationalism is also evident in the new product arena. Recent years, for example, have seen the appearance of numerous anti-product products such as Jolt Cola, which boasts the immortal byline 'all the caffeine and twice the sugar of ordinary colas'; TNT Cider, with its distinctive 'stick of dynamite' packaging; Death brand cigarettes, which come complete with (you'll never guess) a skull and crossbones on the flip-top and categorical assurances – from the manufacturer – that smoking kills; and, incredibly, the burgeoning number of unhealthy lifestyle magazines (e.g. *Cigar*, devoted to the pleasures of smoking and *The Idler*, orientated towards the slothful in society). Likewise, the clothing industry has witnessed the rise of anti-fashion fashions, to which the generic term 'deconstruction' has been applied. These involve the rearrangement and juxtaposition of incompatible garments, materials, styles and shapes (such as a dress over jeans or ribbons and flounces combined with industrial footwear); deliberate foregrounding of the manufacturing process to give an 'inside out' look; and, an overall aesthetic of disproportion, untidiness and impoverishment rather than the traditional emphasis on harmony, neatness and allure.

By far the most important manifestation of this anti-foundationalism, however, is evident in the emergence of the 'green' movement. With its anti-consumption, anti-waste, anti-exploitation outlook, the green movement represents the antithesis of all that marketing stands for, or, rather, is presumed to stand for by the community at large. As Peattie (1992, p.85) rightly points out, 'since green thinking involves reducing the very consumption which marketing aims to stimulate . . . this makes the concept of "green marketing" appear to be a contradiction in terms'. Some marketing organisations, admittedly, have responded to the (re-)appearance of green issues on the consumer agenda by emphasising the environmentally friendly nature of their products, their conservation mindedness and the verdancy of their credentials generally. Others, such as The Body Shop and The Nature Company, which did much to raise consumer consciousness in the first place, are indissolubly associated with environmental protection in the public mind and have benefited accordingly. For more than twenty years, moreover, marketing academics have stressed the importance of human and environmental issues – in the shape of the societal marketing concept and the macro-marketing school of thought – and emphasised that the success of marketing-orientated organisations is not measured by profits alone.

Be that as it may, surveys have shown that many consumers remain sceptical about the 'caring, sharing', deep green image that marketing organisations increasingly attempt to portray, regard the bulk of environmentally friendly claims to be little more than cynical sales promotion gimmicks and consider such companies and their products to be part of the problem rather than part of the solution (Ryan and Skipworth 1993). Notwithstanding the genuine concerns that many organisations express about green issues, and the significant advances which have been made in recent years, it is undeniable that there is something profoundly paradoxical – not to say morally questionable – about vilifying the market, adopting an anti-business ethos and condemning overconsumption, while purveying consumables, being in business and profiting from the anti-market market (Shenk 1993).

Paradox, however, appears to be an inevitable concomitant of the *pluralism* inherent in the postmodern condition, with its characteristic fusion of fragmentation, de-differentiation, hyperreality, chronology, pastiche and anti-foundationalism. Although they have been treated separately for the purposes of explication, it is important – in conclusion – to re-emphasise that all of the above 'distinguishing features' of postmodernism are tightly interwoven into the pluralistic maelstrom of contemporary marketing practices. Thus, the recent decision by Heinz, as manufacturers of archetypal mass market products, to adopt a micro-marketing strategy, is a fine example of *both* fragmentation and anti-foundationalism; Center Parcs, an amalgam of holiday camp, health farm, country club and theme park, exemplifies hyperreality *and* de-differentiation; and, indeed, chronology-cum-pastiche is evident in Harry Enfield's Ealing Comedy-esque pseudo-retro advertisements for Mercury Communications or the mock 1960s cinema commercials – all split screen, Hammond organ accompaniment and pompous voiceover – for Fisherman's Friend lozenges. In a similar pluralist vein, pastiche *plus* anti-foundationalism is illustrated by Kamikasi confectionary cigarettes, which parody the Death brand while paralleling its subversiveness, by the increasing number of anti-advertising campaign advertising campaigns (for example, the Vauxhall Corsa episode was itself lampooned by Volkswagen), and, moreover, by Boots' recently launched Natural Range of cosmetics. With names like 'South Sea Bubbles', 'Polar Bear Soap' and 'Fistful of Peanuts', the product range remains true to the green agenda but, at the same time, gently mocks the perceived self-righteous, do-gooding, portentousness of the pioneer of natural cosmetics, The Body Shop.

In addition to the foregoing combinations, it is possible to itemise a host of more complex postmodern marketing interactions, though to do so inevitably invites charges of imposing a reductive modernist framework on the unconstrained, genre-busting exuberance of postmodern promiscuity. Indeed, as I know you're just itching for this chapter to end, three brief concluding combinations will have to suffice. First, after banning a series of Embassy Regal cigarette adverts, featuring 'Reg', a disembodied head dispensing irreverent opinions on current affairs and the meaning of life (which research showed were proving very popular with teenagers), the Advertising Standards Authority responded to the protests of the pro-smoking lobby by advertising itself in a Reg-style campaign. This comprised the disembodied heads of 'real' ASA employees with the singularly appropriate strapline, 'ASA, keeping tabs on ads' (Summers 1993). When, moreover, the hyperreal vegetable fat spread *I Can't Believe It's Not Butter!* was banned from advertising on television in October 1991 (as a result of protests from the food lobby concerning the illegal use of the word 'butter'), its newspaper-based campaign centred on the existence and nature of the advertising ban. More importantly perhaps, not only did the newspapers concerned publicise the ban and the company's response, but the success of the product was subsequently employed *by newspapers* to advertise the power of newspaper advertising. The ban was eventually lifted in August 1992 and, as you might expect, this too was publicised and newspaper ads were taken out by Van den Berg to celebrate the ending of its advertising apartheid and to advertise the forthcoming television ads. Indeed, so successful has the product been that it has since spawned several own-label look-alikes (e.g. Tesco's Unbelievable!)

If our first examples comprised a combination of pastiche, anti-foundationalism and hyperreality, the second represents a sublime fusion of hyperreality, de-differentiation, pastiche and chronology. Disneyland's Main Street USA is not only an integral part of the theme park experience and an extremely successful retailing environment (for Disney spin-off merchandise) in its own right, but it brings together, in an astonishing self-referential arabesque, almost everything that the Disney organisation stands for. And all in a retro setting. As Kowinski (1985, pp.66–7) rightly notes, 'Walt Disney based Main Street USA on the main street of Marceline, Missouri, as it was when he was a boy growing up there. . . . But there were no sleazy bars, dingy luncheonettes, seedy pool halls or dirty jail cells . . . there were only pleasant, clean, colorful and nostalgic small town stores which seemed to shimmer with remembered magic'. In these circumstances, it is little wonder that many prominent commentators, Eco, Baudrillard and Harvey among them, consider Disneyland to be the absolute epitomé of postmodernism.

Disneyland may be the mother-ship of postmodern marketing for an earlier generation of cultural commentators, but the closest contemporary encounter is unquestionably the much-debated Benetton controversy (e.g. Mead 1993; Schonstrom 1992). The world-wide attention, condemnation and outright prohibition that has accompanied the company's eschewal of conventional product/corporate advertising in favour of a fleeting parade of deeply disturbing images – multi-coloured condoms, dying AIDS victim, newborn child, oil-covered bird, terrorist bombing incident, nun kissing priest, nude company chairman, etc. – has led to accusations that, in its attempts to stimulate the consumption of casual wear through images of human immiseration, the organisation is morally bankrupt. It has also been accused of a profoundly cynical desire to generate controversy – on a minuscule advertising budget – in order simply to reap the benefits of the massive accompanying free publicity. In reply, the company maintains that it is endeavouring to raise, in a purely philanthropic fashion, consumer awareness of serious social issues and counters with the suggestion that conventional advertising is at fault for selling fake images and unattainable illusions, for portraying a perfect world which does not exist and never will exist.

Regardless of the rights and wrongs of the Benetton campaign, it represents a deeply affecting postmodern fusion of fragmentation, antifoundationalism, hyperreality, pastiche and, indeed, de-differentiation. After all, is it not the case that, in its shocking and uncomfortable series of adverts, Benetton has effectively assumed the mantle of modern art, the license to disturb and unsettle bourgeois sensibility that the process of canonization and institutionalisation has effectively emasculated and which the postmodern artistic community has abandoned in favour of marketability and popular appeal? As one commentator pointedly pointed out (in Bell 1993a, p.29), '58 sets of genitalia are perfectly at home in the Tate Gallery, but when they appear on an advertising hoarding for casual wear, some people are going to get very upset about it' (what was that I said in Chapter 1 about the risk of descent into indecorum and priapism?).

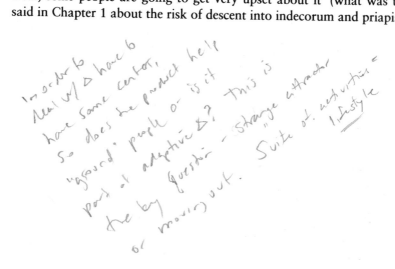

5 Is that an epistemology in your pocket, or . . . ?

Yesterday I bought a new car. It was Wittgenstein's 100th birthday. I did not, of course – lest logicians among you begin rooting around for distributed middles – buy the car for Wittgenstein, who hasn't needed a car these 38 years past. I bought it for me.

When I ordered the car in February, I requested a radio; yesterday, there it was.

'One Pioneer KE 3060B,' said the dealer, ticking his dispatch sheet. 'Detachable'.'

'What?' I said.

'It comes out,' said the dealer. 'It is an anti-theft measure. Also stops the bastards smashing the window. Park the car, take the radio out. Bastard looks in, all he sees is the gap where the radio was.'

'I don't want to carry a radio about,' I said.

'You don't have to,' said the dealer. 'You lock it in the boot.'

I thought for a moment. A bit longer, perhaps, than Wittgenstein would have needed to, but not much.

'Hang on,' I said, 'When the, er, bastard sees the gap where the radio was, won't he force open the boot where the radio is?'

'He won't know you're not carrying it about,' said the dealer.

'He can find out whether I am or not by forcing open the boot,' I said.

'You could always leave it where it was and chance him not knowing it's detachable,' said the dealer.

'Then wouldn't I be better off with a non-detachable one he'd have trouble getting out?'

The dealer looked at me, and he looked at the radio, and he coughed.

Whereof one cannot speak, thereof one must be silent (Wittgenstein).

(Coren 1989, pp.153–4)

Invasion of the Body Snatchers

We saw in the previous chapter how the postmodern condition has infiltrated all manner of contemporary marketing practices from customer care
to sales promotions. It is, of course, possible to explain such occurrences
in traditional, perfectly 'rational' terms. The infamous Marlboro price cut
can be interpreted as an extremely robust but singularly appropriate
response to the growing threat of own-label cigarettes; the British penchant
for wry, self-referential advertising campaigns as a reflection of the reputed
national disdain for commercial life in general and the hard sell in particular; and Heinz's promotional shift from mass to micro-marketing as an
inevitable outcome of the availability of low-cost computing power, appropriate database-handling software, the proliferation of advertising media
and the increasing unpredictability of consumer behaviour. Equally plausible explanations can doubtless be found for the rise of hyperreal or retro
products, the unconventional Vauxhall Corsa or Coca-Cola 'Always'
campaigns, the Benetton or Hoover controversies, and the popularity of
Barcode Battler or *Fly Fishing* by J.R. Hartley. Nevertheless, it is undeniable that many occurrences on the current marketing scene appear to
match the postmodern mood, accord with postmodern sentiment, resonate
on the postmodern wavelength.

There is more to postmodern marketing, however, than attempts to
discern parallels between the day-to-day detritus of extant marketing practices and the distinguishing features of postmodernism. A substantial academic literature pertaining to marketing and postmodernism now exists.
Broadly speaking, this body of literature can be divided into four
contrasting, but by no means mutually exclusive, categories (Figure 5.1).
The first consists of discussions of marketing phenomena by non-marketing
scholars (and cultural commentators), many of whom are closely associated with, or have expressed opinions on, the postmodern movement. The
second category involves academic marketers' analyses of issues which
form part of the postmodern project, though the authors concerned choose
not to emphasise or may not be fully aware of the connection. The third
category of contributions, by contrast, makes frequent use of 'postmodern'
terminology and idiom, but actually rests on epistemological foundations
which are closer to modernism than postmodernism. However, the fourth,
final and, from the perspective of this monograph, arguably the most
important category consists of 'genuine' (for want of a better term)
attempts to grapple with postmodernism and identify its ramifications for
marketing theory and research.

(Before we commence our discussion of the various permutations, it is
necessary to digress once again and point out that the four categories of
postmodern marketing scholarship do not always coincide with the textual
breaks – the film titles – in this particular chapter. I appreciate, and my

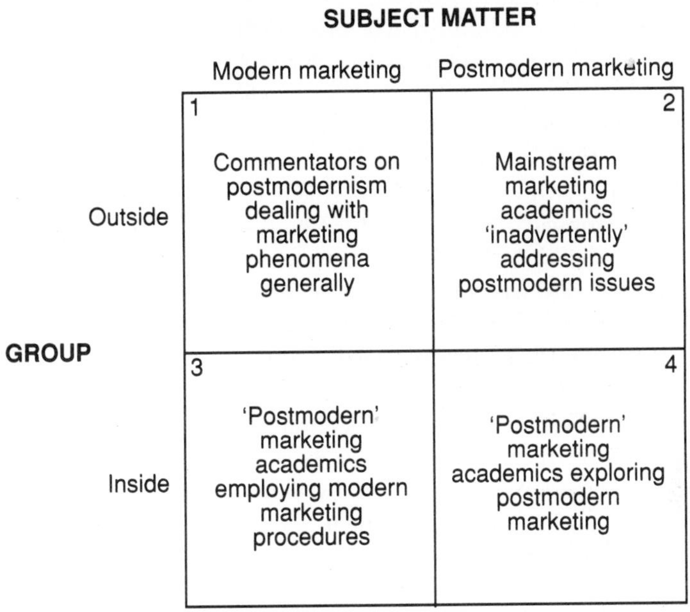

SUBJECT MATTER

Modern marketing   Postmodern marketing

	Modern marketing	Postmodern marketing
Outside	1 Commentators on postmodernism dealing with marketing phenomena generally	2 Mainstream marketing academics 'inadvertently' addressing postmodern issues
Inside	3 'Postmodern' marketing academics employing modern marketing procedures	4 'Postmodern' marketing academics exploring postmodern marketing

GROUP

Figure 5.1 Academic approaches to marketing and postmodernism

test marketing informs me, that this can be a little bit disconcerting for the uninitiated, but I'm afraid I've just about run out of patience. Having survived the fires of post-structuralism, you should be able to cope quite easily with such inconsequential acts of textual terrorism. Granted, you may not be able to grasp, first time round, some of the concepts we'll be dealing with in this chapter – I'm not sure that I understand them myself – but wilful textual subversion shouldn't really be a problem for you by this stage!)

With regard to the first category, perhaps the most striking aspect of the extra-marketing marketing literature, so to speak, is the sheer variety of academic specialisms involved. Contributions come from both long-established disciplines, such as sociology, anthropology, geography and linguistics, and comparative newcomers to the ivory tower (e.g. media studies, cultural studies, communications theory, organisation studies), not to mention a host of quasi-academic columnists and commentators (Judith Williamson, Gilbert Adair, Stephen Bayley, etc.). Clearly, it is impossible to do justice to this extensive body of literature in an essay such as this, but an indication of the nature of these insights can none the less be provided.

- Adair (1993), for example, discusses the cultural significance of sweets, confectionary and chocolate, a seemingly mundane market but one that is worth billions and forms part of the daily lives of literally millions of people. In a wonderfully evocative, skilful and original article, he outlines the various metaphors inscribed in the construction of these products, describes the oral gratification they provide and notes their nostalgic evocation of times past, innocent childhood and a much-loved but long-departed Great Britain of red telephone boxes, friendly policemen and stiff upper lips, a place where everyone knew their place, everything stopped for tea and birdsong was guaranteed at eventide (Table 5.1).

- Williamson (1986) has commented elegantly on the relationship between art and advertising, arguing that the traditional high art/low art categorisation is paralleled by the social stratification classification schemes of advertisers. High art, she argues, is thus particularly prone to appropriation by advertisers because of its ability – as in the celebrated press and poster advertising campaign for Benson and Hedges cigarettes – to imbue mass market products, and by extension their consumers, with an indelible aura of taste, refinement and exclusivity.

- Shields' (1989) postmodern reading of the West Edmonton Mall emphasises its fragmentation of geographical space and historical time, achieved through a bizarre juxtaposition of hyperreal places and settings (Paris, New Orleans, the Pyramids, Spanish Galleon, etc.). For its patrons, this incongruous, de-centred ensemble induces a 'spatio-temporal haze', prompts the loss of geographical and chronological bearings, and encourages the behavioural enactment of a collective fantasy. The mall is a climate-controlled play space, far removed from the quotidian concerns of daily life and the meterological realities of the Canadian prairies.

- Fiske (1989a), furthermore, has explored the cultural meanings of jeans (informal, egalitarian, individualistic, mythical connections with the American west and so on); examined, through a series of binary oppositions, how jean manufacturers introduce subcultural inflections into their promotional campaigns (male/female, east/west, culture/nature); and contended that the wearing of torn, distressed or otherwise disfigured jeans represents a form of 'semiotic guerrilla warfare', a means of resisting the commodification process. Notwithstanding capital's ability to appropriate these oppositional tendencies through the production of pre-torn, pre-faded or pre-washed variants of the product, subordinate social groups continue to evade, expropriate and subvert the hegemony of the capitalist system.

- Kellner's (1992) critical discussion of the function of cigarette advertisements in postmodern society notes how they contribute to identity formation through subject positions, ideological coding and the meanings and values they seek to communicate. Specifically, he deconstructs a sequence of advertisements for Marlboro and shows how the

Table 5.1 Sweet dreams

I suppose the great goal of any newspaper columnist is to discover some subject on which none of his rivals has as yet alit, a subject of small but real significance in the texture of our lives but which ideally has never been written about – in short, a scoop. Well, I fancy I've found just such a subject, one whose most intriguing feature is precisely the conspiracy of columnistic silence that surrounds it. The subject I refer to is sweets.

Why does nobody ever write about sweets? I mean sweets, humble confectionery, as stocked in any ordinary newsagents: Rolos and Polos, Picnic and Yorkie bars, fruit pastilles and liquorice allsorts, coconut ice and marzipan, the sort of sweets that all but monopolised our childhood reveries (remember?), that still constitute an occasional indulgence in most of our adulthoods and that, so it's claimed, are retailed in far greater quantities (if not necessarily qualities) in Britain than in any other country in the world. If chocolate – or rather, that excessive craving for it which is called 'Chocoholism' – has received fairly extensive journalistic coverage, sweets as a general category (instead of as a threat to dental hygiene) have prompted almost no copy at all.

It's the near-inexhaustible variety of sweets that makes one wonder why their metaphorical potential has been so seldom tapped. Scientifically speaking, they variously suggest the molecular (Maltesers, Aero bars), the geological (those chocolate bars with their successive strata of fudge, nougat, caramel, peanut brittle), the topological (Polo mints, whirly liquorice strips), the agricultural (Fruit Gums, jelly beans) and the geographical (the sharp Alpine serration of Toblerone). In a cultural context, they hint at Cubism (Bassett's little Liquorice Allsorts man is almost a breach of Fernand Léger's copyright), primitivism (dolly mixtures, jelly babies), pop art (lollipops, *passim*), op art (old-fashioned candy-striped humbugs) and pure abstraction (what could be more like Carl Andre's notorious installation of bricks in the Tate Gallery than a bar of Cadbury's Dairy Milk?).

Sweets are interesting for several other reasons, too. They have an infallibly Proustian potency for calling up the spirits of one's childhood. They have a tendency to date one (or me, at least) in the generational sense: on the rare occasions when I buy sweets for myself, I invariably remain faithful to those of my own childhood that are still extant, and I'll have no truck with Lion or Dime Bars or any of that new-fangled rubbish. As Adam Thorpe (in his novel *Ulverton*) understood, sweets operate as a vivid signifier of a long-vanished Britain – a Britain of village shops with shiny copper weights and small white paper packets which you opened by blowing into and enormous glass jars which had to be fetched down from the topmost shelf with a step-ladder and whose Bakelite lids were devilish hard to unscrew. And, of course, they function as a premature glimmer of the pleasures of oral gratification when indulged in, like certain types of unreproductive sex, for its own sake alone. Sweets are consumed for themselves. They are gratuitous, futile and not too healthy. But they are also little aspirins of contentment – ephemeral contentment, to be sure, but not much more so than any more elevated manifestation of that elusive state.

Source: Adair (1993), p.8

increasingly abstract images continue to signify the brand's traditional connotations of ruggedness, independence, power and masculinity, while requiring consumers to decipher the text and actively construct its meaning or meanings. The pleasurable feeling that this feat of interpretation induces is transferred to the product, he argues, thereby reinforcing Marlboro's association with freedom and creativity.

- Willis (1991), likewise, in a virtuoso analysis of marketing phenomena, ranging from the iconography of plastic, see-through packaging and the craze for Cabbage Patch dolls, to the metamorphosis of various company logos, contends that the neighbourhood supermarket is in fact a theme park manqué, nothing less than a 'postmodern museum of the third world' (p.17). The displays of exotic fruit include museum-like descriptions; simulacra of work, service and management are undertaken (coffee grinding, orange juicing, photographs of rarely-seen management decorating customer service counters); and tableaux of in-store bakeries, delicatessens, florists and gourmet food sections are staffed by store personnel whose uniforms are more dramaturgical than practical. For Willis, indeed, the entire operation of the store is an exercise in theme park theatricality.

These examples, it must be emphasised, could be extended almost indefinitely. A very short shortlist might include (say) Featherstone (1991) or Reekie's (1993) analyses of the cultural significance of the department store; Harvey's (1989) succinct deconstruction of a Citizen Watch advertisement; Jameson's (1984) much-cited discourse on the Bonaventure Hotel in Los Angeles; Adair (1992) on the notorious Benetton promotional campaign; Bowlby's (1985, 1993) literary insights into the nature of shopper behaviour; Eco's (1986) identification of the hyperreal in the Madonna Inn, a theme hotel in California; Davidson's (1992) comparison of British and American advertisements for BMW; du Gay and Negus (1994) on the atmospherics and layout of record shops; Fiske *et al.*'s (1987) exploration of Australian pub, beach and shopping culture; Ferguson (1992) and Morris's (1993b) respective studies of Princes Square speciality shopping centre in Glasgow and Green Hills community centre in Newcastle, New South Wales; Williamson (1986), Schudson (1984), Miller (1987) or Jhally's (1990) investigations into the nature, meaning and ideology of contemporary advertising; and, not least, Ewen (1988), de Certeau (1984), Bourdieu's (1984) and Lefebvre's (1991) classic studies of everyday consumption and consumption-related behaviours.

When this corpus of extra-marketing marketing literature is examined from a marketing perspective, several important points emerge. The first of these is that the analyses are almost totally devoid of empirical evidence and, therefore, the extent to which consumers actually experience the 'decentered hyperspace' of the Bonaventure Hotel, described by Jameson

(1984), the 'spatio-temporal haze' that Shields (1989) identified in West Edmonton Mall, or the 'mythology of domesticity' Davidson (1992) infers from a four-sheet poster for Persil washing powder, is somewhat uncertain, to say the least. As Featherstone (1991, p.5) makes clear, 'while learned references to the characteristic experiences of postmodernity are important we need to work from more systematic data and should not rely on the readings of intellectuals'. Second, the studies are characterised by an incomplete view of marketing in that they concentrate on its most visible manifestations – advertising, retail stores and shopping malls, consumer behaviour and, to a lesser extent, specific products – rather than the entire spectrum of marketing functions, tools and techniques. Extra-marketing investigations of marketing planning, physical distribution and pricing policies, to cite but three examples, are conspicuous by their absence. Third, they are inclined to view marketing phenomena from the outside in, as it were, instead of the company-centred, inside out perspective that prevails among marketing academics,[1] though there is some evidence to suggest that this orientation is changing. Lash and Urry (1994), for instance, have recently explored the organisation, methods and world view of the advertising industry, as has Davidson (1992), and a broadly similar approach to market research organisations has been adopted by Mort (1989). Fourth, it is fair to say that the bulk of these studies concentrate on the activities of marketing practitioners (the trade press and interviews with key informants seem to be the principal sources employed) in preference to the contributions of marketing scholars. Indeed, on the few occasions when the latter are utilised, condemnation is not slow in coming. Thus, Tomlinson (1990, p.24) describes Baker's well-known model of consumer behaviour as a 'triumph of the trite . . . [with] . . . no sense of the centrality of the processes of signification in the marketing process' and Willmott (1993, p.217) dismisses marketing theory and academic research *in toto* as 'uncritically subordinated to the service of corporate values and priorities'.

Finally, and from a mainstream marketing standpoint, perhaps the most problematic aspect of this body of literature, is its oppositional ethos. Marketing in general and advertising in particular are invariably portrayed as the manipulative handmaidens of multinational capital, extremely powerful instruments for stimulating unnecessary wants, raising unfulfillable expectations and seducing gullible, undiscerning individuals onto the treadmill of insatiable consumption from which they will never be released no matter how hard they pedal. This postmodern Sisyphean labour is a direct consequence of marketing's pernicious ability to create imaginary worlds of perfect appearances, perfect personal relationships, perfect families, perfect personalities, perfect careers, perfect holidays, perfect presents, perfect pizzas, perfectly pulled pints and perfect imperfections, to which we are all induced to aspire and invariably seek to identify ourselves. Whereas the 'modern' individual's sense of identity derived from his or her work role – miner, schoolteacher, farmer, etc. – and remained comparatively stable as a consequence, the identities of 'postmodern' individuals are inextricably linked with their patterns of consumption, their possessions, their fashion-consciousness, their conspicuous display of branded goods (cars, clothing, perfume, etc.). Albeit hollow, de-centred and characterised by secular rather than spiritual fulfilment, postmodern identities are extremely fluid, infinitely adaptable and easily changed through the acquisition of new repertoires of products with the requisite marketing-implanted images (Bocock 1993).

In fairness to the present generation of cultural commentators, their stance on marketing and advertising is much more sophisticated than the hostile condescension that characterised their predecessors such as Raymond Williams (1980), Adorno and Horkheimer (1973) or, as we saw in Chapter 1, F.R. Leavis. Consumers are no longer portrayed as malleable, simple-minded dupes held in marketing's mendacious thrall, but as astute, discerning, self-aware individuals who *enjoy* shopping and identity transformation, are fluent in the language of advertising and revel in the whole consumption experience, yet at the same time remain capable of ironic detachment, doughty resistance and subverting rather than succumbing to the machinations of marketing and multinational capital (Fiske 1989a, b; Wernick 1991; Nava 1992). It is no exaggeration to state, however, that this school of thought is implacably opposed to the ideology of the marketplace and, although ready to acknowledge and – prepare to be shocked – *partake* of its attractions (under protest, you understand), continues to seek a secure moral and political platform from which to oppose capital's maleficent but ineluctable commodification process.

Red River

Postmodernism, as Davidson (1992) suggests, may have rendered marketing academically respectable for those on the left of the political spectrum. But for most mainstream marketing practitioners and academics, the left's basic world-view, either in its original hard-line or more recent, less dogmatic variants, is utterly alien and all but incomprehensible. Marketing, like any profession, has its fair share of unethical practices, unprincipled charlatans and barking mad right-wingers. But the left's grand conspiracy theory of rapacious capitalists stoking the flames of consumer desire for their own hegemonic and ideological ends, is a gross distortion at best and arrant nonsense at worst. Most marketing spokespersons, be they practitioners or academics, genuinely believe that they are responding to the needs and wants of consumers; maintain that, all things considered, marketing is a force for the good; and subscribe to the view that, despite its undoubted failings, marketing is socially responsible, ideologically untainted and politically neutral.

Now, you don't need me to tell you that marketing is not socially and ideologically unaligned, nor is it value-free and apolitical. It is absurd to suggest that marketing does not induce excessive consumption or that it is necessarily 'a good thing' (see Pollay 1986, 1987; Holbrook 1987a). And many of marketing's more enthusiastic supporters no doubt rightly stand accused of naive realism, false consciousness, failing to distinguish between appearances and essences, and a host of other politically incorrect practices. Nevertheless, as they themselves are the first to acknowledge, it is the left that got it wrong; it is the left that has had to come to terms with the carnivalesque and liminality of the marketplace; it is the left that has been forced to modify its long-time stance of supercilious superiority and lofty disdain; it is the left that has been emasculated, recuperated and commodified by the running dogs of capital. Indeed, the latter-day capitulation of the left is such that only the most cynical, twisted, mean-spirited misanthrope would take advantage of the opportunity presented by its intellectual surrender to point out that none other than Roland Barthes, the scourge of the bourgeoisie, once worked for an advertising agency. As you should know by now, I'm not that sort of person.

The left's loss of intellectual authority, comparatively speaking, might tempt many academic marketers to dismiss such extra-disciplinary intrusions and continue on their merry epistemological way as if nothing untoward had occurred. After all, the left's view of marketing is ill-informed, partial, passé, lacks empirical support and is predicated on an outmoded, morally questionable and historically bankrupt political philosophy. Although this attitude is eminently understandable, and has some basis in fact, it is important to appreciate that many of the extra-marketing marketing analyses are just as informative – arguably much more informative – as their equivalents in the marketing literature. For example, you only have to compare Wernick's (1991) astonishing deconstruction of a Marlboro advertisement with that recently proffered by Stern (1993); or Solomon's (1986) symbolic interactionist study of jeans wearers with Fiske's (1989a) above-mentioned *tour de force*; or the contrasting insights into the marketing of places provided by Sack (1992) and Kotler *et al.* (1993) respectively, to appreciate that academic marketing has much to learn from oppositionally inclined researchers. Their ideological agenda, supercilious self-righteousness and traditional disdain for our discipline and practice may be misinformed, unsettling and all too readily dismissed as the death rattle of the loony left, but their standards of scholarship are unsurpassed by anything academic marketing has to offer.

Academic marketers, to be fair, have not ignored the advent of postmodernism. On the contrary, the movement has attracted a great deal of attention, though in many cases the researchers concerned do not *explicitly* place their individual studies within a postmodernist framework. In truth, all of the characteristic features of postmodern pluralism, which were outlined in the previous chapter, have been subject to investigation by marketing academics, some more often than others:

- *Fragmentation* clearly underpins academic reflections on the disinte-gration of mass markets, lies at the heart of the current enthusiasm for 'micro-marketing', 'database marketing', 'one-on-one marketing', etc., and inheres in attempts to comprehend contemporary consumer behav-iour, developments in Eastern Europe, information technology and the world economy (Mueller-Heumann 1992; Thomas 1993; Dussart 1994; Lansley 1994);

- *De-differentiation* is evident not only in copious academic studies of strategic alliances, joint ventures, infomercials, vertical marketing systems and the all-pervasive rhetoric of 'relationships', but it is also implicated in the application of marketing technology – a degraded cultural form – to élite domains such as museums, the arts, religion and so on (Barnes and Stafford 1993; Jennings and Saunders 1993; Hunt 1994);

- *Hyperreality*, if you are inclined to indulge in postmodern proprietor-ship, subsumes almost every study of store, corporate or brand image, price perceptions, advertising effects and store atmospherics, though some of the most interesting work at present involves the scripts, schemata and dramaturgical roles played by participants in the service encounter (Grove and Fisk 1991; Stern 1992; Guiry 1992);

- *Chronology* is apparent in academic investigations of time perception, just-in-time distribution, the advertising implications of television channel hopping, voiceover compression, fifteen second advertising 'spots', etc., and, not least, consumer researchers' new found interest in nostalgia and 'the good old days' (Kaufman *et al.* 1991; Stafford *et al.* 1993; Holbrook 1993);

- *Pastiche*, interestingly, is a category in which comparatively few main-stream academic analyses can be placed, possibly because of its para-digmatic nature – in other words, most research that broaches the topic (e.g. Grafton Small and Linstead's (1985) work on architectural brico-lage; Belk's (1987) tongue-in-cheek suggestions concerning the discipline of consumer research; or Holbrook and colleagues' (1989) 'positivistic' analysis of a short story) tends to do so within a broad 'postmodern marketing' framework;

- *Anti-foundationalism* is part and parcel of the philosophical convulsions that have rocked marketing scholarship in the past decade or so, and the host of questions currently being asked about the continuing utility of the marketing concept, but its most obvious manifestation is in the enormous academic interest being shown in 'green marketing' issues, sustainable development and suchlike (Alwitt and Berger 1993; Troy 1993; Foxall 1994; Simintiras *et al.* 1994).

Apart from such 'inadvertent' postmodern analyses, as it were, a number of more specific instantiations can be identified. By this I mean academic research that deals directly with postmodernism, as discussed in Chapter 3, albeit bereft of the accompanying 'postmodern' lexicon. Dawson (1979, 1982), for example, has described the rapidly changing nature of the retail industry in terms of Bell's post-industrial hypothesis, arguing that we are in the throes of a 'retailing revolution' comparable to the Industrial Revolution of the nineteenth century. Developments in macro-marketing in general and marketing organisation in particular have been accorded broadly similar treatment (e.g. Nason 1985; Rosenberg 1985). Post-Fordism, furthermore, provides the conceptual framework for Freathy and Sparks' (1992) recent research into contemporary patterns of retail change. Not only do they highlight Henry Ford's contributions to modern retailing, in the form of the first supermarket, but they argue that retail organisations, much more so than the manufacturers normally cited by academic researchers, exemplify the distinguishing features of post-Fordism – information technology driven, flexible specialisation, polarised employment patterns, etc. The post-structuralist's preoccupation with metaphorical reasoning is paralleled by manifold published reflections on marketing metaphors (Zikmund 1982; Arndt 1985; van den Bulte 1994) and postmodern science also has its marketing disciples. True, we are eagerly awaiting the first academic marketing treatise on shamanistic drumming, though Gould's (1991) encomium to idiot dancing comes pretty close, but Sheldrake's 'formative causation' (Kohli and Novak 1984), Kapra's *Tao of Physics* (Firat 1989; Olson 1991; Belk *et al.* 1989), Lovelock's Gaia hypothesis (Fisk 1994) and, not least, the implications of chaos theory (McQuitty 1992; Diamond 1993) have all been addressed or referred to in the academic marketing literature.

However, by far the most influential aspect of postmodernism thus far derives from Kuhn and Feyerabend's respective insights into the history and philosophy of science. As with many academic disciplines, Kuhn's 'paradigmatic' terminology and his model of scientific revolutions have attracted a great deal of attention from – and achieved very little consensus among – researchers who have sought to apply them to the development of marketing thought (see Dholakia and Arndt 1985). For some, the model has much to commend it, especially at a time of disciplinary infighting where it holds out the prospect of eventual reconciliation (Roberts 1984; Rassuli 1991). For others, marketing science is still at the pre-paradigmatic stage and hence application of the framework is premature (Uusitalo and Uusitalo 1985). And for yet others, the Kuhnian model is seriously flawed and alternative formulations, such as Lakatos's 'methodology of scientific research programmes' or Laudan's 'reticulated model of scientific rationality' have been explored (Leong 1985; Anderson 1986). Feyerabend's epistemological anarchism also has its marketing adherents,

though many academics are understandably chary of associating themselves unequivocally with a philosophy that, if the onslaught of its opponents is to be believed, places them on a par with satanists, child molesters,
neo-Nazis, lawyers, estate agents and, how can I put this?, marketing practitioners. Noteworthy exceptions include Peter (1983), Arndt (1985) and
Foxall (1990). Indeed, as one of the few marketing scholars who appear
to have taken the trouble to read Feyerabend with an open mind, Foxall
argues persuasively for the active interplay – the deliberate confrontation
– of tenaciously held competing paradigms and demonstrates the utility of
this approach in terms of the behaviourist and cognitive interpretations of
consumer research.

More far-reaching perhaps than direct references to Kuhn and
Feyerabend, the relativism inherent in their positions prompted what has
proved to be the most profound, prolonged and polemical debate in the
history of marketing thought. Although in certain respects a continuation
of the long-running 'art or science' controversy, the confrontation
commenced in 1983 when Paul Anderson challenged the fundamental
philosophical premises of marketing scholarship. The received view,
variously if imprecisely described as 'positivist', 'positivistic' or 'logical
empiricist', rests on the assumption that a single, external world exists,
that this social reality can be empirically measured by independent
observers using objective methods, and that it can be explained and
predicted through the identification of universal laws or law-like generalisations. Anderson, by contrast, sought to demonstrate the shortcomings
of this conventional wisdom: principally, its dependence on the flawed
'verification theory of meaning'; the inadequacies of its falsificationist
procedure; and the difficulties presented by the inherent theory-ladenness
of observation. The verification theory of meaning holds that only empirically verified propositions can be considered meaningful, but, as a
consequence of the problem of induction (the fact that no matter how
many tests a theory passes it can never be considered proven, because the
next test might fail), verification is ultimately unattainable. What is more,
Popper's attempt to circumvent this difficulty through falsification, which
attempts to refute rather than confirm deductively derived theoretical
conjectures, also fails as it is impossible, in practice, to refute a theory
(any number of 'explanations' for an aberrant empirical test can be
constructed).[2] The notion of a secure observational base is equally falla-
cious due to the fact that data are theory-laden; in other words, empirical data only become meaningful within the context of an existing theory.
They are not antecedent to theory, they are determined by it.

In these circumstances, Anderson (1983, 1986, 1989) concluded that
marketing is ill-served by the positivist perspective and that a relativist
approach, subsequently termed 'critical relativism', has much more to
offer. This maintains that, although an external world may well exist 'out

there', it is impossible to access this world independently of human sensations, perceptions and interpretations. Hence, 'reality' is not objective and external to the observer but socially constructed and given meaning by human actors. What counts as knowledge about this world is *relative* to different times, contexts and research communities. Relativism holds that there are no universal standards for judging knowledge claims, that different research communities construct different world views, which are effectively immune from outside criticism, and that science is a social process where consensus prevails about the status of knowledge claims, scientific standards and the like, though these are not immutable. Science is so social, in fact, that Peter and Olson (1983), in their ringing endorsement of the relativist position, concluded that science is a special case of marketing, that successful scientific theories are those which have performed well in the marketplace of ideas thanks to the marketing skills of their proponents.

It almost goes without saying that the relativists' eschewal of the orthodox idea of marketing science – as objectively proven knowledge – and its replacement with the notion of science as societal consensus, provoked a ferocious reaction. The foremost defender of the faith, Shelby Hunt (1984, 1990, 1992), was particularly scathing about relativism, arguing that it leads inexorably to nihilism, irrationalism, incoherence and irrelevance. 'The discipline of marketing', he thundered, 'is hardly advanced by adopting a philosophy that sees no difference between astronomy and medical science on the one hand and astrology and palmistry on the other' (Hunt 1984, p.34). Battle was thus joined and over the next decade or so, marketing's philosophical heavyweights slugged it out on terrain as diverse as demarcation criteria, 'truth', 'reification', 'incommensurability', and quantitative versus qualitative research methodology. The precise assumptions of logical positivists, logical empiricists and falsificationists were clarified; the oft-repeated assertion that marketing is dominated by positivism was challenged; 'scientific realism', which holds that the world external to human cognition is a real world comprising hard, tangible, measurable and ultimately knowable structures, was advanced as a candidate for marketing's philosophical redemption and its differences from positivism and relativism explained. The manifold variants of relativism and realism were also explicated, professional philosophers were called in as putative referees, and, when the combatants eventually battered each other to a standstill, an uneasy truce descended on the battlefield (see Kavanagh 1994).

The smoke, however, has since dispersed, the dead and wounded attended to, and the ultimate, appropriately ironic, outcome of the conflict is now apparent. Shelby Hunt, the indefatigable champion of realism, has done more to advance the cause of relativism than any of its advocates! In his self-appointed role as marketing's philosophical gun-slinger – the fastest epistemologist in the west – Hunt's intemperate invective, vituper-ative rejoinders and, it has to be said, disingenuous dogmatism merely served to focus attention on, and thereby helped legitimise, the relativist position. It is quite probable that mainstream marketing research would have continued in its hypothetico-deductive way, all but oblivious to the relativist option, if it were not for the rootin'-tootin' activities of trigger-happy marketing philosophers. Granted, the vast bulk of marketing academics still work within a broadly realist/empiricist/ instrumentalist/positivistic framework, but very few, I suspect, are unaware of the alternative epistemological options that are now available (O'Shaughnessy 1992b).

Weird Science

Regardless of the long-term outcome of the 'realism versus relativism' debate, it opened the door for a host of unconventional approaches to marketing scholarship in general and consumer research in particular. Disillusioned by the traditionalists' mechanistic, hypothetico-deductive search for law-like generalisations concerning consumer decision taking and information processing, a group of avant-garde marketing researchers have sought to comprehend, through a variety of interpretive approaches, the deeply-felt beliefs, emotions and meanings that inhere in the rituals, myths and symbols of consumption behaviour (Hudson and Ozanne 1988). These approaches have been accorded a number of descriptors (e.g. post-positivist, naturalistic, hermeneutic, constructionist, humanistic and, the one I plan to employ, interpretive), none of which does full justice to the multiplicity of contrasting perspectives that form part of this anti-positivist alliance. Indeed, the diversity is such that several commentators have taken to using the term 'postmodern', with all its polysemic and ecumenical over-tones, to describe the movement. For example, in his introduction to the June 1989 issue of the *Journal of Consumer Research*, which contains the apotheosis of interpretive consumer research, Belk, Wallendorf and Sherry's majestic exposition of the Consumer Odyssey project, the editor of the journal, Richard J. Lutz, describes their work as 'post-modern'. Hirschman and Holbrook's (1992) recent, exemplary monograph on interpretive consumer research places *humanistic, hermeneutic, semiotic, phenomeno-logical, existential* and several other approaches under the 'postmodern' umbrella. And, Sherry's (1991) seminal summary of the 'postmodern alter-natives' available to interpretive consumer researchers situates *critical theory, literary theory* and *historical perspectives* within postmodernism's capacious domain. Even critics of the interpretive turn, most notably Shelby Hunt (1994), have taken to using 'postmodern' in a catch-all sense.

Although, as we noted at the start of Chapter 3, the appropriation of the term 'postmodern', with all its cutting-edge connotations, is a fairly common practice among academic disciplines engaged in internecine warfare, the epistemological positions espoused by many 'postmodern' marketing and consumer researchers do not accord with *our* version of postmodernism. If, admittedly, we imagine a conceptual continuum with (say) logical empiricism at one end and Baudrillard's apocalyptic postmodernism at the other, then it is undeniable that the bulk of interpretive marketing research lies toward the latter end of the spectrum. Nevertheless, most of the positions championed by 'postmodern' marketing scholars have been specifically rejected by the leading lights of the postmodern moment – Derrida, Lyotard, Foucault, Baudrillard and the rest. Indeed, in some cases, such as humanism and critical theory, their stances are almost diametrically opposed.

For example, the *humanistic* perspective, according to its principal adherent in marketing and consumer research, involves an 'orienting strategy' (a basic set of beliefs which cannot be validated as true or false and is rarely, if ever, replaced) made up of the following assumptions: that human beings construct multiple realities; that the researcher and the phenomenon under study are mutually interactive; that research inquiry is directed towards the development of idiographic knowledge; that causes and effects cannot be separated; that research is inherently value-laden; and that the outcome of research – i.e. knowledge – is socially constructed, not discovered. Clearly, this is a world away from the controlled experiments and mathematical models of the traditional marketing metaphysic, which holds that there is a single tangible reality, the researcher and the researched are independent, generalisable truth statements are identifiable, causes and effects can be distinguished, and objective, value-free knowledge can be discovered (Hirschman 1986).

Be that as it may, Hirschman's humanism is *not*, and cannot be construed as, postmodernism, because it presupposes an autonomous human subject, the free-thinking, self-conscious individual that post-structuralists, such as Derrida and Foucault, categorically repudiated and considered to be essentially an epiphenomenon of language. In fact, this 'death of the subject' thesis is captured in one of the most frequently cited passages in the entire postmodern canon, Foucault's (1972, p.387) famous 'wager' that in the forthcoming (postmodern) era, 'man would be erased, like a face drawn in sand at the edge of the sea'. As Rosenau (1992, p.47) emphatically points out, albeit not without exaggeration, postmodernists consider humanism to be a,

> logocentric meta-narrative, seeking to provide answers based only on its own unquestioned, internally validated, fixed frame of reference. It propels the human subject to the centre and implies 'man as master of the universe, dominating, controlling, deciding'. . . . While claiming to better the human condition . . . humanism has misled humankind

into Marxism, National Socialism and Stalinism . . . [and] . . . has been used to justify Western superiority and cultural imperialism.

The *Critical Theory* of the Frankfurt School is also often cited as an example of postmodernism in marketing and consumer research (Hetrick 1989; Sherry 1991). A number of prominent marketing scholars have extolled the virtues of critical theory (Rogers 1987; Firat 1989; Iyer 1991) and at least one well-known authority on the subject, Mark Poster, has addressed an audience of marketing academics (Poster and Venkatesh 1987). However, perhaps the fullest expression of this perspective is found in a paper by Murray and Ozanne (1991), who, in a somewhat emasculated exposition (presumably the more radical denunciations of consumer society made by critical theorists, were deemed too inflammatory for mainstream consumer researchers), presented a brief history of the Institute for Social Research and outlined critical theory's principal principles. These include the belief that research should comprise a critique of society; that this criticism should be interdisciplinary; that theory and practice are inseparable; that orthodox Marxism should be rejected and the proletariat abandoned as an agent of change; that facts and values are interdependent; and that genuine knowledge is a potential instrument of emancipation. Whereas, in other words, the positivistically inclined hold that reality is objective, singular and divisible, and interpretivists consider it to be socially constructed, multiple and holistic, critical theorists see reality in its dynamic, historical totality, as a 'force field' between subject and object. Where positivism is predicated on nomothetic, context-independent, value-free and ahistorical knowledge, and interpretivism assumes idiographic, context-dependent, value-laden and time-bound knowledge structures, critical theory is forward-looking, practical, imaginative and committed to unmasking false consciousness, hidden epistemological assumptions and the forms of domination that lurk behind supposedly 'scientific', 'rational', 'objective' and 'value-free' knowledge claims. And where, finally, positivists seek explanation and interpretivists understanding, critical theorists pursue the holy grail of human emancipation (Murray and Ozanne 1991).

While marketing has much to learn from critical theory, not least the opportunity it provides to unpack 'the myth of market freedom and with it the myth of marketing itself' (Morgan 1992, p.136), it is quite incorrect to conclude that postmodernism and critical theory are one and the same. On the contrary, the foremost contemporary figure in the Frankfurt School tradition, Jürgen Habermas, is far and away postmodernism's most formidable critic. Habermas (1985, 1987, 1992), in complete contrast to Lyotard, firmly believes in the continuing importance of the Enlightenment project, though he acknowledges that its record is far from unsullied and that knowledge has undoubtedly become computerised, compartmentalised, commodified and fragmented. He argues, nevertheless, that to abandon the emancipatory aspirations of modernity, to give it up as a lost cause, or to deny the genuine progress that has been made since the pre-modern period, is merely to acquiesce to anti-modernists like Lyotard, Foucault and Derrida, which can only result in disillusion, entropy and neo-conservatism. Most importantly perhaps, Habermas maintains that his own theory of communicative action (in which an ideal speech situation of egalitarianism, rationality and free, undistorted communication between individuals and social groups obtains, and where the views of minorities, the oppressed and marginalised are recognised, and treated in a just, demo-cratic fashion) provides a way of circumventing the situation, described by Lyotard, of knowledge fragmentation into an infinite number of hetero-geneous and incompatible language games (see White 1988; Burrell 1994). Yet, despite Habermas's doughty attempts to hold back the tides of irrationality – and the irrationalists' tart rejoinders (see Rorty 1985; Foucault 1991) – it is generally accepted that the credibility of critical theory has been severely dented by the advent of the postmodern project and attempts to rethink the movement are underway (e.g. Bannet 1993). As Ray (1993, p.ix) acknowledges, 'the notion of historically grounded reason, which offers both the legitimisation for Critical Theory and the impetus behind the resistance of oppression, has become unfashionable in an intellectual milieu informed by relativism and postmodernism.'

Closely aligned with critical theory, in so far as Habermasian insights are dependent on a modification of the procedure, is the so-called 'linguistic turn' in consumer and marketing research (O'Shaughnessy and Holbrook 1988). Frequently portrayed as an essential part of the postmodern marketing moment, this comprises *hermeneutics*, *semiotics* and several analogous positions (see Mick 1986), all of which are premised on what Hirschman and Holbrook (1992) term, a 'linguistic construction of reality'. Originally a method for recovering the meaning of ancient texts, and regarded by Dilthey as the key to the human sciences' ultimate aim of 'understanding', hermeneutics was extended by Gadamer and Ricoeur to the interpretation of the entire gamut of human activities (see Silverman 1991). In effect, every human action or artefact can be 'read' as if it is a 'text' and an understanding of its meaning derived by recourse to the appropriate methodology, namely the 'hermeneutic circle'. For Gadamer, this is a self-correcting cycle of interpretive interplay between the whole of the text and its parts, whereby understanding derives from the fusion of the researcher's preconceptions and the context-dependent meanings of the text under consideration (Outhwaite 1985).

This interpretation of meanings is equally central to semiotics, the study or science of signs. Derived, on the one hand, from Ferdinand de Saussure's subdivision of the linguistic sign into 'signifier' and 'signified' (see Chapter 3) and indebted, on the other hand, to US philosopher C.S. Pierce's triadic distinction between 'sign', 'interpretant' and 'designatum', semiotics (or semiology, for those in the European tradition) involves the analysis of systems of signification, the means by which human beings communicate or attempt to communicate through gestures, music, language itself and, of course, food, clothing, possessions, advertisements, etc. (Culler 1981). Although the development of semiotics owes much to the methodical, 'neo-positivistic' endeavours of Mills (Holbrook and Hirschman 1993), the semiological artiste *par excellence* was the early Roland Barthes (1973). In a series of dazzling analyses of French popular culture – wrestling, soap powder, steak and chips, the Citroen DS 19 – he stripped away the surface level of denotative meaning (e.g. a photograph in *Paris-Match* of a black soldier saluting the French flag) to expose a second level – the 'what-goes-without-saying' – of connotation and proceeded to examine its underlying ideological implications (i.e. French imperialism).

Roshomon

The marketing devotees of hermeneutics/semiotics/semiology occasionally complain of their maltreatment at the hands of unsympathetic reviewers (Holbrook and Hirschman 1993), but it is fair to say that such perspectives are now widely regarded as a legitimate, if not entirely mainstream, approach to consumer and marketing research. Indeed, for philosophies that have been described as 'unsubstantiated rantings' and 'lazy cultural relativism' (Thorne 1993, p.243), hermeneutic and semiotic approaches are proving surprisingly popular, having been applied to cinematic consumption, advertising, Japanese package designs, fashion, shopping behaviour, the service encounter and several others besides (e.g. Holbrook and Grayson 1986; McQuarrie and Mick 1992; Sherry and Camargo 1987; Solomon 1983; Deighton 1992). The procedures, of course, are far from perfect. Concern is frequently expressed about the role of the researcher, the validity of the interpretations, the indiscernible impact of deeper social forces and power relations on individual behaviour, and the reliability of protocol statements (Firat 1989; O'Shaughnessy 1992b). However, for the purposes of our present discussion, these shortcomings are inconsequential compared to the simple fact that semiotics and hermeneutics should *not* be confused with postmodernism. As we noted in Chapter 3, the late Roland Barthes eschewed the science of semiology, abandoned his search for deep, underlying structures of meaning and in 'The death of the author', acknowledged the multiplicity of meanings in a text, the sheer profusion of potential interpretations (see Rylance 1994). Foucault and Derrida, furthermore, regarded hermeneutics as old-fashioned, logocentric and predicated on the western metaphysic of progress (metaphysical in so far as it treats the text in a holistic fashion and progressive in its assumption that a closer and closer approximation to true meaning is possible). Nor, it must be emphasised, is this simply a matter of allowing multiple meanings – Ricoeur recognised this possibility, after all. Derrida's deconstruction demonstrates that meaning is indeterminate, that texts are saturated with unresolvable ambiguities, with innumerable, conflicting meanings that operate simultaneously and are disseminated across the iridescent surface of the text. In fact, Jackson and McLeish (1993) go so far as to suggest that deconstruction is the complete opposite of hermeneutics and Holub (1994, p.382) concludes, 'hermeneutics and post-structuralism can be reconciled only by limiting the infinite play of signification while at the same time maintaining the impossibility of determinacy'.

Besides the 'linguistic construction of reality' championed by hermeneuticists and semioticians, a number of marketing exponents of 'individual construction of reality', in the shape of *existentialism* and *phenomenology*, are also evident (Hirschman and Holbrook 1992). Existentialism, as formulated by Kierkegaard in the nineteenth century, elaborated by Heidegger in the 1930s and popularised by Jean-Paul Sartre in the early post-war period, is a philosophical movement which holds that humans are self-creating beings, creatures who are not initially endowed with characters and goals, but who can choose them and what they want to be by an act of pure decision. Whereas everything else in existence merely exists, humans are – uniquely – aware of their existence and consequently have the potential to understand and (possibly) control it. Knowledge resides in the Gestalt, the totality of human existence, and the key to knowledge is an on-going process of self-understanding, which is continually evolving, inherently unstable and never completed (Warnock 1970; Silverman 1988).

If, to paraphrase Jean-Paul Sartre, existence precedes understanding, phenomenology provides a means of comprehending the peculiarities of the human condition. According to its founding father, Edmund Husserl, phenomenology is nothing less than the 'science of the subjective'. It assumes that even though we cannot be certain about the independent existence of objects in the external world, we can be certain about how they appear to us in consciousness. Objects, therefore, are not regarded as things in themselves but as things posited, or intended, by consciousness and hence the act of thinking and the object of the thought are interdependent. For phenomenologists, the external world is reduced to the contents of consciousness alone and it is the exploration of individual human consciousness, either through introspection or third-person accounts of others' experiences, that enables genuine, meaningful knowledge to be attained (Kearney 1986; Macann 1993).

As Eagleton (1983, p.61) caustically notes, however, Husserl's 'transcendent' phenomenology is highly abstract – 'a question of intuiting the universal essence of what it is to be an onion'. In practice, it was Heidegger's 'hermeneutical' phenomenology, coupled with Sartre's mordant prognostications on the meaning of life and Schutz's (1967) studies of the social world that did much to provide phenomenology with an existential grounding. Irrespective of its intellectual forebears, the existential/phenomenological perspective has quite a few contemporary adherents in the academic marketing community. Holbrook (1985, 1986, 1987b, 1988) has written several introspective accounts of his diverse consumption activities; Brown (1989) has penned a broadly similar overview of the international marketing research experience; Thompson *et al.* (1990) assembled third person reports on the shopping practices of married women; Mick and Buhl (1992) have focused on the advertising experiences and contrasting life worlds of three Danish brothers; Hirschman (1990, 1991, 1992) has offered a number of distressing accounts of her personal problems; and, in what will no doubt go down as a monument to male mid-life libidinal angst, Gould (1991) has penned an astonishing introspective essay on his perceived vital energy and its relationship to product use (see also Fennell 1985; Thompson *et al.* 1989; Mick and DeMoss 1990).

Like the hermeneutic/semiotic standpoint, the existentialist/phenomenological position is not short of shortcomings. These include its emphasis on human agency rather than the limitations imposed by socio-economic structures, its aprioristic tendencies (the notion that the mind is endowed with innate ideas or concepts which it has not derived from experience) and its propensity for description, uncontrolled hypotheses and emergent research designs over the explanatory orientation beloved by devotees of positivism (O'Shaughnessy 1992b; Wallendorf and Brooks 1993). From our current perspective, however, the most serious difficulty is that it is not postmodernism. More than almost any other philosophical position, existentialism/phenomenology is predicated on the 'transcendental ego', on free-thinking, autonomous human subjects. In Eagleton's (1983, p.58) words, it 'restored the transcendental subject to its rightful throne. The subject was to be seen as the source and origin of all meaning. . . . The world is what *I* posit or "intend": it is to be grasped in relation to *me*, as a correlate of *my* consciousness'. In fact, it was the outmoded existentialism of Sartre and Camus that French structuralist and post-structuralist thinkers, with their emphasis on the constitutive effects of language and their attempts to de-centre the human subject, were reacting to and stood four-square against (Hawkes 1977; Sturrock 1979a). To conclude, therefore, that existentialism/phenomenology is a postmodern position, as Thompson *et al.* (1989, 1990) have done, is to stretch the concept some way beyond its elastic limit, ductile though it undoubtedly is.

Another approach that is often subsumed under the umbrella of 'postmodern' marketing research is *literary criticism* (Sherry 1991; Hirschman and Holbrook 1992). The most prominent exponent of this perspective is Barbara B. Stern, a consumer researcher who was trained in literary theory

(Hirschman 1989b). In a detailed, and highly illuminating, explication of magazine and television advertisements, which treats them, in effect, as works of literature, Stern (1989a) has demonstrated the importance of prosody (rhythm, metre, rhyme, euphony and cacophony) in effective advertising communication. On another occasion she subjected a single advertisement, a 1929 magazine ad for Ivory Soap Flakes, to a variety of contrasting readings from the manifold schools of literary theory – psychoanalytical, reader-response, Marxist and so on (Stern 1989b). Interestingly, however, although she described the 'deconstructive' approach to literary criticism (post-structuralism, remember, is often termed 'deconstruction' in American literary circles), the Ivory Flakes advertisement was *not* subject to a deconstructive reading. Granted, one of Stern's (1993) subsequent papers has proffered a postmodern feminist deconstruction of various cigarette advertisements, but to suggest that her body of work, or literary criticism generally, is an instantiation of postmodern marketing is clearly an overgeneralisation. Not only does she range across several schools of literary theory, only one of which can legitimately be described as postmodern, but Stern's preferred approach – New Criticism – is about as far from post-structuralist literary theory as it is possible to be. American New Criticism, as espoused by Ransom, Wimsatt, Brooks and the lit-crit establishment of the 1940s, 1950s and 1960s, treated the literary text as an autonomous object, isolated from its historical and social context, or indeed authorial intention and reader response (Robey 1986; Selden and Widdowson 1993). The text, in other words, meant what it meant and an array of objective, rigorous, 'scientific' techniques were developed for the process of its critical interrogation. As Eagleton (1983, p.49) points out, New Criticism's 'battery of critical instruments was a way of competing with the hard sciences on their own terms, in a society where such science was the dominant criterion of knowledge'. It is indeed ironic that this essentially modernist (or realist, in so far as the literary work was treated as an object in itself) approach to literary criticism should be cited as an example of postmodern marketing (see Searle 1994). Not only was American New Criticism the very citadel of literary orthodoxy that fell to Jacques Derrida in his famous 1966 presentation at Yale, 'Structure, sign and play in the discourse of the human sciences', but post-structuralism once went under the epithet, New, New Criticism (Hawkes 1977).

If literary theory has attracted the attention of comparatively few marketing and consumer researchers thus far, the same cannot be said for *historical analysis*. As a result of the pioneering endeavours of Stanley Hollander and his colleagues at Michigan State University, which has led to the establishment of a dedicated, biennial conference and a quarterly newsletter, *Retrospectives in Marketing*, marketing history comprises perhaps the single largest sub-field of 'postmodern' marketing scholarship (see, for example, Hollander and Rassuli 1993). Sherry (1991) goes so far as to suggest that historical perspectives, with their inherently interpretive world view, provide the key to comprehending postmodern developments in contemporary consumer research. Nevett (1991), moreover, maintains that as there are many similarities between the problems that face practising marketing managers and those typically encountered in the study of history, an historical orientation provides a useful antidote to the sterility of the positivistic standpoint which continues to pervade academic marketing. And, according to Lavin and Archdeacon (1989), marketing's latter-day intellectual shift in the direction of relativism/interpretivism has been facilitated by – and has facilitated in turn – the growth of an historical consciousness.

Like literary theory, however, historical perspectives are many and varied. Although most (but by no means all) of these are idiographic in orientation, emphasise the importance of unique events and specific contexts, and are as one in their desire to respect the integrity of the 'facts', there are numerous schools of historical thought – positivist, Marxist, hermeneutic, psychoanalytic, structuralist, idealist, narrative and so on (Jones 1991). While the majority of these contrast sharply with mainstream marketing scholarship, to intimate that historical approaches *per se* count as 'postmodern marketing' is a gross exaggeration. Postmodernism, if anything, endorses the 'end of history' thesis, cultivates a *posthistoire* attitude or, like Foucault, champions an historical world-view consisting of radical discontinuities and iconoclastic revisionism (Rosenau 1992; Niethammer 1992; Goldstein 1994). There is, admittedly, a postmodern movement within historical scholarship – several papers on the implications of postmodernism for history have been published and the 'new historicism' paradigm of contemporary literary theory is broadly postmodernist in ethos (e.g. Ankersmit 1989; Zagorin 1990; Veeser 1989) – but, as far as I am aware, none of this material has materialised in the marketing and consumer research literature. In fact, the one and only reference (to Hayden White's (1989) assessment of the New Historicism movement) specifically dismisses this particular line of thought (Smith and Lux 1993).

Star Trek 2: The Wrath of Kant

The foregoing discussion, it must be stressed, should not be construed as a criticism of marketing's interpretive research community. After all, if it were not for their pioneering endeavours and determination to break the iron grip of the received view, a monograph such as this would never have been possible (yes folks, they have a lot to answer for!). Nor is the above an attempt to denigrate or undermine the marketing insights that have been attained through the adoption of humanism, critical theory, semiology, phenomenology, literary theory or whatever. On the contrary, marketing is a much richer discipline thanks to the perseverance of the interpretivists. The Consumer Odyssey, to name but one of their achievements, will undoubtedly be remembered as a seminal moment of post-war marketing scholarship. What is more, if the deeply hostile tenor of its literature can be tolerated, it is undeniable that marketing has much to gain from critical theory – from a more fully informed, self-reflexive stance than has been apparent hitherto.

Nor, for that matter, do the two previous sections mean to imply that interpretive marketing academics are unaware or somehow ignorant of the extant literature on postmodernism. Nothing could be further from the case. As a glance at the recent publications of (say) Belk, Hirschman, Holbrook, Sherry or Stern amply testify, the holy trinity of Derrida, Foucault and Baudrillard are routinely referred to, albeit usually in passing, and few would deny that Roland Barthes is presently enjoying a whole new lease of life in the marketing literature, the (literal) death of the author notwithstanding. Indeed, the ultimate irony is that any postmodernistically informed attempt to denigrate the interpretivists, the very act of expressing a purist, 'holier than thou' evaluation of this self-styled body of 'postmodern' marketing research, founders on the very rock of postmodernism[3] with its emphasis on the inherent and irreducible undecidability of meaning. If some marketing scholars choose to employ the term 'postmodern' for perspectives – such as McCracken's (1988, 1990) anthropology – which would be considered essentially 'modern' in the original discipline (cf. Tyler 1987; Sangren 1988), or which bear little or no relation to postmodernism as *we* have come to understand it, then so be it. It is a perfectly postmodern thing to do, and for a postmodernist to deny them this freedom is to repudiate the very position he or she purportedly espouses. Silence, as Baudrillard rightly reminds us, is the only appropriate postmodern reaction.

Galling as the interpretivists' appropriation of postmodern terminology seems to be for some card-carrying postmodernists (see for example Costa 1993; Grafton Small 1993a), and confusing as the vacillations of Venkatesh and Sherry undoubtedly are for the uninitiated,[4] such studies are at least redeemed by their very high standards of scholarship. Interpretive research may not be what it claims to be – it's postmodern, Jim, but not as we know it – but it is undeniably insightful. The same, regrettably, cannot be said for another group of marketing researchers who appear to be wielding 'postmodern' terminology somewhat indiscriminately at present. At worst, this involves its use for research which has little or no discernible relationship to postmodernism. Examples include Kropp's (1993) Delphi study of changing consumer values, G. Johnson's (1993) quantitative analysis of managerial cognitions and Nyeck's (1992) investigation into consumer attitudes and orientations. At best, it comprises the use of 'postmodern' in an epochal sense, as a fashionable synonym for 'changed', 'complex' or 'new', often with respect to the dramatic political and economic upheavals of recent years – events in Eastern Europe, the rise of protectionism, environmentalism, religious fundamentalism, etc. Soderlund (1990), for instance, argues that as a result of the new world order, most marketing intelligence systems are incapable of meeting the demands they now face in our postmodern world of chaos, disorder and doubt. Rothman (1992) maintains that a postmodern array of research methods is now required, though the tried-and-tested techniques he advocates – personal interviews, self-completion questionnaires, direct observation and so on – intimates that at most he has a form of retro-marketing research in mind. McDonald (1994), moreover, subscribes to the view that a renewed commitment to the original marketing concept is *the* key to success in the postmodern business environment of the late twentieth century. Although these epochal and vernacular uses of the term contribute to the confusion over postmodernism's domain, described earlier, this tendency is by no means confined to marketing. The term has been employed in this loose sense by the 'fashion victims of thought' (Beaumont 1993, p.43) in many other disciplines and, indeed, this interpretation is also evident in the best-selling books by management gurus and futurologists like Peters (1992), Drucker (1993), Toffler (1990) and Popcorn (1992).

Besides the heroic endeavours of the interpretivists and the abominations of postmodern poseurs – Brown (1993c) in particular – another group of academics (one would be tempted to call them 'authentic' postmodern marketers if it were not for the sheer inauthenticity of the subject matter) has commented extensively on postmodernism in a marketing context. While the group is comparatively few in number and hails largely from the consumer research end of the marketing spectrum, it is growing very rapidly. Its contributions, moreover, are many and varied, but for the purposes of our present discussion these can be divided, yet again, into four rough categories: *general* overviews of postmodernism and its implications for marketing *practice*; analyses of *specific* aspects of the postmodern condition in relation to marketing *practice* or *practices*; general discussions of the *theoretical* ramifications of postmodern marketing; and investigations of the meaning of postmodernism for *specific* marketing *theories* and concepts (Figure 5.2).

With regard to the first category, it is interesting to note that the term 'postmodern' has a surprisingly long history in the management and marketing literature. According to Best and Kellner (1991), it was first used by our old friend Peter Drucker in a 1957 volume entitled *Landmarks of Tomorrow*. Another early exponent was Weldon J. Taylor (1965) who, in a contribution to the perennial 'art versus science' debate, described the nature of marketing science in a postmodern world. Significant though

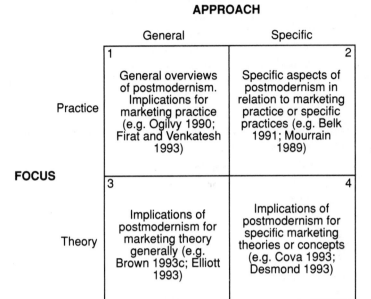

Figure 5.2 Postmodern marketing: approaches and foci

they were, however, these usages comprised little more than adaptations of Toynbee's celebrated temporal schema, which we referred to in Chapter 1 (though Ostergaard (1993) considers Taylor to be a forerunner of Lyotard). Contemporary versions of postmodernism, so to speak, date from the late 1980s–early 1990s, when several important marketing-orientated introductions to the postmodern appeared. By far the best and quite the most accessible of these was written by James Ogilvy (1990), a philosopher and practising market researcher. After dismissing the notion that postmodernism is a passing fad with little to say to the business community, he contended that the modern/postmodern divide revolved around contrasting interpretations of five key issues: the modern idea of progress versus the postmodern rejection of western-style historicism; modernity's faith in science versus postmodernity's utter disillusion; mass manufacturing versus flexible specialisation; bureaucratic hierarchies versus de-layered heterarchies; and the all-encompassing nation state versus the individually orientated private sector. This led Ogilvy to conclude that, in practical marketing terms, postmodernism implies that segmentation strategies should take precedence over global marketing, the dominance of established brands will increase, a greater emphasis on environment-friendly messages is likely to prove necessary and consumer behaviour could become increasingly eclectic and unpredictable in years to come.

Standing shoulder-to-shoulder with Ogilvy's seminal overview is the definitive academic analysis of postmodern marketing practicalities by Firat and Venkatesh (1993). A refinement of several earlier statements by the authors (e.g. Firat 1989; Venkatesh 1989; Firat and Venkatesh 1991), this contribution contends that, with its emphasis on the creation, manipulation and reproduction of images, marketing has taken centre-stage in today's postmodern world of hyperreality, fragmentation, reversed consumption and production, de-centred subjects and paradoxical juxtapositions of opposites. Modern marketing is already a postmodern institution and the ultimate social practice of postmodernity. Indeed, in their enthusiasm for the potential insights provided by postmodern marketing perspectives, Firat and Venkatesh (1993, p.246) actually suggest that marketing represents a new meta-narrative for postmodernism and, hence, 'the new metaphor for life!'. While this may or may not turn out to be the case, the practical implications of marketing's position at the heart of contemporary culture and society are none the less profound. According to Firat and Venkatesh, these range from the dissolution of formerly sacrosanct boundaries (high and low culture etc.) and marketing's ultimate responsibility for the plight of the state education system, to a need for much greater sensitivity to customer heterogeneity. For far too long, they argue, marketing has been content to portray images of the normal, the mainstream, the stereotypical, the beautiful, the perfect. Greater awareness of consumer diversity, difference, heterogeneity and the 'other' is thus urgently required.

Apart from their broad insights into the implications of the postmodern moment, Firat and Venkatesh have sought to explore, in their separate writings, the practical marketing ramifications of certain *specific* aspects of postmodernism. Drawing upon Debord and Baudrillard, Venkatesh (1992) stresses the significance of 'spectacle', 'pastiche', 'liminality', 'affect', 'carnivalesque' and the overall emphasis on the visual in contemporary consumption experiences (e.g. vivid adverts, rock concerts). Firat (1992a), furthermore, examines the nature of 'fragmentation' in the postmodern, arguing that it is everywhere apparent – short television ads, disconnected images on billboards, the separation of products from their contexts, consumer life experiences, gender roles, body parts and the fragmentation of the de-centred self. So much so, that he considers fragmentation to be the universal – the new meta-narrative, no less – of postmodernism. Firat (1992b) has also explored the prevalence of hyperreality on the postmodern marketing scene, as have several other commentators. In fact, it is fair to say that Baudrillard's ruminations on the hyperreal have attracted more comment among academic researchers than almost any other aspect of the postmodern marketing condition. Wright (1989), for instance, discerns evidence of hyperreality in several theme restaurants; Belk (1991) reports on fake representations of the past in consumer sites like Heritage

Village USA and Colonial Williamsburg, which despite their staged inauthenticity and carefully sanitised versions of history, are actually preferred to the real thing; and, in an entertaining parody of Baudrillard's convoluted syntax ('The ecstatic celebration of the synthetic' etc.), Mourrain (1989) identifies the hyperreality that inheres in representations of Californian wine with their paradoxical fusion of incompatible elements, most notably science/technology and history/aesthetics.

Above and beyond analyses of the component parts of postmodernism, a number of postmodern analyses of specific marketing practices can be identified. One of the earliest of these was Grafton Small and Linstead's (1985) identification and deconstruction of the western metaphysic of progress inscribed in a British food manufacturer's promotional literature. This pioneering study has since been followed by a series of elegantly written, elegiac essays on characteristically postmodern marketing themes – gift giving, ethics, nostalgia, personal loss and organisational structures (Grafton Small and Linstead 1989; Linstead and Grafton Small 1990, 1992; Grafton Small 1993b, c). The representation and blurring of gender stereotypes, especially the so-called 'new man', in television advertisements for household cleaning products have also been examined (Elliott *et al.* 1993), as has the relationship between compulsive consumption and the empty postmodern self (Elliott 1994), young people's playful subversion of television advertising (O'Dohonoe 1994), the creation of cult status in innovative consumer products by means of postmodern marketing management techniques like artistic entrepreneurship and enlightened paternalism (Cova and Svanfeldt 1993), the place of fashion, design and perpetual change in postmodern society (Hetzel 1994) and, not least, investigations of the characteristic features of postmodern consumption – spectacle, surfaces, carnivalesque, fragmentation, schizophrenia and the nature of the self – as portrayed in cinematic representations (Belk and Bryce 1993). Perhaps the single most important contribution to our understanding of postmodernism in a specific marketing setting, however, is Linda Scott's (1992) post-structuralist reading of several US magazine advertisements. In an expositional *tour de force*, she effectively moved beyond the structuralist and semiotic approaches which dominate interpretive investigations of the 'postmodern' marketing condition, and revealed the intricate, inchoate and irreducible interplay of intertextual meanings that inhere in even the most literal advertisements.

Hear My Song

The parallels between contemporary marketing practices and the precepts of postmodernism are comparatively clear cut. As a consequence, they have been explored in some detail and with not a little enthusiasm. Commentators on the relationship between marketing *theory* and postmodernism are much less ebullient, however. Although relatively few in number, almost all of those who have examined this issue have come to the conclusion that the implications of the postmodern moment for existing marketing theories and models are *extremely serious* if not fatal. Granted, some of these comments are 'off the cuff', as it were, and others appear to be predicated on a particularly Baudrillardian brand of nihilistic postmodernism. Nevertheless, the effective abandonment of decades of mainstream scholarship and academic endeavour appears to be the price of entry into the ephemeral, idiographic, ambiguous, provisional, schizophrenic world of postmodern marketing. It can, of course, be argued that postmodernism merely reinforces what is already widely acknowledged – that the principles of marketing are far from established. But, it is important to emphasise that whereas most modern marketers maintain that, with a modicum of additional research, superior versions of marketing principles are attainable, postmodernists consider such endeavours to be both unnecessary and futile.

Elliott (1993) typifies this standpoint, in so far as he contends that in a postmodern world characterised by the consumption of symbolic meaning and construction of multiple realities, many of our traditional marketing concepts concerning consumer behaviour, consumption activities and marketing research are in need of fundamental reassessment. Meaning is not determined by marketers but negotiated by consumers. Highly individual, and often inconsistent, interpretations are the norm. In these circumstances, established marketing techniques are inappropriate, customary rules of logic, cause and effect, or sense and sensibility, do not necessarily apply, and language may not be the most appropriate medium for attaining understanding of consumer cognitions. While 'scientific' marketing can continue to be pressed into epistemological service, the outcomes of these endeavours are likely to be superficial and uninsightful. Postmodern marketing scholarship, as Elliott sees it, must learn to tolerate incompatible alternatives, cope with paradox, accept that there is more than one perspective and encourage the contradictory juxtaposition of opposites.

Broadly similar evaluations of the place of marketing theory in postmodernity have been expressed by Hetrick and Lozada (1993) and Brown (1993c). The former authors, in a paean to marketing's need for greater self-consciousness and critical awareness, contend that the discipline is all but incapable of developing postmodern marketing theories. With its traditional emphasis on the 'normal', the 'same', the 'conventional', the 'homogeneous', the 'mainstream' (male/white/heterosexual/professional/affluent, etc.), marketing is likely to have trouble conceptualising or accommodating postmodernism's preoccupation with the 'other', the 'marginalised', the 'disqualified', the 'disenfranchised', the 'deviant', the 'silenced' (female/coloured/homosexual/unqualified/unwaged and so on). The latter commentator simply provides an inventory of marketing models and principles predicated on the modernist assumptions of analysis, planning and control – the 4Ps, SWOT analysis, hierarchy of advertising effects, classification of goods typologies, the strategic matrices of Ansoff, Porter or the BCG, etc. – and deems them unsuitable in a postmodern marketing milieu of intuition, spontaneity and disorganisation. What is more, whereas contemporary marketing practices are manifestly postmodern in ethos, marketing theory remains mired in a futile modernist search for laws, regularities and predictability. According to Brown (1993c, p.25), post-modernism,

> highlights the inherent limitations of many extant marketing models and theories. It asks not only whether exposure to the Boston matrix causes 'cows' to be milked and 'dogs' put to sleep unnecessarily, or whether the inordinate failure rate of new products is due, not to the inadequacies of the products themselves, but to companies' adherence to marketing's misconceptualisation of the NPD process. It also asks the all-important question of whether companies/products/campaigns, etc. succumb because they stray from the path of marketing righteous-ness, as marketers are wont to assume, or because the path itself is heading in the wrong direction.

Clearly, this is an extreme interpretation of the situation, with few crumbs of comfort for the disorientated survivors of postmodernism's conceptual holocaust. This view, however, seems to be shared by most commentators on the implications of postmodernism for *specific* marketing models, frameworks, principles and generalisations. Thus, the marketing concept itself has been subject to several postmodern readings, which have vari-ously concluded that it is 'a classic meta-narrative' (Brown 1994c, p.87), 'failing' (Tornroos and Ranta 1993, p.166), and needs to be 're-examined, recast or even abandoned' (Firat *et al.* 1995, p.54).[5] In a similar vein, the stages model of internationalisation, the production–sales–marketing eras typology and the manifold 'growth of the firm' frameworks (Figure 5.3) have been dismissed as a marketing manifestation of the discredited western metaphysic of inexorable human progress (Brown 1993c). Retail location theory, fashion theory, market segmentation, the new product development process, consumer behaviour theory, image studies, strategic marketing theory and the search for a general theory of marketing have also received short shrift from postmodernistically inclined academics (Firat 1991; Cova 1993; Brown 1993d; Desmond 1993; Tornroos and Ranta 1993; Firat *et al.* 1993). Even the celebrated realism versus rela-tivism debate – the very nature of scientific truth in marketing – has been explored from a broadly postmodernist perspective and the dubious assumptions and rhetorical strategies of the defenders of the marketing faith thereby exposed (Thompson 1993).

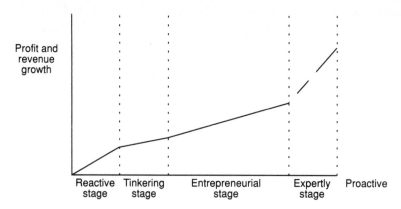

Figure 5.3 The growth of marketing in the firm
Source: Carson (1985)

Disconcerting as the above assessments probably are for mainstream marketing researchers, it must be emphasised that not every model or theory has been swept aside by the tidal wave of postmodernism. Concepts predicated on a cyclical, rise and decline metaphor may be exempt according to some – but by no means all – authorities on the postmodern condition (e.g. Jencks 1989; Burrell 1993; Debord 1994). In this respect, a detailed study of the wheel of retailing theory illustrates postmodernism's ambivalence towards cyclical models of change (Brown 1993e). On the one hand, the wheel theory is universalist, in so far as it assumes the same low-cost, trading-up pattern applies to every retailing institution in every socio-economic setting; it is subject-centred, in that it is predicated on the actions of conscious, free-thinking, self-determining, individual human beings; and it presupposes that history has a pattern or shape. All of these assumptions are anathema to the adepts of postmodernism. On the other hand, the wheel is a prime example of the metaphorical thinking that post-modernists frequently espouse. As one of the most frequently cited concepts in marketing thought, its 'performativity' (to employ Lyotard's key crite-rion) in the marketplace of academic ideas is unimpeachable. Most impor-tantly perhaps, it is premised on the notion of cyclical time (time's cycle), as opposed to the linear interpretation of time that underpins the western world-view (time's arrow). While postmodernists may be opposed to the idea that history has a pattern or shape, the shape they particularly revile is time's arrow – the idea of progress, the ascent of man, the triumphal, ever-upward trajectory of human achievement, which underpins both Marxian and liberal democratic consciousness alike. Even Michel Foucault, widely regarded as *the* historian of discontinuity, does not dismiss the notion of cyclical time completely. On the contrary, in *The Order of Things* he emphasises that the radical breaks discernible in the history of thought (*epistemes* in his terminology) actually exhibit elements of recurrence. Foucault (1972) argues, in short, that when one *episteme* replaces another, certain patterns repeat themselves – changing only in the arrangement of the elements – and do so again during succeeding epistemological transmutations. The parallels with the wheel theory are thus clear: albeit premised on a cyclical analogy, the wheel does not contend that (say) department stores and supermarkets are locked in a continual low-cost, high-cost cycle. The wheel stresses radical discontinuity, the periodic emergence of new, dynamic retail formats that challenge moribund incumbent institutions, but which go through broadly similar patterns of development and decline.

Not everyone, it must be emphasised, would accept Brown's assessment of the place of the wheel theory (or analogous cyclical metaphors) in a postmodern marketing world. In fact, it is fair to say that his reading of the wheel theory represents a desperate attempt to wrest a dubious concept – the one upon which he has built an insubstantial academic career – from the all-consuming flames of postmodernism. It is a sad day for marketing scholarship when such blatant acts of self-interest and academic distortion take the place of reasoned, rational, rigorous, disinterested and (naturally) entirely objective research endeavour.

6 I'll be back!

Perrier has been doing time. It has been banged up. Caught with its hand in the benzene, it has been paying its debt to society. Furthermore, in consequence of that debt, it has been having itself sorted out. Behind the crenellated walls, the caring society has been at it. It has been doctored. It now wears a little bottle-badge which reads 'New production', though it is gamely trying to bear the stigma with pride. In full-page press ads and television commercials, it is winsomely murmuring 'Helleau again'. It is, in short, asking for the forgiveness it has done everything in its power to justify. It is trying to persuade me to give it another chance.

But shall I grant it? I ask because I have just returned from the off-licence, where, sprung only this morning from chokey, Le Perrier Nouveau was sitting expectantly on the shelf, yet what I have come back with is Highland Spring. Not because I hold any brief for Highland Spring, nor for Badoit, nor yet for Malvern, Evian, Volvic, or anything else I have been knocking about while Perrier was doing its bird, but simply because absence makes the heart grow fickle, and promiscuity breeds indiscrimination. If it bubbles, these days, it'll do.

I lie, even to myself. It is a characteristic of the unfaithful. If I think about it honestly, I am forced to recognise that for some time before the tragedy at Vergeze I had been looking for an excuse to part the ways with Perrier. I know the signs now. I have been there before, and more than once. Call them mineral watersheds. . . .

'Eau revoir,' I cried loyally, in the wake of the departing paddy-wagon. But in my heart I knew it was really cheerieau.

(Coren 1990, pp.202–3)

Apocalypse Now

Few would deny that marketing is an enormously important activity. Apart from the millions of people who are directly employed in what may loosely be described as the marketing industry – brand managers, advertising copy-writers, design consultants, market researchers, storekeepers, salesmen, truck drivers, shelf stackers, bill posters, shop assistants, university lecturers and so on – the marketing system impinges upon and affects the everyday lives of literally billions more. It is something that we all encounter on a daily basis, whether it be purchasing a paper from the local newsagent, cursing the trucks and delivery vehicles as they impede our journeys to work, mulling over the messages on the roadside advertising hoardings as they recede rapidly into the distance, binning the junk mail with which we are all ceaselessly inundated, queuing in the express checkout line for the service encounter and our few precious 'moments of truth', associating the inept performance of our favourite football team with its hapless but optimistic sponsors, slumping in front of the television set, surfing through the channels in search of the latest instalment of our favourite advertising soap opera, or scanning the titles of the latest literary blockbusters which offer a one-word solution to our current managerial problems – 'excellence', 'quality', 're-engineering' and, er, 'postmodernism'. The marketing system, moreover, has been held responsible for such diverse occurrences as the modern conception of Christmas, global warming and the collapse of the communist regimes in Eastern Europe. Even the space shuttle has carried advertising on its ample exterior (ironically, for Schwarzenegger's box-office disaster, *Last Action Hero*).

It is impossible, in short, to exaggerate the importance of marketing. In fact, it is fair to say that the sheer extent of marketing's influence and pervasiveness is limited only by the imaginations of those who write about the extent of marketing's influence and pervasiveness. As we saw in Chapter 2, vivid imaginations are not exactly in short supply among marketing fundamentalists and zealots. If the claims in introductory textbooks are taken at face value, marketing is not only the secret of business success and personal accomplishment, but it holds the key to socioeconomic development, world peace and human understanding. However, in order to attain this utopian vision of plenitude, in order to enter this land of marketing milk and honey, you *must* become a true believer, you *must* refuse to stray from the logical empiricist straight and narrow, you *must* resist the epistemological temptations that are placed in your path. Only then will the celestial city open its gates and permit you to enter. The eschaton of marketing orientation can be yours but only if you subscribe to the teachings of the prophets and the four commandments of analysis, planning, implementation and control.

At first glance, the apostles of marketing seem to have discovered the ark of the management covenant. The holy writ of marketing has been accepted by captains of industry and government ministers alike. Successful organisations attribute their achievements to their superior marketing wisdom and knowhow. The receipt of venture capital or start-up finance is invariably dependent upon the existence of a comprehensive and workable marketing plan. Every management consultant worth their (pillar of) salt – or should that be 4Ps of silver? – emphasises the importance of market orientation. A multitude of training courses is now available; centres of marketing scolasticism have been established; undergraduate and postgraduate degree programmes are offered in every self-respecting tower of academic Babel; marketing professors are genuflected to by students and practitioners alike (or so they think); and the flood of marketing publications is becoming almost uncontrollable. After crying in the wilderness for many years, marketing seems to have become acceptable to academics in adjacent disciplines – economics, psychology, geography, sociology, etc. Even those heretics on the left of the political spectrum, intellectual unbelievers who once treated marketing with suspicion, derision and disdain, now regard it with grudging admiration and accord it the respect it undoubtedly deserves.[1] It would appear that marketers have inherited the earth. Indeed, it is said that when businessmen go to management heaven, they often remark on the apparent lack of marketing people. St Peter then tells them that the marketers are kept in a separate compartment, because 'they think they're the only ones here'.

If, to switch from a theological to dramaturgical analogy, the public face of marketing is one of fixed grins, boundless optimism and an irrepressible ethos of 'can do', the private face – the face behind the mask – is deeply troubled, decidedly uncertain and in danger of complete collapse. According to numerous academic authorities and leading practitioners, marketing is in, or teetering on the brink of, a very serious *crisis of representation*. It is characterised by an all-pervasive air of doubt, directionlessness and despair. The vigorous, thrusting project – the marketing revolution – of forty years ago which knew no bounds, took no prisoners and swept all before it has, depending upon which metaphor you prefer, come to a halt, stalled, lost its way, seen better days, fallen from grace, run aground/out of steam/into the sand. Described in detail in Chapter 2, doubts are increasingly being cast on the continuing veracity of the marketing concept. Marketing principles no longer appear relevant to the real world and, if anything, seem to do more harm than good. Leading figures in our field are marketing's most outspoken critics rather than the propagators of the marketing message. Facile conceptual frameworks, which are little more than diluted or rehashed versions of the original marketing concept, are paraded as the answer to marketing's current malaise. Reports on the plight of marketing scholarship are periodically produced and their recommendations routinely ignored. Original research which seeks to extend existing conceptual frameworks is greeted with a resounding 'so what?' or dismissed as 'me-too' or 'minor twist'. The sense of academic cohesion, solidarity and commitment to the marketing cause that once prevailed has been torn asunder by a series of bitter philosophical disputes and declarations of epistemological independence. In these depressing circumstances, it is little wonder that the enthusiasm of marketing's early proponents – or contemporary textbook writers – now strikes us as supremely naive; that the seminal contributions of our discipline's foremost thinkers are treated with irreverence, cynicism and derision (heaven forfend, they'll be disparaging Wroe Alderson or Ted Levitt next); and that many believe the marketing concept is an anachronism, an aberration, a throwback to a bygone age of mass markets and mass marketing. Not everyone, admittedly, would concur with this disconcerting diagnosis of marketing's current state of health (e.g. Bass 1993; Little *et al.* 1994),[2] but the vast majority of contemporary commentators maintain that marketing is in the throes of a 'mid-life crisis', a fundamental crisis of representation (e.g. Freeling 1994; Anderson 1994; McDonald 1994).

The Verdict

It is the contention of this book that marketing's crisis of representation – the widespread belief that something is seriously amiss, that its once solid foundations are by no means secure – is paralleled by postmodernism, which in many respects comprises a crisis of representation in cultural, social and intellectual life generally. Notwithstanding the lack of consensus on the nature of the postmodern moment, most authorities agree that it represents some kind of reaction to or departure from modernism and modernity. As we noted in Chapter 3, the project of modernity dates from the Enlightenment of the eighteenth century and the debate between the ancients and the moderns. Broadly speaking, this comprised an extensive effort to develop rational science, universal laws, absolute truths and, through the accumulation of objective knowledge, overthrow the irrationality of myth and religion (Turner 1990; Hall *et al.* 1992). Although the modern movement was far from monolithic, its archetypal exemplars – the architecture of Le Corbusier and Mies van der Rohe, the novels of Lawrence and Joyce, the poetry of Eliot and Pound, the economics of Marshall and Keynes, the philosophy of Russell and Popper, the management principles of Taylor and Ford etc. – were all characterised by objectivity, rationality and universality. Modernism, in essence, embraced the idea of progress, rejoiced in the power of reason, lauded scientific discovery and technological innovation, espoused the ascent of man, anticipated freedom from oppression and held that, once its fundamental laws and mechanisms were understood, the physical and social world as we know it could be analysed, planned and controlled (Smart 1992).

Postmodernists, by contrast, reject attempts to impose order and coherence on the chaos and fragmentation of 'reality'. Instead, they argue, we should accept that knowledge is bounded, that our capacity to establish meaningful generalisations is limited and, rather than seeking the impossibility of universal truths, we should rejoice in the ephemerality, contingency and diversity of the physical and human worlds as we experience them, be comfortable in the absence of certainty, learn to live without definitive explanations and recognise that the objectives of the Enlightenment project are utopian and unattainable (Rosenau 1992). Whereas, in other words, modernism stands for the so-called 'scientific' virtues of objectivity, rigour, detachment, precision, logic and rationality, postmodernism champions the ostensibly 'artistic' attributes of intuition, creativity, spontaneity, speculation, emotion and involvement. Indeed, in its assertion that everything – be it a haircut, holiday, personal crisis or political upheaval – is a 'text', to be interrogated, interpreted and deconstructed as the reader, not the author, sees fit, postmodernism in many respects represents a repudiation of the natural science model of academic attainment and an espousal of the philosophical principles of the humanities in general and post-structuralist literary theory and linguistics in particular (Rosenau 1992). It positions itself, in Rorty's (1989, p.8) resonant phrase, 'as auxiliary to the poet rather than the physicist'.

Above all else, then, postmodernism is a way of looking at the world. It is a way of looking askance at the world. Postmodernists offer ambiguity where modernists offered certainty, they seek complexity where their predecessors sought simplification, they find disorder where their forebears found order, they see a glass that is half-empty instead of half-full and they challenge convention by refusing to accept the accepted. Postmodernists espouse individuality as opposed to universality, advocate plurality instead of consensus, place heterogeneity above homogeneity, emphasise dissent rather than conformity, and champion difference where modernists stressed similarity. In short, they replace the traditional modernist emphasis on reason, objectivity and control, with unreason, subjectivity and emancipation, with paradox, uncertainty and instability, with a rationale that rejects rationality.

While the postmodern project is not above criticism (see below), its preoccupation with ambiguity, undecidability and chaos cannot fail to strike a chord with observers of the contemporary business and marketing arena. Its juxtaposition of centre and periphery, propinquity of sacred and profane, melding of truth and fiction, conjunction of time and space, interpenetration of old and new, amalgam of natural and human, synthesis of superficial and profound, fusion of male and female, blend of east and west, mixture of ecstasy and tedium, combination of protean and sublime, and union of quotidian and eternal, is very much in tune with today's contradictory business environment where organisations are variously urged to be both global and local, centralised and decentralised, large and small, and planned yet flexible; where workers are expected to be autonomous team players and managers deemed capable of delegating authority while remaining in complete charge; and where efficiency and effectiveness prevail, consistency and flexibility obtain, low cost and differentiation strategies combine, product variety and standardisation co-exist, and both mass and niche markets are served (Handy 1994; Naisbitt 1994; Hampden-Turner and Trompenaars 1994).

Indeed, as Chapter 4 sought to demonstrate, many of the distinguishing features of postmodern pluralism – fragmentation, de-differentiation, hyperreality, chronology, pastiche and anti-foundationalism – are clearly discernible on the current marketing scene. Postmodernism thus provides a perspective on, and means of conceptualising, the dramatic changes that are taking place in the marketing arena, whether it be the fragmentation and turbulence of markets and competition, the emergence of strategic alliances and boundaryless corporations, the rise of the retro product and parodic advertising, the latter-day preoccupation with authenticity, reality and the nature of time, and, not least, the advent of anarchistic, iconoclastic, anti-marketing marketing practices ranging from shock-horror advertising campaigns to the green marketing 'revolution'. Most importantly perhaps, it is arguable that the basic world view, the ethos, the standpoint, the orientation, the, yes, *Weltanschauung* of postmodernism is very much in tune with contemporary marketing sentiment, with its all-pervasive miasma of doubt, uncertainty, disillusion, ennui and scepticism. Postmodernism possesses many incompatible attributes and is composed of numerous tightly interwoven strands, but it is characterised above all by its air of exhaustion, its decadent 'anything goes' cynicism, its sense of dissipation, languor, impotence, evisceration, etiolation, enfeeblement – call it what you will. As Gilbert Adair (1992, p.15) rightly points out, postmodernism represents 'the last gasp of the past'. Bruno Latour (1993, p.9), likewise, describes a situation where postmodernists 'remain suspended between belief and doubt, waiting for the end of the millennium'.

Just as postmodernism's characteristic air of resignation, equivocation and despair parallels the growing disillusion with marketing's seeming lack of meaningful accomplishments, so too some of the most prominent precepts of postmodernism are readily translatable into marketing terms.

- Foucault's concept of power/knowledge is clearly relevant to channel relationships, especially at a time when retailers' scanning systems enable them to provide or withhold precious product performance information from their suppliers. His emphasis on the positive – as opposed to the coercive – effects of power is in tune with the present marketing emphasis on relationships, networks and alliances. Indeed, his late flirtation with individuality-cum-subjectivity, in the shape of 'technologies of the self', is not far removed from today's preoccupation with micro-marketing, one-on-one marketing, database marketing and the like.
- Baudrillard's suggestion that image is all, that illusion is more important than reality, that fact and fiction are indistinguishable, that *image is reality*, may well have been a revolution in Marxian thinking, but it

is unlikely to disconcert too many marketing academics and practitioners. It is a commonplace, arguably the most basic commonplace, of the contemporary marketing world view, where products are routinely developed to match existing images – cf. Calvin Klein, Ralph Lauren – rather than the other way around.

- Lacan's emphasis on the inexorable slippage of the signifier under the signified is highly relevant to the brand building process and, in an expositional triumph, Desmond (1993) has demonstrated the parallels between the mirror stage and market orientation, arguing that the latter is a misrecognition, a profound myopia, a fundamental misunderstanding of how the world is believed to be.

- Lyotard, likewise, may regard 'performativity' as a sign of the intellectual slackening that typifies the postmodern condition, but, as Little *et al.* (1994) have recently shown, the success of marketing science is premised on, and measured by, this very attribute (see also Scott 1993). Lyotard's emphasis on the Kantian sublime is also pertinent to analyses of hedonic consumption, which, we are reliably informed (e.g. Holbrook and Hirschman 1982), is often described in terms of the indescribable – 'you had to be there', 'I can't put it into words', etc.

- The Derridean notion that meaning derives from differences internal to the sign system, that meanings are inherently unstable and, indeed, that signs contain 'traces' of the other signs in a chain of signs, is virtually a blueprint of positioning theory. Products, after all, derive their meanings in terms of their similarities and differences from other competitive products. Meanings are continually changing as a result of promotional activity, modifications and so on. The entire system is interdependent, in that alterations to one product affect the meanings of every other element in the product field, and because consumers inevitably evaluate a product against its perceived competitors and bring their own idiosyncratic interpretations to bear, it follows that each product carries imperceptible 'traces' of the others and that meanings are ultimately unknowable or indeterminate.

In a similar vein, Gummesson's (1991) recent prediction of the end of marketing as a separate function, and its replacement by a de-centred form of marketing practice, which is, in effect, disseminated across the entire organisational archipelago, could just as easily have been made by Michel Foucault or Jacques Derrida. Marketing, moreover, is incorrigibly intertextual, depending as it does on conceptual quotations and borrowings from adjacent disciplines – though the debt is increasingly being repaid, with interest – and is not the marketing message inherently linguistic? Was it not Kotler and Levy (1969, p.12), after all, who stated that 'everything about an organisation talks'?

Even Barthes' 'death of the author' thesis, which may seem quite shocking in terms of our conventional (untutored) views of literature and criticism, turns out to be anything but. In elevating the interpretations of the reader over the authority of the author, Barthes was merely espousing the marketing concept by another name. After all, the revolutionary aspect of the marketing concept was that it considered the needs of the consumer (reader), not those of the producer (author), to be the key to success in business. Barthes' belief that there are no privileged meanings in a text, that no interpretation is better than any other, makes perfect sense to marketers – we cannot control what consumers think and say – and, when considered in these terms, it is clear that a marketing orientation is characterised by the creation of 'writerly' products and services rather than the 'readerly' products and services that typify product- and sales-orientated organisations. Ironically, however, it is only when we encounter something as 'shocking' as the death of the author thesis that we begin to appreciate the unconventional, counter-intuitive and truly revolutionary nature of the original marketing concept, the magic of which has long since ceased to entrance.

Nightmare on Elm Street 2: Freddy's Revenge

Given the clear relevance of postmodernism to marketing practice and thought, it is hardly surprising that the movement has attracted the attention of a burgeoning number of academic marketing researchers. As has been the case in many other disciplines, however, the term has been used in a variety of ways and taken to refer to several quite different phenomena. In Chapter 5 we noted that the various approaches to postmodern marketing can be divided into three broad categories. Setting aside the 'inadvertent', as it were, studies of chronology, relationship marketing and so on, the first approach comprises 'genuine' attempts to grapple with the complexities of postmodernism and assess its implications for marketing. These range from Ogilvy's (1990) and Firat and Venkatesh's (1993) exemplary overviews of postmodern marketing practices, to the specific insights into Lyotard, Derrida and Baudrillard offered by Scott (1993), Linstead and Grafton Small (1992) and Suerdem (1992) respectively. The second approach comprises the fashion victims of thought, individuals who have applied the term to research which bears little relationship to postmodernism, or are using the designation in an essentially epochal sense. In this respect, when a died-in-the-wool 'modern' marketing academic like Malcolm McDonald (1994), someone who has been advancing the cause of rigorous marketing planning for nigh on twenty years, starts reciting the postmodern lexicon, it is difficult to determine the most appropriate response – amusement, bemusement, admiration (for the sheer effrontery) or a rueful shake of the head over yet another postmodern paradox.

The final, and by far the most common, approach to postmodern marketing stems from the sub-discipline of consumer research, where the term is closely associated with the recent advent of interpretive perspectives on consumption activities and behaviour (Sherry 1991; Hirschman and Holbrook 1992). Although the ethos of postmodernism, with its emphasis on academic ecumenism and epistemological plurality, is compatible with these manifold approaches to consumer research – hermeneutics, existentialism, semiotics, critical theory, etc. – some of the latter's champions are in danger of confusing the consequences of a postmodern outlook with the premises of the postmodern project itself. Indeed, some of the positions embraced by prominent 'postmodern' consumer researchers – Hirschman's (1986) humanism, for example – would be rejected by most postmodernists. More importantly perhaps, some of the suggestions currently being mooted, principally Hetrick and Lozada's (1993) contention that postmodern insights can only be attained through the intermediary of critical theory, are patently absurd. While marketing has much to learn from critical theory, it is neither a staging post on the postmodern trail nor a destination in itself. It would be profoundly ironic if western Marxism in general or critical theory in particular – positions, remember, that are in retreat across the entire front of contemporary social science – were to circle the wagons and attempt to regroup in *marketing* of all places. Marketing is the very locus of 'mass deception', according to Adorno and Horkheimer (1973), a milieu that is peopled by propagandists, fascists, jazz musicians and, worst of all, film producers!

Cynics, the mean-spirited and Foucauldians, of course, might be tempted to conclude that interpretive consumer researchers have appropriated the term 'postmodern', with all its cutting-edge connotations, and used it as a weapon to wield in their hegemonic struggle for control of the sub-discipline. After all, the definition of what constitutes marketing 'knowledge' has enormous practical implications for the pedagogic process, publication opportunities and, not least, the career paths and employment prospects of individual researchers. In fairness, however, there still appears to be a widespread belief among marketing academics that postmodern and interpretive (post-positivist, naturalistic, etc.) approaches are one and the same (see, for example, Hill 1993). The fact of the matter is that postmodernism shares many of the characteristics of hermeneutics, critical theory, structuralism, humanism and so on, but it also has important differences with each. As Rosenau (1992, p.14) emphasises,

> post-modernists . . . do not agree with hermeneutics if, in its search for explanation, it assumes that one interpretation is better than others, if its goal is to recover a singular meaning for any political or social act. They question structuralism's commitment to science, rationality, reason and logic and critical theory's emphasis on extratextual explanations of

EPISTEMOLOGY

	Realist	Relativist
Realist	1 'Traditional' marketing research	2 'Traditional' qualitative research
Relativist	3 Interpretive marketing research	4 Postmodern marketing research

ONTOLOGY

Figure 6.1 Research options available to marketing academics

social phenomena. They see the western marxist project of 'emancipation' as logocentric and humanist, criticise its emphasis on the societal totality at the expense of *le quotidien* (the local or daily life), and consider the critical theorist's search for truth to be naive.

One possible way of demonstrating the foregoing differences is by means of a basic and admittedly oversimplified four-cell matrix. Illustrated in Figure 6.1, this distinguishes between epistemology (the grounds of knowledge) and ontology (the nature of the world) and arbitrarily subdivides these continua along realist and relativist dimensions. The top left hand cell assumes that individuals have direct, unmediated access to the real world and that, notwithstanding the problems associated with sampling, questionnaire design and suchlike, it is possible to obtain hard, secure, objective knowledge about this single external reality. The vast bulk of academic marketing research, from attempts to conceptualise the new product development process to empirical analyses of the shopping behaviour of green consumers, would fall into this category. The top right hand cell also assumes direct, unmediated access to external reality but assumes that people's knowledge of this world is highly individual, subjective, unquantifiable, difficult to access and best illuminated through the use of 'traditional' qualitative research procedures like depth interviews and group discussions. Such studies not only provide hypotheses for subsequent empirical tests, but for some marketing researchers, they also form the basis of meaningful generalisations and model development (e.g. Carson 1989). The bottom left hand cell presupposes that individuals do not have direct access to the real world – language, culture, theory and other distortions are interposed – but that their knowledge of this perceived world (or worlds) is meaningful *in its own terms* and can be understood through careful use of appropriate naturalistic or ethnographic research procedures, though generalisations and universally valid findings are unattainable. Much of marketing's interpretive research tradition, from the celebrated Consumer Odyssey and Hirschman's personal revelations, to Gould's (1991) celebration of sex, drugs and rock 'n' roll, is incorporated within this category. The final, bottom right hand cell represents the postmodern position which not only rejects the notion that individuals have unmeditated access to external reality, but it also questions the very existence of the free-thinking 'subject'. It maintains that the knowledge people imagine they possess is unreliable, dispersed, fragmented, pre-existing and an epiphenomenon of language. In other words, it demotes the human subject from a constitutive to a constituted status and, more to the point, presents very serious practical problems for putative postmodern marketing researchers.

Indeed, according to Baudrillard and like-minded commentators on the sceptical wing of the postmodern movement, empirical research is now impossible due to the implosion of the social into the media. Thus, despite Elliott *et al.*'s contention (1993, p.315) that 'there is a need to derive methodological approaches which can utilise some of the highly abstract postmodernist concepts if they are to gain currency in marketing research', it would appear that undertaking meaningful empirical research of any kind is problematical within a postmodern framework (see Rosenau 1992). In these circumstances, marketing researchers seem to be faced with the choice that has materialised in several other disciplines – sociology and organisation studies, for example – whether to concentrate on postmodern marketing or the marketing of postmodernism. The latter would involve attempts to explain the development, positioning, promotion, distribution and diffusion of the postmodern 'product', and, given the manifold competing epistemological products, account for its undoubted success in the marketplace of academic ideas. The former, by contrast, would be devoted to deconstructing the artefacts of extant marketing discourse, revealing the structural weaknesses of our disciplinary edifice, identifying, tracing and exposing the inherent intertextuality of modern marketing, and generally sitting on the sidelines pouring scorn on the achievements of marketing practitioners and academics alike (can you imagine?).

The difficulties that postmodern marketing raises are not confined to researching the unresearchable or the cavils of dyspeptic scholarly malcontents, postmodernism also poses severe problems for the underpinning philosophy of science in marketing. As a relativist position, postmodernism conceives of the world as a plurality, where morals, manners and mores are specific to individual societies and belief systems, and where no one form of knowledge is deemed superior to any other. Indeed, in its assertion that there are no universal standards of validity, truth and rationality, postmodernism in many ways is relativism *in excelsis*, scepticism in the extreme (Gellner 1992). Although the attractions of relativism are undeniable – the acceptance of difference, an espousal of equality, a refusal to stand in judgement and an emphasis on the 'other', neglected and marginalised groups in society – the standard criticisms of relativism still apply (Hughes 1990; Harris 1992; Hirst 1993). If all norms and rules are equal, then it is impossible to prioritise, compare value systems or make choices between moral alternatives (the bogeys of witchcraft, astrology, Nazism and alternative medicine are usually paraded at this point). More importantly perhaps, relativism is self-contradictory in that to announce that there are no universal standards is, in effect, to make a universal statement on standards. To contend that history has no shape is, as Giddens (1990) points out, to state that history has a shape but that the shape is shapeless. To argue that there are no generalisations, laws or truths is to make a generalisation, law-like or truth statement respectively.

Postmodernism, in short, stands accused of making authoritative announcements on the demise of authority, being absolutist in its denial of the absolute, eschewing theory building whilst adhering to an (anti-theoretical) theoretical stance, employing a metanarrative to demonstrate the end of metanarratives, repudiating the existence of evaluative criteria on the basis of its own evaluative criteria, advocating equality of interpretation yet elevating the interpretations of the 'other', espousing epistemological ecumenism while excluding the Enlightenment project, using the tools of rational thought to advocate the irrational and rejecting the power of reason on the basis of reasoned argument (Best and Kellner 1991). It is profoundly ironic, moreover, that postmodernism's characteristic disillusion with the universal has become all but universal in itself; that postmodernism seems to enjoy enormous popularity, yet hardly anyone (least of all its leading thinkers) is prepared to endorse it without reservation; that postmodernists reject the élitism and impenetrability of high (modern) culture but their own writings and artifacts are hardly models of accessibility or clarity (as you can doubtless testify!); and, that postmodernists' espousal of cynical, playful and irreverent deconstruction seems to apply to everyone's texts but their own.

Above all, however, it is deeply incongruous that postmodernists champion close and detailed readings of texts yet are apparently content to rely on caricature and oversimplification in their own analyses. As the critics of postmodernism are quick to point out, all four component parts of the alleged epochal shift have been subject to detailed scrutiny and found wanting. The characteristic features of artistic postmodernism –

fragmentation, ambiguity, self-referentiality, etc. – were equally evident in the era of high modernism (Harvey 1989). The notion of the post-industrial society has been exposed as a compendium of errors (Frankel 1987), post-Fordism as gross oversimplification (Callinicos 1989) and research suggests, contra-Baudrillard, that people are more than capable of distinguishing between image and reality (Edgar 1993; Elliott *et al.* 1993). The ostensible parallels between postmodern science and postmodern social theory have also been exploded (Best 1991); the contentions of Kuhn, Feyerabend and the SSK subject to detailed rebuttal (Wolpert 1992); and, Rorty's neo-pragmatism has been challenged more than once (Norris 1990, 1993). What is more, the sheer inconsistency of (say) Foucault, who renounced the human subject only to rehabilitate it, or Derrida, who recently repudiated deconstruction and made an eloquent plea for the traditional literary canon (see D'Souza 1993), is also less than confidence inspiring, as are post-structuralist contentions that there can be no systematic knowledge of the human condition. According to Giddens (1990), this is not only unworthy of serious intellectual consideration but if it were true the position itself would be impossible to write about or articulate. It is, in actual fact, a recapitulation of the anti-foundational philosophy propounded by Friedrich Nietzsche and his manifold forerunners in the anti-Enlightenment. Although the postmodern movement is often portrayed as the latest intellectual affectation from France, many of its premises – anti-foundationalism, eschewal of progress, the end of history, relativism, non-systematicity, the relationship between power and knowledge and, not least, the unconventional style of writing – were anticipated by Friedrich Nietzsche. Along with Heidegger, indeed, Nietzsche is widely considered to be a postmodernist *avant la lettre* (Koelb 1990; Magnus *et al.* 1993). Friedrich Nietzsche, as Brown (1994d) has pointed out in his usual hyperbolic fashion, was a postmodernist before there were modernists to be post.

The Last Picture Show

In light of the demonstrable shortcomings, contradictions and aporias of postmodernism, many of you may be reluctant to welcome, and wholeheartedly embrace, the postmodern marketing moment. Many of you may be troubled by Venkatesh *et al.*'s (1993, p.215) uncritical advocation of postmodernism; disconcerted by their contention that marketers must board this conceptual bandwagon 'before it is too late'; unconvinced by their justification of this extraordinary leap of faith ('isn't it a fact that the marketing discipline prides itself in being in the vanguard of new ideas?'); astonished by their veiled threats to unbelievers ('anyone who considers postmodernism a passing fancy will do so at considerable peril to oneself'); and, not least, dismayed by their disparaging *ad hominem* remarks on marketing scholars ('many of whose intellectual positions are ideologically motivated but are concealed behind the facades of disinterested pursuit of knowledge'). In these circumstances, you may well alight, with considerable relief, on Kavanagh's (1994, p.33) emphatic assertion that, 'postmodernism will merely paralyse us into inaction', or even Scott's (1992, p.611) ultimate conclusion that, 'our own disciplinary concerns with communication and persuasion would find poststructuralism lacking'. And, having given postmodern marketing your due and careful consideration, you can proceed to go about your business as if nothing untoward had occurred, albeit you now realise that interpretive researchers are a model of circumspection, rectitude and *sotto voce* scholarship, compared to the deranged ululations of postmodernists, with their pretentious philosophising, bogus insights, sardonic insouciance, fetid maliciousness and ostentatious attempts to shed pseudo-light on nonproblems.

These concerns are perfectly reasonable and, in many ways, quite legitimate. Make no mistake, buying into postmodernism does not come cheap. As we noted in Chapter 5, it exacts a very heavy price from any prospective purchasers. It challenges the very premises of marketing understanding. It topples the illustrious edifice of marketing principles constructed over generations of academic endeavour. It espouses a relativist position which, despite its ecumenism, catholicism and flexibility, is riven with internal contradictions and a refusal to distinguish between right and wrong. It may breed a blank generation of sardonic, world-weary researchers with no respect for themselves, their forebears or the achievements of the marketing academy (whatever next?). It opens the door to obscurantism, relativism and an unhealthy preoccupation with the ironies, aporias, inconsistencies and intertextuality of the marketing literature rather than the generalising social science ambitions of the discipline. 'In the end', as Rosenau (1992, p.137) points out, 'the problem with post-modern social science is that you can say anything you want, but so can everyone else. Some of what is said will be interesting and fascinating, but some will also be ridiculous and absurd. Post-modernism provides no means to distinguish between the two.'

Set against this, however, postmodernism *does* offer a number of very significant attractions for the marketer and provides a means of comprehending several difficulties with which the discipline is currently endeavouring to grapple. In the first instance, postmodernism holds out the prospect of a *rapprochement* between marketing theory and practice. If, as we noted in Chapter 4, the practices of marketing are becoming increasingly postmodern in character, there is a danger that continuing, blind pursuit of traditional, modernist marketing conceptualisations will become further divorced from 'reality' than they already are. Although some scholars appear to welcome the prospect of a 'pure' and 'applied' disciplinary bifurcation (e.g. Hirschman, Holbrook), the consequences of such a rupture are likely to prove very serious if marketing practitioners then turn to other academic specialisms which appear to offer more meaningful insights into (say) the consumption behaviour of 'post-shoppers'. In this respect, it is worth recalling that postmodernism emphasises creativity, intuition, spontaneity, ad-hocery, emotion, involvement, uniqueness, local narratives (e.g. case studies and company myths), which the general management literature increasingly elevates over the once pervasive postulates of rigour, planning and predictability (Waterman 1990; Mintzberg 1989; Morgan 1993; Kay 1993).

The second attraction of the postmodern project pertains to its broad compatibility with many of today's much-vaunted marketing restoratives – 'micro-marketing', 'maxi-marketing', 'database marketing', 'new marketing', 'wrap-around marketing', 'value-added marketing', 'relationship marketing' and so on (refer to Table 2.5). Although the premises of these panaceas are many and varied, they all possess one of two basic components: (a) an emphasis on dealing with the customer *as an individual*; or (b) a desire to *retain existing* customers, products or services rather than creating them anew. With regard to the former, however, the primacy of the individual – 'different strokes for different folks', 'do your own thing', 'anything goes', 'there is no fashion only fashions', etc. – is precisely what 'affirmative' postmodernism presupposes (Rosenau 1992). Whereas modern marketing is predicated on the development of meaningful generalisations about consumers in the mass (or sizeable segments thereof), 'affirmative' postmodernism emphasises the uniqueness, diversity, plurality and idiosyncrasy of each and every individual. In terms of the latter, likewise, postmodernism is characterised by a predisposition towards the old, the established, the tried-and-tested, the recycled and, in Jameson's (1985) celebrated phrase, the 'perpetual present'. The complete opposite, in other words, of the progressive, modernist odyssey for the new and improved, the innovative, the futuristic, the revolutionary, the 'washes whiter' and so on.

The third opportunity on offer pertains to marketing's perennial search for academic respectability (Cannon 1991). As a result possibly of the discipline's lowly standing in the scholarly caste system, which descends from the illustrious, Nobel Prize garlanded 'hard' sciences like physics and chemistry, through the softer and intellectually suspect social and historical sciences (economics excepted), to the academic 'untouchables', those concerned with the pursuit of profit and commercial activity, marketing has long felt obliged to prove itself 'more scientific than science', aspire to the most rigorous standards of research and, not infrequently, apologise for the inadequacy or immaturity of its conceptual accomplishments.[3] Yet, in endeavouring to emulate the (seemingly) logical, rigorous, model building, law seeking and nomothetic standards of the physical sciences, academic marketing has effectively downplayed and de-emphasised the creativity, spontaneity, adaptability and individual insight that often characterise successful marketing practices (see Carson 1985; *The Economist* 1989; Cova and Svanfeldt 1992). Postmodernism not only provides the (anti-conceptual) conceptual foundations for the individualistic, idiographic and intuitive end of the 'art–science' continuum, but, in its espousal of heterarchy (flat or overlapping organisational structures) rather than hierarchy, it repudiates the premises of the academic caste system. In a postmodern world, therefore, marketing would no longer occupy the lowest level of the academic firmament, with its necessity for periodic *apologia* and a more scientific than science outlook. A self-confident marketing, secure in the knowledge that it is the equal of any discipline, physical or human, would be the ultimate outcome.

A fourth advantageous aspect of the postmodern condition is its emphasis on metaphor or, strictly speaking, metonymy.[4] As we saw in Chapter 3, postmodernists often resort to metaphorical reasoning – cf. Baudrillard's fondness for 'scientific' analogies (black holes, fractals, DNA) or Foucault's preference for spatial tropes (site, carceral archipelago, heterotopia) – and place great store by the metaphorical nature of truth, meaning and human understanding. Postmodernism suggests that we need to create fresh marketing metaphors, play different tunes and new games, envision alternative worlds, reconceptualise the marketing concept and, as other disciplines have done (e.g. McCloskey 1985; Tyler 1987), pay due attention to the essentially rhetorical nature of marketing discourse. Metaphors, admittedly, may distort as much as they enlighten (van den Bulte 1994), but they shape how we see and interpret our environment. Consider, for example, the various analogies that have been employed by commentators on latter-day developments in the philosophy of marketing science. Almost without exception, these are predicated on the notion of conflict, schism or warfare, thereby emphasising the differences between the two 'sides'. For example, the long-running dispute between the respective champions of realism and relativism, Hunt and Anderson, has been depicted as a sixteen-round boxing contest (Kavanagh 1994). A religious trope – true believers versus heretics – has also been employed (Brown 1993f) and a prayer for the 4Ps of peace has even been proffered (Hirschman and Holbrook 1992). Sherry (1991), similarly, describes the situation of interpretive researchers as being akin to the accused in a court case or the defenders of an isolated frontier outpost surrounded by positivists on the warpath. Indeed, our own discussion of these events in Chapter 5 utilised a wild west, 'quick on the draw' analogy.

The state of contemporary marketing scholarship, however, could just as easily be compared to a multi-screen cinema. After all, it can legitimately be argued that marketing research has been transformed in recent years from a drab, down-at-heel, monolithic 'picture palace', with only one theoretical programme – positivism/empiricism – on show, to a fashionable, glittering multiplex offering a wide choice of innovative research programmes. These programmes vary considerably in their content and certification, with some aimed at a mainstream audience, others reliant on art-house appeal, and yet others – mentioning no names – only suitable for the delinquent, institutionalised or suitably restrained. What is more, as many of the programmes are (arguably) incommensurable, they cannot be viewed simultaneously, though they are at least showing under the same roof, *which we call marketing*. The multiplex metaphor, in other words, retains the differences that are central to the warfare analogy but replaces conflict and estrangement with shared values, complementarity, mutual tolerance and the understanding that 'anything goes'. Well, almost anything.

The final and arguably the most fundamental implication of postmodernism, however, is the unavoidable process of critical self-examination that it imposes upon the marketing discipline. Postmodernism draws our attention to the unassailability of the marketing concept, in that successful marketing practices are invariably lauded as exemplars of the concept in action and marketplace disasters summarily dismissed for failing to adhere to the 'proper' approach. It reminds us that the propagation of unproven or debatable principles, be it the product life cycle, Boston matrix or stages theory of internationalisation, is counterproductive at best and pernicious at worst. After all, part of the reason for (say) the latter-day fragmentation of markets is *the rise of marketing* with the enormous stress it places on segmentation, targeting and positioning. The micro-marketing/database marketing/maxi-marketing revolution has *spawned* not simply served the much-prophesied 'markets of one', the prospect of which is causing so much anguish and heart-searching among marketing practitioners. Even the popular notion of 'science', the ideal to which marketing scholarship aspires but will never gain admittance, is partly a marketing *creation* thanks to generations of washing powder, cosmetics, shampoo and patent medicine commercials (white coats, spotless labs, all-pervasive air of rigour and objectivity). Postmodernism, in other words, reminds us of the reflexive or circular nature of social knowledge, where the very existence of a concept influences and alters the phenomena to which it pertains. As Giddens (1990, pp.41–153) points out,

> new knowledge (concepts, theories, findings) does not simply render the social world more transparent, but alters its nature, spinning it off in novel directions. . . . Concepts . . . are not merely handy devices whereby agents are somehow more clearly able to understand their behaviour than they would do otherwise. They actively constitute what that behaviour is and inform the reasons for which it is undertaken.

Postmodernism, in sum, may not provide us with any answers, but it certainly makes us think. It makes us think about marketing thinking. It forces us to ask questions about the nature of marketing 'knowledge'. In Rorty's (1980) apt phraseology, it is edifying rather than systematic. Postmodernism may be a relativist position, yet not only can relativism be defended (e.g. Smith 1988; Clark 1990), but the alternatives – realism, conventionalism, instrumentalism or whatever – are equally flawed. Part of the attraction of relativism, as the prominent realist philosopher Harvey Siegel (1992, p.429) openly acknowledges, is, 'the difficulty of formulating a defensible conception of non-relativism'. Postmodernism, moreover, may necessitate the elision of many of marketing's intellectual achievements, but it can be contended that, in light of their manifest inadequacies, most of the incumbents of marketing's conceptual hall of fame aren't worth maintaining anyway. Is it not time, after Barthes, for 'marketing degree zero' or a Foucauldian archaeology of marketing discourse? Isn't it strange that, at a time when science is witnessing a shift from truth to performativity (according to Lyotard), marketing science is being exhorted to move from performativity to truth (by Shelby Hunt)? Should we not be thinking, *à la* Derrida, of placing ~~marketing~~ *sous rature* (under erasure) and admitting that it is necessary but hopelessly inadequate?

Postmodern marketing, to conclude, tells us that the proponents of marketing orientation have become product orientated. It suggests that if being different is the secret of marketing success, then the marketing concept ought to be abandoned, given its virtual ubiquity. Above all, postmodernism implies that the fundamental issue to which we should address ourselves is not marketing myopia but the *myopia of marketing*.

(The Terminator)

Now, some of you may be wondering where I stand in all of this, if there are any of you left that is. What, you may well be saying to yourself, do *you*, the author, think you are playing at? Why do you keep shifting your position? Are you for postmodernism or against it? You told us at the outset how you were a closet postmodernist, yet you have just served up a root-and-branch critique. How can you expect marketers to espouse postmodernism when you're not prepared to espouse it yourself? And, come to think of it, where do you stand on marketing? One minute you're defending the discipline from the disparaging comments of left wing intellectuals or lauding our academic achievements, the next you're making snide remarks about the foremost marketing authorities or recommending the abandonment of almost everything we've achieved hitherto. You complain about marketing being caricatured, yet you caricature marketing yourself. You tell us that most modern marketing concepts are about to be swept away, but that the precepts of postmodernism are readily translatable into contemporary marketing terms. How, for that matter, do you expect us to take you seriously when you make your case in such an intemperate manner? We have had just about enough of this and we want answers to the following simple questions: are you a postmodernist or not?; is marketing postmodern or not?; and, what kind of book is this supposed to be anyway?

Faced with these courteous inquiries, it is tempting to state that my position on postmodernism is that I have no position on postmodernism. However, I suspect that you are all too well versed in the wiles of the postmodern project to be fooled by the speciousness of such a pronouncement. Conversely, I could remind you of the post-structuralist assertion that authorial intentions are immaterial and that it is for you to bring your own interpretations to bear upon the text, thereby introducing a temporary stability and coherence. In short, if you find the text paradoxical, irritating, pretentious, disquieting or whatever, that's your problem (sorry, prerogative), not mine. According to Barthes' 'always already written', indeed, I have merely woven this text together from the threads of existing texts – *your texts* – and, as such, you have no one to blame but yourselves. Alternatively, and in a final desperate attempt to shake you off, I could simply dismiss myself as an epiphenomenon of language, a de-centred, fragmented subject position, a gendered construct of patriarchy, the mouthpiece of discursive ventriloquism, or an unstable artefact of power relations and regimes of truth. I could then conclude with Scruton's (1994, pp.478–9) charming observation that, 'Deconstruction deconstructs itself, and disappears up its own behind, leaving only a disembodied smile and a faint smell of sulphur', and proceed to live happily ever after (though not on my royalties, I suspect). Appealing though such evasions and circumlocutions undoubtedly are, they are unlikely to stem the ensuing tide of irate personal correspondence, the flood of abusive letters written in green ink or, because sharp objects are prohibited in the institution concerned, in multi-coloured crayon or felt-tip (and that, dear reader, is only from the publishers).

For what it's worth then, let me confess in this little textual coda that my position on postmodernism is unequivocally equivocal. As I mentioned in Chapter 1, I enjoy postmodern films, literature, music, television, etc. and have amassed an embarrassingly large collection of volumes on what we described as 'postmodern science' (anyone for the *Dancing Wu Li Masters* or *The Metaphysics of Virtual Reality*?). I am perfectly comfortable with Baudrillard's remorseless cynicism – in truth I find him hilariously funny – and reading Barthes is like witnessing a literary firework display. I admire Foucault for the sheer bravura of his unorthodox, counter-intuitive interpretations, though his syntax is impenetrable and sentences interminable. Lyotard's polemic is insufficiently polemical in my opinion – too much Kant, not enough cant – and, much as I respect Rorty, he is excessively avuncular, too *laissez-faire*, for my taste. Nietzsche, however, I adore. I may not have learned much from my walk on the wild side, but at least it exposed me to Nietzsche. As it is true confessions time, I have to admit that I am still baffled by Derrida and Lacan, slightly less so in the case of the former, though I suspect that my appreciation will develop in due course (the first time I read Jameson's (1985) celebrated essay on postmodernism I was totally lost, but I now consider it to be a model of lucidity and perspicacity).

Yet, despite my admiration for most things postmodern, I realise in my heart of hearts that it is ultimately inadequate. Style is not enough in itself, there must be some content. Call me old-fashioned, call me faint-hearted, call me a modernist post-modernist, if you prefer, but I suspect that people expect answers, a sense of direction, an indication of the way forward, however rocky the road might be. To argue that the answer is that there are no answers; or that the answer is that you're wasting your time looking for answers; or that the answer is that you should do what you think is right for you or your organisation; is insufficient in the final analysis. A Gallic shrug and pass the Gauloises is just not good enough, I'm afraid. Postmodernism, in sum, is like eating chocolate éclairs. They are delicious, indulgent and subversive, but in the end it's back to the exercise bike.

When it comes to marketing, I am equally ambivalent. I have enormous admiration for practising marketers and the undoubted academic achievements of our discipline. I feel marketing has been misrepresented by many outside commentators and oppositionally inclined intellectuals. Notwithstanding my earlier remarks, I have great respect for the works of Ted Levitt, Wroe Alderson, Shelby Hunt and, especially, interpretive marketing researchers, whose accomplishments in the face of considerable hostility and misunderstanding speak for themselves (would I lie to you?). Most importantly, perhaps, I earn my living by disseminating the marketing message and have no sense of guilt – none whatsoever – in doing so. At the same time, I am chary about chanting the tired old marketing mantra. I don't think marketing has all, or even many, of the answers; I don't think the marketing concept can be applied to everything under the sun (Luck was right, you know); and I suspect that whereas many marketing practices are becoming increasingly 'postmodern', marketing theory seems resolutely stuck in a modernist time-warp. A serious re-think is long overdue. Worse still, I believe that our continuing propagation of unproven marketing principles is both dangerous and irresponsible (and irresponsibility must be avoided at all costs). While many people share Professor Michael Thomas's (1994) concerns about the fate of marketing, it is my belief that the discipline and profession is ill-served by mindless regurgitation of obsolescent marketing ideology. Being critical is not being disloyal. Quite the reverse. Bringing ridicule and hyperbole to bear is vitally necessary, because reasoned argument is all too easily ignored. Granted, some marketers may contend that as the discipline is well aware of its shortcomings, it is unnecessary to use the sledgehammer of postmodernism to crack the marketing nut. In my opinion, modern marketing is a very tough nut indeed. It is a veritable conceptual cyborg – 'it can't be bargained with, it can't be reasoned with . . . it will not stop, ever' – which requires extreme measures if it is to be destroyed and, in due course, reconstituted.

Having read the preceding paragraphs, some of you may be on the point of exasperation with my continuing failure to adopt a definitive position on postmodern marketing. I can assure you, it gives me no pleasure either (yes, I'm even ambivalent about being ambivalent). In my defense, I can only say that it is at least postmodern. You see, postmodernism is not about espousing a position, postmodernism is characterised by equivocation (though being equivocal about equivocation is also acceptable, as is equivocation about being equivocal about equivocation . . .). Postmodernism does not endorse any one approach, *not even postmodernism*, and, if it were not decidedly un-postmodern to say so, nothing could be more un-postmodern than the passionate advocation of postmodernism (see Soper 1993). This book, then, has tried to capture the spirit of postmodernism, with all its ironies, inconsistencies, irreverences, paradoxes and equivocations. It has endeavoured to meld form and content by means of its 'double coded' cinematic metaphor; its, admittedly contrived, self-referential ethos (what Holbrook (1994, p.16) rightly describes as 'behold the beholder beholding the beholded'); and, its attempted postmodern fusion of scholarship and journalism, sycophancy and sarcasm, enthusiasm and scepticism, entertainment and edification, self-satisfaction and self-deprecation, humour and hostility, erudition and sedition, hyperbole and humility, discourse and figure, and superficiality and, well, superficiality. Cognisant of the old joke, (Q) 'What's the difference between a postmodernist and the Mafia? (A) 'A postmodernist makes you an offer you can't understand!', this monograph has sought to make postmodernism understandable. It has tried to explain a phenomenon that was once described as, 'something everyone has heard of but no-one can quite explain what it is'. It has tried to avoid the obfuscation of 'decentred hegemonic strategies', 'phallogocentric narratological polypony', 'meta-critical heteroglossian valorisation' and the like, which are regrettably *de rigueur* in the postmodern literature, as indeed are pretentious terms like *de rigueur*, *Zeitgeist* and *Weltanschauung* (well, nobody's perfect). Above all, the book has tried to make postmodernism sufficiently interesting for you, as marketing practitioners, students or researchers, to want to explore it and its implications in much more detail (and, not least, to petition the publishers about my proposed follow-up volume, *Postmodern Marketing 2: The Return of the Shamanistic Drummer*).

Let me leave you, however, with one final postmodern thought: if you believe any of the foregoing, you'll believe anything. *Hasta la vista*, baby!

I love the smell of napalm in the morning

1 You talkin to me?

1 Footnotes, in my opinion, are the 'dark continent' of academic discourse. Everyone knows they are there, but as no one pays any serious attention to them, they comprise an essentially unexplored continent, a virgin territory occupied by hostile asides, carnivorous arguments, diseased pronouncements, hectares of impenetrable textual thicket capable of deterring all but the most determined explorers and (presumably) Prester John. Footnotes, however, are also a land of opportunity, in that they encourage freedom of expression and permit the types of scurrilous or defamatory statements that would be deemed unacceptable in the civilised textual world of polite academic society. Footnotes, furthermore, are happy hunting grounds for mean-spirited book reviewers, because it is in the footnotes (and appendices) that unwary authors lower their defences, make inadvertent remarks and let slip information which, if exposed to critical scrutiny, can serve to undermine the most carefully constructed scholarly facade. Consider, for example, Shelby D. Hunt's (1990) bizarre footnote which sought to draw parallels between post-positivist marketing researchers and the perpetrators of the Tiananmen Square massacre, but which has only served to reflect very badly on the author himself. Rather than continuing to dwell on the unsavoury side of footnotes, however, let us turn to (the Harvard biologist) Stephen Jay Gould's observation that 'genuine' scholars are driven by one overwhelming ambition. This desire does not pertain to fame, fortune, the Nobel Prize, membership of the Royal Society, the trappings of academic superstardom or whatever, but to writing a footnote which takes up a full page of text. Unfortunately, most of us are denied this aspiration as publishers are increasingly inclined to gather footnotes together into a textual ghetto, though I suppose a full-page 'note' still counts for something. There is, of course, another possibility – another sublime scholarly achievement – and that is to write a book (or paper) where the list of references is longer than the body of the text. In my previous book, I tried and failed to attain this apogee of academic life, and I can tell that even if I were to pad this footnote out with cogitations on the weather we've been having lately, descriptions of my recent holiday experiences or showing you photographs of my wife and family, I'm still not going to get a full page out of it. Of course, I could take this opportunity to apologise at length for my ludicrous textual comparison between myself and the giants of postmodernism (Foucault, Barthes, Derrida, Baudrillard, etc.). I am the first to acknowledge that I am an intellectual ant to their elephant, an amoeba to their homo sapiens, a Ratners to their Tiffanys, Poundstretcher to Harrods, Aldi to Takashimaya, Happy Eater to *Le Manoir aux Quat' Saisons*. Drat, I can't think of any more. I'm not going to make it. Failed again. The story of my life.

2 It may be more appropriate to describe this as a geo-political problem, in that it isn't simply a question of postmodernism's left-wing political inclination. Most

commentators on the postmodern moment draw inspiration from the grand, speculative tradition of Continental philosophy rather than the horny-handed empiricism of Anglo-American schools of thought. As Barry Barnes (1985b, p.85) emphasises, 'We have never been able to accept the frankly speculative approach of the Continental philosophers, or their grand metaphysical theories. In Anglo-Saxon philosophy we have always kept our feet on the ground, and refused to accept any but the most securely established claims'. In a similar vein, Gore Vidal (1993, p.122) has recently argued that, 'the French mind is addicted to the postulating of elaborate systems in order to explain everything, while the Anglo-American mind tends to shy away from unified-field theories. We chart our courses point-to-point; they sight from the stars. The fact that neither really gets much of anywhere doesn't mean that we haven't all had some nice outings over the years'.

2 I coulda been a contender!

1 The complete lack of brand names in the equivalent chapters of this particular volume, gives you a fair indication of the author's commercial appeal and inherent marketability. I remain, nevertheless, optimistic and open to offers – any offers!

2 Keith's (1960) celebrated paper also mentions an impending fourth era, of 'marketing control', where marketing permeates, underpins and drives the entire organisation. But, as this marketing utopia has yet to be fully attained, his final phase seems to have been conveniently forgotten.

3 It is worth stressing that this era did not simply witness the emergence of the modern marketing concept, but saw the efflorescence of a great many of marketing's most celebrated theoretical principles – the 4Ps, the marketing mix, the wheel of retailing, channels theory, the hierarchy of advertising effects, the product life cycle, the gravity model, the classification of goods, etc. Some of these concepts, admittedly, have extensive antecedents, yet they were all reformulated and came to prominence in that remarkable purple patch of marketing scholarship, the late 1950s–early 1960s.

4 Strictly speaking, the 'broadening' debate preceded Kotler and Levy's (1969) deathless discussion in the *Journal of Marketing*. As Hunt (1976) points out, it actually dates from a 1965 Ohio State University position paper. Kotler and Levy, however, are generally credited with bringing the issue to a head and, after a ferocious academic altercation, of winning the day.

5 In this respect, it is interesting to contrast the approaches adopted by the authors of introductory marketing textbooks with those of commentators on marketing theory and thought. Whereas the former are inclined to commence with a morality tale about the benefits of marketing orientation, a whiggish summary of western economic history, a denunciation of the misconceptions of misguided non-believers or a synoptic overview of marketing's enormous influence on our everyday existence, the latter tend to exhibit a touching modesty, an endearing admission of our academic inadequacies. However, just as the over-inflated claims of marketing's adepts are untenable, so too the inclination to scholarly self-abasement is arguably no longer necessary (see Brown 1994e).

3 What have they got in there, King Kong?

1 A celebrated example of such national identity inducing activity is the Scottish kilt. Contrary to popular perception, the kilt is not an ancient or traditional Celtic costume, but the creation of Thomas Rawlinson, an enterprising mid-eighteenth century ironmaster – and an Englishman to boot (see Trevor-Roper 1983).

2 In postmodern dance, for example, the early post-war penchant for reduction, minimalisation and the abandonment of the expression of meaning (through the eschewal of character, narrative and representation) has been superseded – in the work of Trisha Brown, for instance – by the reintroduction and retrieval of meaning in the form of pastiche, irony, playfulness, radical juxtaposition and sheer theatricality (see Banes 1987). Postmodern theatre emphasises impro-visation, a seams-showing, work-in-progress quality, the foregrounding of the 'theatricality' of the performance, an effacement of the barrier between audi-ence and actors, and, as in performance art, the fusion of genres coupled with multimedia experimentation (Connor 1989). In music and opera, meanwhile, the rhythmic complexity, discordance and atonality that characterised high modernism (Stravinsky, Schoenberg) has provoked a reaction 'against intellec-tual complexity' (Nyman), an emphasis on aleatory, or chance, procedures (Cage), controlled indeterminacy (Reich) and old-fashioned melody (Gorecki) (see Sporre 1989).

3 The sheer extent of this 'micro-political' transformation is amply illustrated by the fact that, in Britain, the Royal Society for the Protection of Birds has more members than the three main political parties combined.

4 For Jameson, 'pastiche' involves an acknowledgement of the fact that stylistic innovation is no longer possible and thus the only remaining alternative is to combine, recycle or evoke already existing formats or genres (e.g. *Star Wars* as an evocation of 'the Saturday afternoon serial of the Buck Rogers type'). On the other hand, 'schizophrenia' refers, not to the clinical condition, but to the characteristically postmodern sense of time, the supposed loss of historical depth which is analogous to the schizophrenic's inability fully to distinguish between past, present and future. Postmodern life is thus lived in a depthless, yet overwhelmingly vivid, 'perpetual present'.

5 At the risk of oversimplifying a highly complex and internally variegated intel-lectual movement, the important thing to remember about post-structuralism and its predecessor, structuralism, is that they are characterised above all by their tendency to treat the subject matter of the investigation, whether it be food, fashion or fables, as if it were a language. According to the traditional structuralist approach, first developed in the linguistics of Ferdinand de Saussure and subsequently applied to all manner of academic specialisms, the analyses of language should concentrate on *langue*, the complete system of language and its rules of organisation, rather than *parole*, the individual utter-ance or speech act. Language, moreover, is a system of signs which has to be studied 'synchronically', as a complete system at a given point in time, rather than 'diachronically', in terms of its historical development (Culler 1988; Jackson 1991). By holding the system steady, so to speak, it becomes possible to identify the distinctive elements that make up its structure and the rela-tionships between them. For Saussure, meaning derives entirely from the differ-ences between the elements of the sign system itself. As we noted in an earlier

section, 'night' becomes meaningful in respect of its difference from 'day', a 'blue' object is not one that is red, brown or purple, and a green traffic signal derives meaning from the other alternative combinations of the three light system. (Different languages, of course, possess sign systems that are structured in contrasting ways – in Passmore's (1985, p.24) apt dictum, they 'differ by differentiating differently'.) The importance of this point cannot be overemphasised. Saussure explains meaning not in terms of the relationship between a linguistic sign like 'dog' or 'cat' and the furry, four-legged creatures in the 'real' world (the referents), but in terms of the relationship – the difference – between the linguistic signs themselves (dog, dot, cot, cat, etc.). The most important aspect of a linguistic sign is 'being whatever the others are not. . . . Concepts . . . are purely differential, that is to say they are concepts defined not positively, in terms of their content, but negatively by contrast with the other items in the same system' (de Saussure 1983, p.115). In Saussure's system of linguistic meaning, the 'real' world – the world of the referent – is effectively set aside. As Derrida subsequently pointed out, there is nothing outside the text.

6 Another, more recent, example of this emphasis on indeterminacy is 'fuzzy logic', which rejects the western binary system of exclusionary logic (black *or* white, right *or* wrong, 1 *or* 0, all *or* nothing) with one that sanctions contradiction, endorses ambiguity and revels in uncertainty (see Kosko 1993). However, as the inclusion of a discussion of fuzzy logic is likely to be too much of a temptation for any potentially hostile reviewers of this monograph – logic doesn't come much fuzzier than mine, after all – I've decided to bury it in the comparative safety of the footnotes. If, of course, any reviewers are reading this, all I can say is that your thoroughness, diligence and perspicacity is a credit to the book reviewing profession. You won't say anything nasty about me, will you? Can we come to some sort of financial arrangement? Are we in a negotiating situation here?

7 Although he does not mention him by name, Lyotard (1984) is clearly thinking about Kuhn in his discussion of 'postmodern science'.

8 Needless to say, Derrida's deconstruction of Lacan's deconstruction of Poe's celebrated essay has been deconstructed in turn by Barbara Johnson (1981).

4 You can't handle the truth!

1 The restorers of the Vieux Carre in New Orleans, for instance, were not averse to replacing dilapidated wrought iron balustrades with plastic versions of the same, leading Relph (1987) to describe it as a 'Creole Disneyland' and Lewis (1975, p.40) to conclude that it 'looked less and less like Louis Armstrong and more and more like Colonel Saunders'.

2 In a recent article on Las Vegas, Pullinger (1994, pp.2–3) writes as follows, 'I love Vegas because it's audacious, self-referential, ironic, grotesque and 24-hour. It's American free enterprise at its most pure – the casinos want your money, you give it to them. Vegas is completely straightforward and utterly, flamboyantly surreal . . . I stayed at the Luxor [Hotel] this time . . . [which has] . . . a 36 storey Great Pyramid with a larger-than-the-original Sphinx crouched over the valet parking out front. . . . Hotel rooms line the glass exterior of the pyramid; the interior is a vast atrium, home to a casino floor "big enough to park nine 747 airplanes", virtual reality attractions, restaurants,

cafes, bars, [and] a vast reproduction of a Mayan step pyramid. . . . Why go as far as Egypt, or even Mexico for that matter, and risk local insurrection and bilharzia when you can see it all, much more safely, right here?'

5 Is that an epistemology in your pocket, or . . . ?

1 Many marketers, of course, might argue that the very essence of the marketing concept is the ability to view an organisation from the outside, from its customers' perspective. This is true, but the marketer's vantage point still remains within the organisation.

2 Falsification, furthermore, does not accord with the historical record, as there are many instances of flawed theories being accepted by the scientific community, despite falsification, and the initial rejection of theories that are now widely accepted. Indeed, if the falsificationist procedure were applied as Popper recommended, few if any theories of the physical world would pass muster.

3 I fully appreciate that the 'rock' metaphor is totally inappropriate for postmodernism. It is perhaps best described as a spider's web, a vortex, a hall of mirrors, a cascade of soap bubbles or an implosive Black Hole. But the very incongruity of the metaphor highlights the all-important part played by figurative thinking in the conceptualisation process. As Rorty (1980) points out (metaphorically of course) the important thing is not whether an analogy is 'right' or 'wrong', but our reaction to it, our decision whether to savour the metaphor or spit it out.

4 In their early papers on the subject, both Venkatesh (1989) and Sherry (1991) consider interpretive research to be part and parcel of the postmodern moment. They subsequently contended that 'postmodernism is not a synonym for postpositivism or interpretivism for these two concepts are very much embedded within the discourse on modernism' (Venkatesh *et al.* 1993, p.217).

5 It should be pointed out, however, that Ostergaard (1993) considers the broadened marketing concept, particularly in its application to organised religion, to be representative of the postmodern marketing condition.

6 I'll be back!

1 Discussing the latter-day crisis in Marxian sociology, for example, Hebdige (1989, p.89) acknowledges that 'marketing has provided the dominant and most pervasive classifications of social types in the 1980s'. Hebdige, admittedly, considered this state of affairs to be both morally repugnant and indicative of the bankruptcy of radical sociology, nevertheless it illustrates the extent to which marketing perspectives are being disseminated and the seriousness, if not respect and admiration, with which they are now treated.

2 As a glance at (say) Bass (1993) or Little *et al.* (1994) amply testifies, there is no shortage of marketing optimists, individuals who are happy to expound on the discipline's illustrious lineage and exciting prospects. In the main, however, these people are fully paid up members of marketing's macho-modelling community, those who appear to take enormous pride in wrestling with structural equations and matrix algebra, boast about the size of their hard discs, doubtless tear telephone directories in half or inflate hot water bottles as their party pieces, and take every opportunity to kick sand (or silicon chips at least)

in the faces of the seven stone weaklings of qualitative research. In fairness, and in a cowardly attempt to avoid the pummelling that the macho-modellers are probably planning for me, I should perhaps add that these diehard marketing enthusiasts may well have a point. Many contemporary commentators are referring to marketing's so-called 'crisis of representation', but it is equally important to raise questions about and indeed challenge these "representations of crisis" (who are the crisis mongers?; why are they propounding this perspective?; what's in it for them?).

3 Consider, for instance, the remarks of the AMA Task Force (1988, p.13), 'marketing remains a field of study scorned by its parent disciplines and by the major foundations and funding agencies'. Consider also Greenley's (1986, p.61) comments on marketing planning, 'the planning body of knowledge is still at an early stage of development, within a management science body of knowledge which itself is still poorly developed when compared to other disciplines'. Or, indeed, those of Baker (1983, pp.27 and 30) on marketing theory, 'to date . . . theory is poorly developed in marketing. . . . Many of the major problems involved in using and developing theory are interrelated with . . . the . . . youth of the discipline and the nature of marketing phenomena'.

4 If you read any of the literary or cultural studies literature on postmodernism (e.g. Hassan 1985), you may be slightly confused by the metaphor/metonymy duality as the former is usually described as 'modern' and the latter as 'postmodern'. Clearly, this is contrary to the position argued in this monograph, where the emphasis on metaphor is considered to be characteristic of the postmodern moment. It is important to stress, however, that this essay is simply contrasting the postmodern emphasis on *figurative* thinking with the essentially *literal* world-view of the logical positivists/empiricists. Both metaphor and metonymy are examples of figurative thinking and if we focus our attention solely on the continuum of figurative thought, then it is true that metaphor, with its holistic emphasis ('Boddington's, the Cream of Manchester') is 'modern', whereas metonymy, with its stress on the part, on taking something related to stand for the whole thing ('Miller, the champagne of bottled beers') is much more 'postmodern' in ethos. I would argue, none the less, that both are 'postmodern' in a marketing context, with metonymy being slightly *more* postmodern than metaphor.

Look into your heart

Achrol, R.S. (1991) 'Evolution of the marketing organisation: new forms for turbulent environments', *Journal of Marketing* 55, 4: 77–93.

Adair, G. (1992) *The Postmodernist Always Rings Twice*, London: Fourth Estate.

Adair, G. (1993) 'Sweet dreams', *The Sunday Times*, 14 March, 9: 8.

Adams, W. (1991) 'Aesthetics: liberating the senses', in T. Carver (ed.) *The Cambridge Companion to Marx*, Cambridge: Cambridge University Press, 246–74.

Adorno, T. and Horkheimer, M. (1973 [1944]) *Dialectic of Enlightenment*, trans. J. Cumming, London: Verso.

Allen, J. (1992) 'Post-industrialism and post-Fordism', in S. Hall, D. Held and T. McGrew (eds) *Modernity and its Futures*, Cambridge: Polity, 169–220.

Allen, J., Braham, P. and Lewis, P. (eds) (1992) *Political and Economic Forms of Modernity*, Cambridge: Polity.

Alwitt, L.F. and Berger, I.E. (1993) 'Understanding the link between environmental attitudes and consumer product choice: measuring the moderating role of attitude strength', in L. McAlister and M.L. Rothschild (eds) *Advances in Consumer Research, Volume XX*, Provo: Association for Consumer Research, 189–94.

American Marketing Association Task Force (1988) 'Developing, disseminating and utilizing marketing knowledge', *Journal of Marketing* 52, October: 1–25.

Anderson, L.M. (1994) 'Marketing science: where's the beef?', *Business Horizons* 37, January–February: 8–16.

Anderson, P.F. (1983) 'Marketing, scientific progress and scientific method', *Journal of Marketing* 47, Fall: 18–31.

Anderson, P.F. (1986) 'On method in consumer research: a critical relativist perspective', *Journal of Consumer Research* 13, September: 155–73.

Anderson, P.F. (1989) 'On relativism and interpretivism – with a prolegomenon to the "why" question', in E.C. Hirschman (ed.) *Interpretive Consumer Research*, Provo: Association for Consumer Research, 10–23.

Andrews, N. (1993) 'Review of "Last Action Hero"', *Financial Times*, Thursday 29 July: 13.

Ankersmit, F.R. (1989) 'Historiography and postmodernism', *History and Theory* 28: 137–53.

Ansoff, H.I. (1957) 'Strategies for diversification', *Harvard Business Review* 35, 5: 113–24.

Archer, J. (1991) *As the Crow Flies*, New York: HarperCollins.

Arndt, J. (1981) 'The conceptual domain of marketing; an evaluation of Shelby Hunt's three dichotomies model', *European Journal of Marketing* 14, 3: 106–21.

Arndt, J. (1985) 'On making marketing science more scientific: role of orientations, paradigms, metaphors and puzzle solving', *Journal of Marketing* 49, Summer: 11–23.

Aronowitz, S. and Giroux, H.A. (1991) *Postmodern Education: Politics, Culture and Social Criticism*, Minneapolis: University of Minnesota Press.

Aspinwall, L. (1958) 'The characteristics of goods and parallel systems theories', in E.J. Kelley and W. Lazer (eds) *Managerial Marketing*, Homewood: Richard D. Irwin, 434–50.

Bagozzi, R.P. (1975) 'Marketing as exchange', *Journal of Marketing* 39, October: 32–9.

Bagozzi, R.P. (1979) 'Toward a formal theory of marketing exchange', in O.C. Ferrell, S.W. Brown and C.W. Lamb (eds) *Conceptual and Theoretical Developments in Marketing*, Chicago: American Marketing Association, 431–47.

Baker, M.J. (1983) *Marketing: Theory and Practice*, Basingstoke: Macmillan.

Baker, M.J. (1987) 'One more time – what is marketing?' in M.J. Baker (ed.) *The Marketing Book*, London: Heinemann, 3–9.

Baker, M.J. (1989) 'Marketing – a new philosophy of management', *The Quarterly Review of Marketing* 14, 2: 1–4.

Baker, M.J. (1991) *Marketing: An Introductory Text*, Basingstoke: Macmillan, fifth edition.

Baker, M.J. (1992) *Marketing Strategy and Management*, Basingstoke: Macmillan, second edition.

Baker, M. J. and Hart, S.J. (1989) *Marketing and Competitive Success*, Hemel Hempstead: Philip Allan.

Banes, S. (1987) *Terpsichore in Sneakers: Postmodern Dance*, Wesleyan: Wesleyan University Press.

Bannet, E.T. (1993) *Postcultural Theory: Critical Theory After the Marxist Paradigm*, Basingstoke: Macmillan.

Barger, H. (1955) *Distribution's Place in the American Economy Since 1869*, Princeton: Princeton University Press.

Barksdale, H.C. and Darden, B. (1971) 'Marketers' attitudes toward the marketing concept', *Journal of Marketing* 35, October: 29–36.

Barnes, B. (1982) *Kuhn and Social Science*, London: Macmillan.

Barnes, B. (1985a) *About Science*, Oxford: Blackwell.

Barnes, B. (1985b) 'Thomas Kuhn', in Q. Skinner (ed.) *The Return of Grand Theory in the Human Sciences*, Cambridge: Cambridge University Press, 83–100.

Barnes, J.W. and Stafford, E.R. (1993) 'Strategic alliance partner selection: when organisational cultures clash', in D.W. Cravens and P.R. Dickson (eds) *Enhancing Knowledge Development in Marketing, Volume 4*, Chicago: American Marketing Association, 424–33.

Barsoux, J–L. (1993) 'When the jokes start to wear thin', *Financial Times*, Thursday 29 July: 12.

Bartels, R. (1951) 'Influences on the development of marketing thought, 1900–1923', *Journal of Marketing* 16, July: 1–17.

Bartels, R. (1962) *The Development of Marketing Thought*, Homewood: Richard D. Irwin.

Bartels, R. (1974) 'The identity crisis in marketing', *Journal of Marketing* 38, October: 73–6.

Barthes, R. (1970 [1953, 1965]) *Writing Degree Zero and Elements of Semiology*, trans. A. Lavers and C. Smith, Boston: Beacon Press.

Barthes, R. (1973 [1957]) *Mythologies*, trans. A. Lavers, London: Paladin.

Barthes, R. (1977a [1968]) 'The death of the author', in R. Barthes, *Image Music Text*, trans. S. Heath, London: Fontana, 142–8.

Barthes, R. (1977b [1971]) 'From work to text', in R. Barthes, *Image Music Text*, trans. S. Heath, London: Fontana, 155–64.

Barthes, R. (1990a [1973]) *The Pleasure of the Text*, trans. R. Miller, Oxford: Basil Blackwell.

Barthes, R. (1990b [1973]) *S/Z*, trans. R. Miller, Oxford: Blackwell.

Bass, F.M. (1993) 'The future of research in marketing: marketing science', *Journal of Marketing Research* 30, February: 1–6.

Baudrillard, J. (1983 [1981]) *Simulations*, trans. P. Foss, P. Patton and P. Beitchman, New York: Semiotext(e).

Baudrillard, J. (1985) 'The ecstacy of communication', in H. Foster (ed.) *Postmodern Culture*, London: Pluto Press, 126–34.

Baudrillard, J. (1987 [1977]) *Forget Foucault*, trans. N. Dufrense, New York: Semiotext(e).

Baudrillard, J. (1988a) *Jean Baudrillard: Selected Writings*, ed. M. Poster, Oxford: Blackwell.

Baudrillard, J. (1988b [1986]) *America*, trans. C. Turner, London: Verso.

Baudrillard, J. (1988c) 'The year 2000 has already happened', in A. Kroker and M. Kroker (eds) *Body Invaders: Panic Sex in America*, Montreal: The New World Perspectives, 35–44.

Baudrillard, J. (1989) 'The anorexic ruins', in D. Kamper and C. Wulf (eds) *Looking Back on the End of the World*, trans. D. Antal, New York: Semiotext(e), 29–45.

Baudrillard, J. (1990a [1987]) *Cool Memories*, trans. C. Turner, London: Verso.

Baudrillard, J. (1990b [1983]) *Fatal Strategies*, trans. P. Beitchman and W.G.J. Niesluchowski, London: Pluto.

Baudrillard, J. (1993a [1976]) *Symbolic Exchange and Death*, trans. I.H. Grant, London: Sage.

Baudrillard, J. (1993b [1990]) *The Transparency of Evil: Essays on Extreme Phenomena*, trans. J. Benedict, London: Verso.

Bauman, Z. (1987) *Legislators and Interpreters: On Modernity, Postmodernity and Intellectuals*, Cambridge: Polity Press.

Beadle, J.J. (1993) *Will Pop Eat Itself?*, London: Faber and Faber.

Beaumont, P. (1993) 'Postmodernism', *The Observer*, Sunday 9 May: 43.

Belk, R.W. (1984) 'Against thinking', in P.F. Anderson and M.J. Ryan (eds) *Scientific Method in Marketing*, Chicago: American Marketing Association, 57–60.

Belk, R.W. (1987) 'A modest proposal for creating verisimilitude in consumer-information-processing models and some suggestions for establishing a discipline to study consumer behaviour', in A.F. Firat, N. Dholakia and R.P. Bagozzi (eds) *Philosophical and Radical Thought in Marketing*, Lexington: Lexington Books, 361–72.

Belk, R.W. (1989) 'Materialism and the modern U.S. Christmas', in E.C. Hirschman (ed.) *Interpretive Consumer Research*, Provo: Association for Consumer Research, 115–35.

Belk, R.W. (1991) 'Possessions and the sense of past', in R.W. Belk (ed.) *Highways and Buyways: Naturalistic Research from the Consumer Behaviour Odyssey*, Provo: Association for Consumer Research, 114–30.

Belk, R.W. and Bryce W. (1993) 'Christmas shopping scenes: from modern miracle to postmodern mall', *International Journal of Research in Marketing* 10, 3: 277–96.

Belk, R.W. and Coon, G.S. (1993) 'Gift giving as agapic love: an alternative to the exchange paradigm based on dating experiences', *Journal of Consumer Research* 20, December: 393–417.

Belk, R.W., Wallendorf, M. and Sherry, J.F. (1989) 'The sacred and the profane in consumer behaviour: theodicy on the odyssey', *Journal of Consumer Research* 16, June: 1–38.

Bell, D. (1973) *The Coming of Post-industrial Society: A Venture in Social Forecasting*, New York: Basic Books.

Bell, D. (1976) *The Cultural Contradictions of Capitalism*, New York: Basic Books.

Bell, E. (1992) 'Superdrug sparks perfume war', *The Observer*, Sunday 4 October: 29.

Bell, E. (1993a) 'Is hanging too good for them?', *The Observer*, Sunday 20 June: 29.

Bell, E. (1993b) 'Sega serves cod with its chips', *The Observer*, Sunday 9 May: 27.

Bell, J. (1994) 'The role of government in small firm internationalisation: a comparative study of export development in Finland, Ireland and Norway, with specific reference to the computer software industry', unpublished PhD thesis, Glasgow: University of Strathclyde.

Bell, M.L. and Emory, C.W. (1971) 'The faltering marketing concept', *Journal of Marketing* 35, October: 37–42.

Benjamin, A. (ed.) (1989) *The Lyotard Reader*, Oxford: Blackwell.

Bennett, H. (1993) 'Marx is dead. Long live Marxism', *The Higher*, Friday 12 March: 48.

Bennett, R.C. and Cooper, R.G. (1981) 'The misuse of marketing: an American tragedy', *Business Horizons* 24, 6: 51–61.

Bennington, G. (1988) *Lyotard: Writing the Event*, Manchester: Manchester University Press.

Berger, P.L. (1963) *Invitation to Sociology: A Humanistic Perspective*, Harmondsworth: Penguin.

Berman, M. (1983) *All That is Solid Melts Into Air: The Experience of Modernity*, London: Verso.

Berry, P. and Wernick, A. (eds)(1992) *Shadow of Spirit: Postmodernism and Religion*, London: Routledge.

Best, S. (1991) 'Chaos and entropy: metaphors in postmodern science and social theory', *Science as Culture*, 11: 188–226.

Best, S. and Kellner, D. (1991) *Postmodern Theory: Critical Interrogations*, Basingstoke: Macmillan.

Betts, P. (1993) 'Branson bets on flutter-as-you-fly', *Financial Times*, Saturday 25 September: 1.

Bloom, A. (1987) *The Closing of the American Mind*, Harmondsworth: Penguin.

Bocock, R. (1993) *Consumption*, London: Routledge.

Bocock, R. and Thompson, K. (eds) (1992) *Social and Cultural Forms of Modernity*, Cambridge: Polity.

Borgmann, A. (1992) *Crossing the Postmodern Divide*, Chicago: University of Chicago Press.

Bourdieu, P. (1984 [1979]) *Distinction: A Social Critique of the Judgement of Taste*, trans. R. Nice, London: Routledge.

Bowie, M. (1991) *Lacan*, London: Fontana.

Bowlby, R. (1985) *Just Looking: Consumer Culture in Dreiser, Gissing and Zola*, New York: Methuen.

Bowlby, R. (1993) *Shopping With Freud*, London: Routledge.

Bowler, P.J. (1989) *The Invention of Progress: The Victorians and the Past*, Oxford: Blackwell.

Boyne, R. (1990) *Foucault and Derrida: The Other Side of Reason*, London: Unwin Hyman.

Boyne, R. and Rattansi, A. (1990) 'The theory and politics of postmodernism: by way of an introduction', in R. Boyne and A. Rattansi (eds) *Postmodernism and Society*, Basingstoke: Macmillan, 1–45.

Bracewell, M. (1994) 'Obscure objects of desire', *The Observer Life*, Sunday 20 February: 4–5.

Bradley, H. (1992) 'Changing social structures: class and gender', in S. Hall and B. Gieben (eds) *Formations of Modernity*, Cambridge: Polity, 177–228.

Bradshaw, P. (1993) 'Keywords: POST-', *The Modern Review* 1, 11: 23.

Brady, J. and Davis, I. (1993) 'Marketing's mid-life crisis', *McKinsey Quarterly* 2: 17–28.

Briggs, J. and Peat, F.D. (1989) *Turbulent Mirror: An Illustrated Guide to Chaos Theory and the Science of Wholeness*, New York: Harper and Row.

Brinkworth, L. (1993) 'Housewives ad nauseam', *The Sunday Times, Style and Travel*, 28 November: 12–13.

Britt, D. (ed.) (1989) *Modern Art: Impressionism to Postmodernism*, London: Thames and Hudson.

Broadbent, G. (1991) *Deconstruction: A Student Guide*, London: Academy Editions.

Brown, R. (1987) 'Marketing – a function and a philosophy', *The Quarterly Review of Marketing* 13, Spring–Summer: 25–30.

Brown, S. (1989) 'I'd rather be in Philadelphia', *ARE Newsletter* 1: 15–22.

Brown, S. (1992) *Retail Location; A Micro-scale Perspective*, Aldershot: Avebury.

Brown, S. (1993a) 'Micro-scale retail location; cinderella or ugly sister?', *International Journal of Retail and Distribution Management* 21, 7: 11–19.

Brown, S. (1993b) 'A beginner's guide to book reviewing', *Irish Marketing Review* 6: 143–7.

Brown, S. (1993c) 'Postmodern marketing?' *European Journal of Marketing* 27, 4: 19–34.

Brown, S. (1993d) 'Postmodernism and central place theory: deconstruction/reconstruction', in S. Burt and L. Sparks (eds) *Seventh International Conference on Research in the Distributive Trades*, Stirling: Institute for Retail Studies, 447–56.

Brown, S. (1993e) 'Retailing thought in a postmodern era: re-aligning the wheel', in G. Davies and P.J. McGoldrick (eds) *ESRC Seminars: Research Themes in Retailing Theme III: Strategic Issues in Retailing*, Manchester: Manchester Business School, 1–31.

Brown, S. (1993f) 'Postmodernism . . . the end of marketing?', in D. Brownlie *et al.* (eds) *Rethinking Marketing*, Coventry: Warwick Business School Research Bureau, 1–11.

Brown, S. (1994a) 'Sex 'n' Shopping', in O. Westall (ed.) *British Academy of Management Annual Conference Proceedings*, Lancaster: Lancaster University, 241.

Brown, S. (1994b) 'Marketing as multiplex: screening postmodernism', *European Journal of Marketing* 28, 8/9: 27–51.

Brown, S. (1994c) 'Marketing and postmodernism: opportunity or aporia?', in M.J. Baker (ed.) *Perspectives on Marketing Management, Volume 4*, Chichester: Wiley, 73–96.

Brown, S. (1994d) 'Nietzsche marketing', in J. Bell *et al.* (eds) *Marketing: Unity in Diversity*, Coleraine: Marketing Education Group Conference Proceedings, 123.

Brown, S. (1994e) 'Sources and status of marketing theory', in M.J. Baker (ed.) *Marketing: Theory and Practice*, Basingstoke: Macmillan, in press.

Brown, S. (1995) *Postmodern Marketing*, London: Routledge.

Brown, S. and Quinn, B. (1993) 'Re-inventing the retailing wheel: a postmodern morality tale', in P.J. McGoldrick (ed.) *Cases in Retail Management*, London: Pitman, 26–39.

Brownlie, D. and Saren, M. (1992) 'The four Ps of the marketing concept: prescriptive, polemical, permanent and problematical', *European Journal of Marketing* 26, 4: 34–47.

Bucklin, L.P. and Sengupta, S. (1993) 'Organising successful co-marketing alliances', *Journal of Marketing* 57, 2: 32–46.

Burchill, J. (1994) 'The terrible spoof', *The Sunday Times*, 22 May, 10: 4–5.

Burgin, V. (1986) *The End of Art Theory: Criticism and Postmodernity*, Basingstoke: Macmillan.

Burrell, G. (1988) 'Modernism, postmodernism and organisational analysis 2: the contribution of Michel Foucault', *Organization Studies* 9, 2: 221–35.

Burrell, G. (1993) 'Eco and the Bunnymen', in J. Hassard and M. Parker (eds) *Postmodernism and Organisations*, London: Sage, 71–82.

Burrell, G. (1994) 'Modernism, postmodernism and organizational analysis 4: the contribution of Jürgen Habermas', *Organization Studies* 15, 1: 1–19.

Bury, J.B. (1987 [1932]) *The Idea of Progress: An Inquiry Into its Origins and Growth*, New York: Dover.

Butler, P. and Brown, S. (1994) 'Broadening the concept of relationship marketing: a meta-theoretical perspective', in J. Bell *et al.* (eds) *Marketing: Unity in Diversity*, Coleraine: Marketing Education Group Conference Proceedings, 135–43.

Callinicos, A. (1989) *Against Postmodernism: A Marxist Critique*, Cambridge: Polity.

Callinicos, A. (1990) 'Reactionary postmodernism?', in R. Boyne and A. Rattansi (eds) *Postmodernism and Society*, Basingstoke: Macmillan, 97–118.

Cameron, M., Rushton, A. and Carson, D. (1988) *Marketing*, Harmondsworth: Penguin.

Cannon, T. (1991) 'The new boy in the band', *The Higher*, Friday 15 March: 17.

Carson, D.J. (1985) 'The evolution of marketing in small firms', *European Journal of Marketing* 19, 5: 7–16.

Carson, D.J. (1989) 'Some exploratory models for assessing small firms' marketing performance (a qualitative approach)', *European Journal of Marketing* 24, 11: 1–51.

Caruso, T.E. (1992) 'Kotler: future marketers will focus on customer data base to compete globally', *Marketing News* 26, 12: 21–2.

Cassidy, J. (1993) 'Bell rings multi-media revolution', *The Sunday Times*, 17 October, 4: 2–3.

Caygill, H. (1990) 'Architectural postmodernism: the retreat of an avant-garde?', in R. Boyne and A. Rattansi (eds) *Postmodernism and Society*, Basingstoke: Macmillan, 260–89.

Chen, I.J., Calantone, R.J. and Chung, C-H. (1992) 'The marketing–manufacturing interface and manufacturing flexibility', *OMEGA* 20, 4: 431–43.

Christopher, M. and McDonald, M. (1991) *Marketing: An Introduction*, London: Pan.

Christopher, M., Payne, A. and Ballantyne, D. (1991) *Relationship Marketing*, Oxford: Butterworth-Heinemann.

Clark, G. and Piggott, S. (1990) *Prehistoric Societies*, Harmondsworth: Penguin.

Clark, M. (1990) *Nietzsche on Truth and Philosophy*, Cambridge: Cambridge University Press.

Clegg, S.R. (1990) *Modern Organisations: Organisation Studies in a Postmodern World*, London: Sage.

Coleman, D.C. (1992) *Myth, History and the Industrial Revolution*, London: The Hambledon Press.

Collins, H. and Pinch, T. (1993) *The Golem: What Everyone Should Know About Science*, Cambridge: Cambridge University Press.

Connor, S. (1989) *Postmodernist Culture: An Introduction to Theories of the Contemporary*, Oxford: Blackwell.

Cook, G. (1992) *The Discourse of Advertising*, London: Routledge.

Cooke, P. (1990) *Back to the Future: Modernity, Postmodernity and Locality*, London: Unwin Hyman.

Cooper, R. (1989) 'Modernism, postmodernism and organizational analysis 3: the contribution of Jacques Derrida', *Organization Studies* 10, 4: 479–502.

Cooper, R. and Burrell, G. (1988) 'Modernism, postmodernism and organisational analysis: an introduction', *Organization Studies* 9, 1: 91–112.

Coren, A. (1989) *Seems Like Old Times*, London: Robson Books.

Coren, A. (1990) *More Like Old Times*, London: Robson Books.

Coren, A. (1991) *A Year in Cricklewood*, London: Robson Books.

Coren, A. (1993) *Toujours Cricklewood?*, London: Robson Books.

Costa, J.A. (1993) 'Review of "Postmodern Consumer Research" by E.C. Hirschman and M.B. Holbrook', *Journal of Marketing Research* 30, November: 527–8.

Cotterell, A. (ed.) (1988) *The Penguin Encyclopedia of Ancient Civilisations*, Harmondsworth: Penguin.

Coupland, D. (1992) *Generation X Tales for an Accelerated Culture*, London: Abacus.

Cova, B. (1993) 'Beyond marketing: from marketing to societing', in D. Brownlie *et al.* (eds) *Rethinking Marketing*, Coventry: Warwick Business School Research Bureau, 12–23.

Cova, B. and Svanfeldt, C. (1992) 'Marketing beyond marketing in a post-modern Europe: the creation of societal innovations', in K.G. Grunert and D. Fuglede (eds) *Marketing for Europe – Marketing for the Future*, Aarhus: EMAC, 155–71.

Cova, B. and Svanfeldt, C. (1993) 'Societal innovations and the postmodern aestheticization of everyday life', *International Journal of Research in Marketing* 10, 3: 297–310.

Crimp, D. (1985) 'On the museum's ruins', in H. Foster (ed.) *Postmodern Culture*, London: Pluto Press, 43–56.

Crowther, P. (1990) 'Postmodernism in the visual arts: a question of ends', in

R. Boyne and A. Rattansi (eds) *Postmodernism and Society*, Basingstoke: Macmillan, 237–59.

Culler, J. (1979) 'Jacques Derrida', in J. Sturrock (ed.) *Structuralism and Since: From Lévi-Strauss to Derrida*, Oxford: Oxford University Press, 154–80.

Culler, J. (1981) *The Pursuit of Signs: Semiotics, Literature, Deconstruction*, London: Routledge.

Culler, J. (1983a) *On Deconstruction: Theory and Criticism After Structuralism*, London: Routledge.

Culler, J. (1983b) *Barthes*, London: Fontana.

Culler, J. (1988) *Saussure*, London: Fontana, revised edition.

Cushman, P. (1990) 'Why the self is empty', *American Psychologist* 45, 5: 599–611.

D'Souza, D. (1993) 'Pied pipers of relativism reverse course', *The Wall Street Journal*, Tuesday 27 July: 10.

Davidson, M. (1992) *The Consumerist Manifesto: Advertising in Postmodern Times*, London: Routledge.

Davies, J.M. (1992) *The Essential Guide to Database Marketing*, Maidenhead: McGraw-Hill.

Dawson, J.A. (1979) *The Marketing Environment*, London: Croom Helm.

Dawson, J.A. (1982) *Commercial Distribution in Europe*, London: Croom Helm.

Day, G.S. (1992) 'Marketing's contribution to the strategy dialogue', *Journal of the Academy of Marketing Science* 20, 4: 323–9.

de Certeau, M. (1984) *The Practice of Everyday Life*, trans. S.F. Rendall, Berkeley: University of California Press.

de Jonquieres, G. (1993) 'Growing taste for alliances in the food industry', *Financial Times*, Friday 22 January: 15.

de Saussure, F. (1983 [1916]) *Course in General Linguistics*, trans. R. Harris, London: Duckworth.

Debord, G. (1994 [1967]) *The Society of the Spectacle*, trans. D. Nicholson-Smith, Cambridge: MIT Press.

Deighton, J. (1992) 'The consumption of performance', *Journal of Consumer Research* 19, December: 362–72.

Deleuze, G. and Guattari, F. (1988 [1980]) *A Thousand Plateaus: Capitalism and Schizophrenia*, trans. B. Massumi, London: The Athlone Press.

Deleuze, G. and Guattari, F. (1994 [1991]) *What is Philosophy?*, trans. G. Burchell and H. Tomlinson, London: Verso.

Denzin, N.K. (1991) *Images of Postmodern Society: Social Theory and Contemporary Cinema*, London: Sage.

Derrida, J. (1978a [1967]) *Writing and Difference*, trans. A. Bass, London: Routledge.

Derrida, J. (1978b [1967]) 'Cogito and the history of madness', in J. Derrida, *Writing and Difference*, trans. A. Bass, London: Routledge, 31–63.

Derrida, J. (1986 [1974]) *Glas*, trans. J.P. Leavy and R. Rand, Lincoln: University of Nebraska Press.

Derrida, J. (1987a [1972]) *Positions*, trans. A. Bass, London: The Athlone Press.

Derrida, J. (1987b [1975]) 'Le facteur de la vérité', in J. Derrida, *The Post Card: From Socrates to Freud and Beyond*, trans. A. Bass, Chicago: University of Chicago Press, 411–96.

Derrida, J. (1991) *A Derrida Reader: Between the Blinds*, ed. P. Kamuf, Hemel Hempstead: Harvester Wheatsheaf.

Derrida, J. (1992) *Acts of Literature*, ed. D. Attridge, London: Routledge.

Desmond, J. (1993) 'Marketing: the split subject', in D. Brownlie *et al.* (eds) *Rethinking Marketing*, Coventry: Warwick Business School Research Bureau, 259–69.

Dholakia, N. and Arndt, J. (eds) (1985) *Changing the Course of Marketing: Alternative Paradigms for Widening Marketing Theory*, Greenwich: JAI Press.

Diamond, A.H. (1993) 'Chaos science', *Marketing Research* 5, 4: 9–14.

Dibb, S., Simkin, L., Pride, W.M. and Ferrell, O.C. (1994) *Marketing Concepts and Strategies*, Boston: Houghton Mifflin, second European edition.

Dickinson, R.A. (1992) 'The myths of marketing', unpublished manuscript.

Dickinson, R.A., Herbst, A. and O'Shaughnessy, J. (1986) 'Marketing concept and customer orientation', *European Journal of Marketing* 20, 10: 18–23.

Douzinas, C., Warrington, R. and McVeigh, S. (1991) *Postmodern Jurisprudence: The Law of Text and the Texts of Law*, London: Routledge.

Doyle, P. (1985) 'Marketing and the competitive performance of British industry: areas for research', *Journal of Marketing Management* 1, 1: 87–98.

Doyle, P. (1993) 'Marketing planning: rethinking the core', in D. Brownlie *et al.* (eds) *Rethinking Marketing*, Coventry: Warwick Business School Research Bureau, 86–90.

Drucker, P.F. (1954) *The Practice of Management*, Oxford: Butterworth-Heinemann, 1993 reprint.

Drucker, P.F. (1993) *Post-capitalist Society*, Oxford: Butterworth-Heinemann.

du Gay, P. and Negus, K. (1994) 'The changing sites of sound: music retailing and the composition of consumers', *Media, Culture and Society*, 16, 3: 395–413.

Dussart, C. (1994) 'Capitalism against capitalism: political and economic implications of marketing practice in Europe', in M.J. Baker (ed.) *Perspectives on Marketing Management, Volume 4*, Chichester: Wiley, 119–34.

Dwyer, F.R., Schurr, P.H. and Oh, S. (1987) 'Developing buyer–seller relationships', *Journal of Marketing* 51, April: 11–27.

Eagleton, T. (1983) *Literary Theory: An Introduction*, Oxford: Blackwell.

Easterby-Smith, M., Thorpe, R. and Lowe, A. (1991) *Management Research: An Introduction*, London: Sage.

Eco, U. (1985 [1983]) *Reflections on The Name of the Rose*, trans. W. Weaver, London, Minerva.

Eco, U. (1986 [1973]) *Travels in Hyper-reality*, trans. W. Weaver, London: Picador.

Edgar, D. (1993) 'Seeing isn't believing', *The Sunday Times*, 22 August, 9: 8–10.

Edwards, M. (1993) 'Shaking up the real thing', *The Sunday Times*, 7 March, 9: 2–3.

Elliott, R. (1993) 'Marketing and the meaning of postmodern consumer culture', in D. Brownlie *et al.* (eds) *Rethinking Marketing*, Coventry: Warwick Business School Research Bureau, 134–42.

Elliott, R. (1994) 'Addictive consumption: function and fragmentation in postmodernity', *Journal of Consumer Policy* 17, 2: 159–79.

Elliott, R., Eccles, S. and Hodgson, M. (1993) 'Re-coding gender representations: women, cleaning products and advertising's "new man"', *International Journal of Research in Marketing* 10, 3: 311–24.

Ellis, J.M. (1989) *Against Deconstruction*, Princeton: Princeton University Press.

Elvy, B.H. (1984) *Marketing Made Simple*, London: Heinemann.

Eribon, D. (1991 [1989]) *Michel Foucault*, trans. B. Wing, London: Faber and Faber.

Ewen, S. (1988) *All Consuming Images: The Politics of Style in Contemporary Culture*, New York: Basic Books.

Eysenck, H. (1985) *Decline and Fall of the Freudian Empire*, Harmondsworth: Penguin.

Featherstone, M. (1988) 'In pursuit of the postmodern: an introduction', in M. Featherstone (ed.) *Postmodernism*, London: Sage, 195–215.

Featherstone, M. (1991) *Consumer Culture and Postmodernism*, London: Sage.

Fennell, G. (1985) 'Things of Heaven and Earth: phenomenology, marketing and consumer research', in E.C. Hirschman and M.B. Holbrook (eds) *Advances in Consumer Research, Volume XII*, Provo: Association for Consumer Research, 544–9.

Ferguson, H. (1992) 'Watching the world go round: atrium culture and the psychology of shopping', in R. Shields (ed.) *Lifestyle Shopping: the Subject of Consumption*, London: Routledge, 21–39.

Feyerabend, P. (1970) 'Consolations for the specialist', in I. Lakatos and A. Musgrave (eds) *Criticism and the Growth of Knowledge*, Cambridge: Cambridge University Press, 197–230.

Feyerabend, P. (1987) *Farewell to Reason*, London: Verso.

Feyerabend, P. (1988) *Against Method*, London: Verso, revised edition.

Fielding, H. (1992) 'Teach yourself postmodernism', *The Independent on Sunday*, 15 November: 21.

Fielding, H. (1994) 'Shot in the foot', *The Sunday Times*, 13 February, 9: 8.

Fillingham, L.A. (1993) *Foucault for Beginners*, London: Readers and Writers.

Financial Times (1992) 'The verbiage of creativity that is . . . mad, bad and dangerous to use', *Financial Times*, Saturday 24 December: vi-vii.

Firat, A.F. (1984) 'Marketing science: issues concerning the scientific method and the philosophy of science', in P.F. Anderson and M.J. Ryan (eds) *Scientific Method in Marketing*, Chicago: American Marketing Association, 22–5.

Firat, A.F. (1989) 'Science and human understanding' in T.L. Childers *et al.* (eds) *Marketing Theory and Practice*, Chicago: American Marketing Association, 93–8.

Firat, A.F. (1991) 'Postmodern culture, marketing, and the consumer', in T.L. Childers *et al.* (eds) *Marketing Theory and Applications, Volume 2*, Chicago: American Marketing Association, 237–42.

Firat, A.F. (1992a) 'Fragmentations in the postmodern', in J.F. Sherry and B. Sternthal (eds) *Advances in Consumer Research, Volume XIX*, Provo: Association for Consumer Research, 203–5.

Firat, A.F. (1992b) 'Postmodernism and the marketing organisation', *Journal of Organisational Change Management 5*, 1: 79–83.

Firat, A.F., Dholakia, N. and Venkatesh, A. (1995) 'Marketing in a postmodern world', *European Journal of Marketing 29*, 1: 40–56.

Firat, A.F. and Venkatesh, A. (1991) 'The making of postmodern consumption', unpublished manuscript.

Firat, A.F. and Venkatesh, A. (1993) 'Postmodernity: the age of marketing', *International Journal of Research in Marketing 10*, 3: 227–49.

Fisher, A. (1993) 'Speed is of the essence', *Financial Times*, Tuesday 3 August: 10.

Fisk, G. (1994) 'Understanding imperatives for changing macroperspectives on marketing', paper presented at the nineteenth annual macromarketing conference, Boulder, Colorado, August.

Fiske, J. (1989a) 'The jeaning of America', in J. Fiske, *Understanding Popular Culture*, London: Unwin Hyman, 1–21.

Fiske, J. (1989b) *Reading the Popular*, Winchester: Unwin Hyman.

Fiske, J., Hodge, B. and Turner, G. (1987) *Myths of Oz: Reading Australian Popular Culture*, Winchester: Allen and Unwin.

Fitzgerald, F. Scott (1934) *Tender is the Night*, Harmondsworth: Penguin.

Foster, H. (1985) 'Postmodernism: a preface', in H. Foster (ed.) *Postmodern Culture*, London: Pluto, vii–xiv.

Foucault, M. (1967 [1961]) *Madness and Civilisation: A History of Insanity in the Age of Reason*, trans. R. Howard, London: Routledge.

Foucault, M. (1972 [1966]) *The Order of Things: An Archaeology of the Human Sciences*, trans. A. Sheridan, London: Routledge.

Foucault, M. (1974 [1969]) *The Archaeology of Knowledge*, trans. A.M. Sheridan Smith, London: Routledge.

Foucault, M. (1977 [1975]) *Discipline and Punish: The Birth of the Prison*, trans. A. Sheridan, Harmondsworth: Penguin.

Foucault, M. (1980) *Power/Knowledge: Selected Interviews and Other Writings 1972–1977*, ed. C. Gordon, Hemel Hempstead: Harvester Wheatsheaf.

Foucault, M. (1990 [1984]) *The Care of the Self: The History of Sexuality Volume Three*, trans. R. Hurley, Harmondsworth: Penguin.

Foucault, M. (1991 [1981]) *Remarks on Marx*, trans. R.J. Goldstein and J. Cascaito, New York: Semiotext(e).

Fox, S. and Moult, G. (1990) 'Postmodern culture and management development', *Management Education and Development* 21, 3: 161–268.

Foxall, G.R. (1984a) 'Marketing's domain', *European Journal of Marketing* 18, 1: 25–40.

Foxall, G.R. (1984b) 'Consumers' intentions and behaviour: a note on research and a challenge to researchers', *Journal of the Market Research Society* 26, 3: 213–35.

Foxall, G.R. (1990) *Consumer Psychology in Behavioural Perspective*, London: Routledge.

Foxall, G.R. (1992) 'The consumer situation: an integrative model for research in marketing', *Journal of Marketing Management* 8, 4: 383–404.

Foxall, G.R. (1994) 'Environment-impacting consumer behaviour: a framework for social marketing and demarketing', in M.J. Baker (ed.) *Perspectives on Marketing Management, Volume 4*, Chichester: Wiley, 27–53.

Frain, J. (1983) *Introduction to Marketing*, Estover: McDonald and Evans.

Frankel, B. (1987) *The Post-industrial Utopians*, Cambridge: Polity.

Freathy, P. and Sparks, L. (1992) 'Fordism and retailing: a note on the curious neglect of the Ford commisaries', University of Stirling: Institute for Retail Studies, Working Paper 9203.

Freeling, A. (1994) 'Marketing is in crisis – can market research help?', *Journal of the Market Research Society* 36, 2: 97–104.

Friedberg, A. (1993) *Window Shopping: Cinema and the Postmodern*, Oxford: University of California Press.

Fullerton, R. (1988) 'How modern is modern marketing? Marketing's evolution and the myth of the "production era"', *Journal of Marketing* 52, January: 108–25.

Gellner, E. (1983) *Nations and Nationalism*, Oxford: Basil Blackwell.

Gellner, E. (1992) *Postmodernism, Reason and Religion*, London: Routledge.

Gellner, E. (1993) *The Psychoanalytic Movement*, London: Fontana, second edition.

Giddens, A. (1990) *The Consequences of Modernity*, Cambridge: Polity.

Gleick, J. (1988) *Chaos: Making a New Science*, London: Cardinal.

Goldstein, J. (ed.) (1994) *Foucault and the Writing of History*, Oxford: Blackwell.

Gordon, S. (1991) *The History and Philosophy of Social Science*, London: Routledge.

Gould, S.J. (1991) 'The self-manipulation of my pervasive, perceived vital energy through product use: an introspective-praxis perspective', *Journal of Consumer Research* 18, September: 194–207.

Grafton Small, R. (1993a) 'Review of "Postmodern Consumer Research" by E.C. Hirschman and M.B. Holbrook', *Journal of Marketing Management* 9, 4: 433–5.

Grafton Small, R. (1993b) 'Morality and the market-place: an everyday story of consumer ethics' in D. Brownlie *et al.* (eds) *Rethinking Marketing*, Coventry: Warwick Business School Research Bureau, 270–8.

Grafton Small, R. (1993c) 'Consumption and significance: everyday life in a brand-new second-hand bow tie', *European Journal of Marketing* 27, 8: 38–45.

Grafton Small, R. and Linstead, S.A. (1985) 'Bricks and bricolage: deconstructing corporate image in stone and story', *DRAGON* 1, 1: 8–37.

Grafton Small, R. and Linstead, S.A. (1989) 'Advertisements as artefacts: everyday understanding and the creative consumer', *International Journal of Advertising* 8, 3: 205–18.

Greenley, G.E. (1986) 'Interface of strategic and marketing plans', *Journal of General Management* 12, 1: 54–62.

Griffin, D.R. (ed.) (1988a) *The Reenchantment of Science: Postmodern Proposals*, Albany: State University of New York Press.

Griffin, D.R. (1988b) 'Introduction: the reenchantment of science', in D.R. Griffin (ed.) *The Reenchantment of Science*, Albany: State University of New York Press, 1–46.

Groonos, C. (1990) 'Relationship approach to marketing in service contexts: the marketing and organisational behaviour interface', *Journal of Business Research* 20, 1: 3–11.

Gross, A.G. (1990) *The Rhetoric of Science*, Cambridge: Harvard University Press.

Grove, S.J. and Fisk, R.P. (1991) 'The theatrical framework of service encounters: a metaphorical analysis', in M.C. Gilly *et al.* (eds) *Enhancing Knowledge Development in Marketing, Volume 2*, Chicago: American Marketing Association, 315–17.

Guilliatt, R. (1992) 'Kiddy cocaine', *The Sunday Times Magazine*, 1 November: 30–5.

Guiry, M. (1992) 'Consumer and employee roles in service encounters', in J.F. Sherry and B. Sternthal (eds) *Advances in Consumer Research, Volume XIX*, Provo: Association for Consumer Research, 666–72.

Gummesson, E. (1987) 'The new marketing – developing long-term interactive relationships', *Long Range Planning* 20, 4: 10–20.

Gummesson, E. (1991) 'Marketing-orientation revisited: the crucial role of the part-time marketer', *European Journal of Marketing* 25, 2: 60–75.

Gurney, O.R. (1990) *The Hittites*, Harmondsworth: Penguin.

Habermas, J. (1985) 'Modernity – an incomplete project', in H. Foster (ed.) *Postmodern Culture*, London: Pluto Press, 3–15.

Habermas, J. (1987 [1985]) *The Philosophical Discourse of Modernity*, trans. F. Lawrence, London: Polity.

Habermas, J. (1992 [1988]) *Postmetaphysical Thinking: Philosophical Essays*, trans. W.M. Hohengarten, Cambridge: Polity.

Hall, S. (1992) 'The west and the rest: discourse and power', in S. Hall and B. Gieben (eds) *Formations of Modernity*, Cambridge: Polity, 275–331.

Hall, S. and Gieben, B. (eds) (1992) *Formations of Modernity*, Cambridge: Polity.

Hall, S., Held, D. and McGrew, T. (eds) (1992) *Modernity and its Futures*, Cambridge: Polity.

Hampden-Turner, C. and Trompenaars, F. (1994) *The Seven Cultures of Capitalism*, London: Piatkus.

Handy, C. (1994) *The Empty Raincoat: Making Sense of the Future*, London: Hutchinson.

Harland, R. (1987) *Superstructuralism: The Philosophy of Structuralism and Post-structuralism*, London: Routledge.

Harris, J.F. (1992) *Against Relativism: A Philosophical Defense of Method*, LaSalle: Open Court.

Hart, N. and Stapleton, J. (1992) *The Marketing Dictionary*, Oxford: Butterworth-Heinemann.

Harvey, D. (1969) *Explanation in Geography*, London: Edward Arnold.

Harvey, D. (1989) *The Condition of Postmodernity*, Oxford: Blackwell.

Harvey, D. (1993) 'Class relations, social justice and the politics of difference', in J. Squires (ed.) *Principled Positions: Postmodernism and the Rediscovery of Value*, London: Lawrence and Wishart, 85–120.

Haskell, F. (1993) *History and its Images: Art and the Interpretation of the Past*, London: Yale University Press.

Hassan, I. (1985) 'The culture of postmodernism', *Theory, Culture and Society* 2, 2: 119–31.

Hassard, J. (1993) *Sociology and Organisation Theory: Positivism, Paradigms and Postmodernity*, Cambridge: Cambridge University Press.

Hattenstone, S. (1992) 'All mod cons', *The Observer Magazine*, Sunday 23 August: 7.

Hawkes, T. (1977) *Structuralism and Semiotics*, London: Routledge.

Hawking, S. (1988) *A Brief History of Time*, London: Bantam.

Hebdige, D. (1986) 'Postmodernism and "The Other Side"', *Journal of Communication Inquiry* 10, 2: 78–98.

Hebdige, D. (1989) 'After the masses', in S. Hall and M. Jacques (eds) *New Times: The Changing Face of Politics in the 1990s*, London: Lawrence and Wishart, 76–93.

Held, D. (1980) *Introduction to Critical Theory: Horkheimer to Habermas*, Cambridge: Polity.

Heller, A. (1993) *A Philosophy of History in Fragments*, Oxford: Blackwell.

Hesse, M. (1980) *Revolutions and Reconstructions in the Philosophy of Science*, Brighton: Harvester Press.

Hetrick, W.P. (1989) 'The ideology of consumerism: a critique', in T.L. Childers et al. (eds) *Marketing Theory and Practice*, Chicago: American Marketing Association, 40–3.

Hetrick, W.P. (1993) 'Comments in "postmodernism" session of *Rethinking Marketing* symposium', Coventry: University of Warwick, July.

Hetrick, W.P. and Lozada, H.R. (1993) 'From marketing theory to marketing anti-theory: implications of ethical critique within the (post)modern experience', in D. Brownlie *et al.* (eds) *Rethinking Marketing,* Coventry: Warwick Business School Research Bureau, 279–90.

Hetzel, P. (1994) 'The role of fashion and design in a postmodern society: what challenges for firms?', in M.J. Baker (ed.) *Perspectives on Marketing Management, Volume 4,* Chichester: Wiley, 97–118.

Hill, R.P. (1993) 'Ethnography and marketing research: a postmodern perspective', in D.W. Cravens and P.R. Dickson (eds) *Enhancing Knowledge Development in Marketing, Volume 4,* Chicago: American Marketing Association, 257–61.

Hirschman, E.C. (1983) 'Aesthetics, ideologies and the limits of the marketing concept', *Journal of Marketing* 47, Summer: 45–55.

Hirschman, E.C. (1986) 'Humanistic inquiry in marketing research: philosophy, method and criteria', *Journal of Marketing Research* 23, August: 237–49.

Hirschman, E.C. (1987) 'People as products: analysis of a complex marketing exchange', *Journal of Marketing* 51, January: 98–108.

Hirschman, E.C. (1989a) 'Afterword', in E.C. Hirschman (ed.) *Interpretive Consumer Research,* Provo: Association for Consumer Research, 209.

Hirschman, E.C. (1989b) 'Foreword', in E.C. Hirschman (ed.) *Interpretive Consumer Research,* Provo: Association for Consumer Research, ix–x.

Hirschman, E.C. (1990) 'The day I almost died: a consumer researcher learns some lessons from a traumatic experience', in E.C. Hirschman (ed.) *Research in Consumer Behaviour, Volume 4,* Greenwich: JAI Press, 109–23.

Hirschman, E.C. (1991) 'Secular morality and the dark side of consumer behaviour: or how semiotics saved my life', in R.H. Holman and M.R. Solomon (eds) *Advances in Consumer Research, Volume XVIII,* Provo: Association for Consumer Research, 1–4.

Hirschman, E.C. (1992) 'Recovering from drug addiction: a phenomenological account', in J.F. Sherry and B. Sternthal (eds) *Advances in Consumer Research, Volume XIX,* Provo: Association for Consumer Research, 541–9.

Hirschman, E.C. (1993) 'Ideology in consumer research, 1980 and 1990: a Marxist and feminist critique', *Journal of Consumer Research* 19, March: 537–55.

Hirschman, E.C. and Holbrook, M.B. (1992) *Postmodern Consumer Research,* Newbury Park: Sage.

Hirshey, G. (1993) 'The snooty dame at the block party', *New York Times Magazine,* Sunday 24 October: 113–157.

Hirst, P. (1993) 'An answer to relativism?', in J. Squires (ed.) *Principled Positions: Postmodernism and the Rediscovery of Value,* London: Lawrence and Wishart, 50–66.

Hodock, C.L. (1991) 'The decline and fall of marketing research in corporate America', *Marketing Research* 3, 2: 12–22.

Holbrook, M.B. (1984) 'Theory development is a Jazz solo: Bird lives', in P.F. Anderson and M.J. Ryan (eds) *Scientific Method in Marketing,* Chicago: American Marketing Association, 48–52.

Holbrook, M.B. (1985) 'The consumer researcher visits Radio City: dancing in the dark', in E.C. Hirschman and M.B. Holbrook (eds) *Advances in Consumer Research, Volume XII,* Provo: Association for Consumer Research, 28–31.

Holbrook, M.B. (1986) 'I'm hip: an autobiographical account of some musical consumption experiences', in R.J. Lutz (ed.) *Advances in Consumer Research, Volume XIII,* Provo: Association for Consumer Research, 614–18.

Holbrook, M.B. (1987a) 'Mirror, mirror, on the wall, what's unfair in the reflections on advertising?', *Journal of Marketing* 51, July: 95–103.

Holbrook, M.B. (1987b) 'The study of signs in consumer esthetics: an egocentric view', in J. Umiker-Sebeok (ed.) *Marketing and Semiotics: New Directions in the Study of Signs for Sale*, Berlin: de Gruyter, 73–121.

Holbrook, M.B. (1988) 'The psychoanalytic interpretation of consumer behaviour: *I am an animal*', in E.C. Hirschman and J. Sheth (eds) *Research in Consumer Behaviour, Volume 3*, Greenwich: JAI Press, 149–78.

Holbrook, M.B. (1993) 'Nostalgia and consumption preferences: some emerging patterns of consumer tastes', *Journal of Consumer Research* 20, September: 245–56.

Holbrook, M.B. (1994) 'Review of "Postmodernism and Social Theory" by S. Seidman and D.G. Wagner', *Journal of Macromarketing*, in press.

Holbrook, M.B. and Grayson, M.W. (1986) 'The semiology of cinematic consumption: symbolic consumer behaviour in "Out of Africa"', *Journal of Consumer Research* 13, December: 374–81.

Holbrook, M.B. and Hirschman, E.C. (1982) 'The experiential aspects of consumption: consumer fantasies, feelings and fun', *Journal of Consumer Research* 9, September: 132–40.

Holbrook, M.B. and Hirschman, E.C. (1993) *The Semiotics of Consumption: Interpreting Symbolic Consumer Behaviour in Popular Culture and Works of Art*, Berlin: de Gruyter.

Holbrook, M., Bell, S. and Grayson, M.W. (1989) 'The role of the humanities in consumer research: Close Encounters and Costal Disturbances', in E.C. Hirschman (ed.) *Interpretive Consumer Research*, Provo: Association for Consumer Research, 29–47.

Hollander, S.C. (1986) 'The marketing concept: a déjà vu', in G. Fisk (ed.) *Marketing Management Technology as a Social Process*, New York: Praeger, 3–29.

Hollander, S.C. and Germain, R. (1992) *Was There a Pepsi Generation Before Pepsi Discovered It?: Youth Based Segmentation in Marketing*, Lincolnwood: NTC Business Books.

Hollander, S.C. and Rassuli, K.M. (eds) (1993) *Marketing: Volumes I and II*, Brookfield, Vermont: Edward Elgar.

Hollinger, P. (1993) 'An attempt at reviving the Habitat habit', *Financial Times*, Monday 18 October: 20.

Holub, R.C. (1994) 'Hermeneutics', in M. Groden and M. Kreiswirth (eds) *The Johns Hopkins Guide to Literary Theory and Criticism*, Baltimore: The Johns Hopkins University Press, 375–82.

Honomichl J. (1992) '"Hypertargeting" scenario not as farfetched as it seems', *Marketing News* 26, 23: 11–12.

Hooley, G.J. (ed.) (1993) 'Marketing in Eastern and Central Europe', *European Journal of Marketing* 27, 11/12: 6–120.

Hooley, G.J. and Lynch, J.E. (1985) 'Marketing lessons from the UK's high-flying companies', *Journal of Marketing Management* 1, 1: 65–74.

Hooley, G.J. and Saunders, J. (1993) *Competitive Positioning: The Key to Market Success*, Hemel Hempstead: Prentice Hall.

Houston, F.S. (1986) 'The marketing concept: what it is and what it is not', *Journal of Marketing* 50, April: 81–7.

Houston F.S. and Gassenheimer, J.B. (1987) 'Marketing and exchange', *Journal of Marketing* 51, October: 3–18.

Hoy, D. (1985) 'Jacques Derrida', in Q. Skinner (ed.) *The Return of Grand Theory in the Human Sciences*, Cambridge: Cambridge University Press, 41–64.

Hoyt, F.B. (1991) 'We don't do marketing here anymore', *Marketing News* 25, 1: 4.

Huczynski, A.A. (1993) *Management Gurus: What Makes Them and How to Become One*, London: Routledge.

Hudson, L.A. and Ozanne, J.L. (1988) 'Alternative ways of seeking knowledge in consumer research', *Journal of Consumer Research* 14, March: 508–21.

Hughes, J. (1990) *The Philosophy of Social Research*, Harlow: Longman.

Hughes, R. (1991) *The Shock of the New: Art and the Century of Change*, London: Thames and Hudson, second edition.

Hughes, R. (1993) *Culture of Complaint: The Fraying of America*, Oxford: Oxford University Press.

Hunt, S.D. (1976) 'The nature and scope of marketing', *Journal of Marketing* 40, July: 17–28.

Hunt, S.D. (1984) 'Should marketing adopt relativism?', in P.F. Anderson and M.J. Ryan (eds) *Scientific Method in Marketing*, Chicago: American Marketing Association, 30–4.

Hunt, S.D. (1989) 'Naturalistic, humanistic and interpretive inquiry: challenges and ultimate potential', in E.C. Hirschman (ed.) *Interpretive Consumer Research*, Provo: Association for Consumer Research, 185–98.

Hunt, S.D. (1990) 'Truth in marketing theory and research', *Journal of Marketing* 54, July: 1–15.

Hunt, S.D. (1991a) 'The three dichotomies model of marketing revisited: is the total content of marketing thought normative?', in T. Childers *et al.* (eds) *Marketing Theory and Applications*, Volume 2, Chicago: American Marketing Association, 425–30.

Hunt, S.D. (1991b) 'Positivism and paradigm dominance in consumer research: toward critical pluralism and rapprochement', *Journal of Consumer Research* 18, June: 32–44.

Hunt, S.D. (1991c) *Modern Marketing Theory: Critical Issues in the Philosophy of Marketing Science*, Cincinnati: South-Western Publishing.

Hunt, S.D. (1992) 'For reason and realism in marketing', *Journal of Marketing* 56, April: 89–102.

Hunt, S.D. (1993) 'Objectivity in marketing theory and research', *Journal of Marketing* 57, 2: 76–91.

Hunt, S.D. (1994) 'On rethinking marketing: our discipline, our practice, our methods', *European Journal of Marketing* 28, 3: 13–25.

Huyssen, A. (1984) 'Mapping the postmodern', *New German Critique* 33, Fall: 5–52.

Hyman, M.R., Skipper, R. and Tansey, R. (1991) 'Two challenges for the three dichotomies model', in T. Childers *et al.* (eds) *Marketing Theory and Applications*, Volume 2, Chicago: American Marketing Association, 417–22.

Imrie, R. and Morris, J. (1992) 'A review of recent changes in buyer–supplier relations', *OMEGA* 20, 5/6: 641–52.

Ingene, C.A. (1993) 'Comments at 'Meet the Editors' session', Miami Beach: Academy of Marketing Science Annual Conference, May.

Iyer, G. (1991) 'Marketing and development: perspectives from critical theory', in M.C. Gilly *et al.* (eds) *Enhancing Knowledge Development in Marketing*, Volume 2, Chicago: American Marketing Association, 651–8.

Jackson, E.M. and McLeish, K. (1993) 'Hermeneutics', in K. McLeish (ed.) *Bloomsbury Guide to Human Thought*, London: Bloomsbury, 342–3.

Jackson, L. (1991) *The Poverty of Structuralism*, Harlow: Longman.

Jameson, F. (1984) 'Post-modernism or the cultural logic of late capitalism' *New Left Review* 146: 52–92.

Jameson, F. (1985) 'Postmodernism and consumer society', in H. Foster (ed.) *Postmodern Culture*, London: Pluto Press, 111–25.

Jameson, F. (1988) *The Ideologies of Theory: Essays 1971–1986*, Minneapolis: University of Minnesota Press.

Jameson, F. (1991) *Postmodernism, or, The Cultural Logic of Late Capitalism*, London: Verso.

Jefkins, F. (1993) *Modern Marketing*, London: Pitman, third edition.

Jencks, C. (1987) *Post-modernism: The New Classicism in Art and Architecture*, London: Academy Editions.

Jencks, C. (1989) *What is Postmodernism?* London: Academy Editions, third edition.

Jenkins, K. (1991) *Re-thinking History*, London: Routledge.

Jennings, D. and Saunders, J. (1993) 'Can the church look out the window? Marketing the church in England today', in M. Davies *et al.* (eds) *Emerging Issues in Marketing*, Loughborough: Marketing Education Group Conference Proceedings, 527–33.

Jhally, S. (1990) *The Codes of Advertising: Fetishism and the Political Economy of Meaning in the Consumer Society*, London: Routledge.

Johnson, B. (1981) 'The critical difference: Balzac's "Sarrasine" and Barthes's "S/Z"', in R. Young (ed.) *Untying the Text: A Post-structuralist Reader*, London: Routledge, 162–74.

Johnson, C. (1993) *System and Writing in the Philosophy of Jacques Derrida*, Cambridge: Cambridge University Press.

Johnson, G. (1993) 'Keynote address', Marketing Education Group Annual Conference, Loughborough University, July.

Johnson, P. (1991) *The Birth of the Modern: World Society 1815–1830*, London: Weidenfeld and Nicolson.

Johnston W.M. (1991) *Celebrations: The Cult of Anniversaries in Europe and the United States Today*, New Brunswick: Transaction.

Jones, D.G.B. (1991) 'Historiographic paradigms in marketing', in C.R. Taylor *et al.* (eds) *Marketing History – Its Many Dimensions*, East Lansing: Michigan State University, 3–12.

Jones, D.G.B. and Monieson, D.D. (1990) 'Early development of the philosophy of marketing thought', *Journal of Marketing* 54, January: 102–13.

Kaldor, A.G. (1971) 'Imbricative marketing', *Journal of Marketing* 35, April: 19–25.

Kaufman, C.F., Lane, P.M. and Lindquist, J.D. (1991) 'Exploring more than 24 hours a day: a preliminary investigation of polychronic time use', *Journal of Consumer Research* 18, December: 392–401.

Kavanagh, D. (1994) 'Hunt versus Anderson: round 16', *European Journal of Marketing* 28, 3: 26–41.

Kay, J. (1993) *Foundations of Corporate Success*, Oxford: Oxford University Press.

Kearney, R. (1986) *Modern Movements in European Philosophy*, Manchester: Manchester University Press.

Kehoe, L. (1993) 'Turn on, tune in and print out', *Financial Times*, Thursday 14 October: 11.

Keith, R.J. (1960) 'The marketing revolution', *Journal of Marketing* 24, January: 35–38.

Kellaway, L. (1994) 'The personnel touch', *Financial Times*, Thursday 6 January: 9.

Kellner, D. (ed.) (1989) *Postmodernism/Jameson/Critique*, Washington: Maisonneuve Press.

Kellner, D. (1992) 'Popular culture and the construction of postmodern identities', in S. Lash and J. Friedman (eds) *Modernity and Identity*, Oxford: Blackwell, 141–77.

Kenney, M. and Florida, R. (1992) *Beyond Mass Production: The Japanese System and its Transfer to the US*, Oxford: Oxford University Press.

Kerr, J. (1994) *A Most Dangerous Method: The Story of Jung, Freud, and Sabina Spielrein*, London: Sinclair-Stevenson.

Kheir-El-Din, A. (1991) 'The contribution of marketing to competitive success', in M.J. Baker (ed.) *Perspectives on Marketing Management, Volume 1*, Chichester: Wiley, 1–28.

King, S. (1994) 'Brand building and market research', in M. Jenkins and S. Knox (eds) *Advances in Consumer Marketing*, London: Kogan Page, 119–35.

Klotz, H. (1988 [1984]) *The History of Postmodern Architecture*, trans. R. Donnell, Cambridge: MIT Press.

Knorr-Cetina, K.D. (1981) *The Manufacture of Knowledge: An Essay on the Constructivist and Contextual Nature of Science*, Oxford: Pergamon.

Koelb, C. (ed.) (1990) *Nietzsche as Postmodernist: Essays Pro and Contra*, Albany: State University of New York Press.

Kohli, A.K. and Jaworski, B.J. (1990) 'Market orientation: the construct, research propositions and managerial implications', *Journal of Marketing* 54, April: 1–18.

Kohli, A.K. and Novak, J.A. (1984) 'The hypothesis of formative causation: implications of an alternative paradigm for marketing theory', in P.F. Anderson and M.J. Ryan (eds) *Scientific Method in Marketing*, Chicago: American Marketing Association, 35–8.

Kosko, B. (1993) *Fuzzy Thinking: The New Science of Fuzzy Logic*, London: HarperCollins.

Kotler, P. (1972) 'A generic concept of marketing', *Journal of Marketing* 36, April: 46–54.

Kotler, P. (1988) *Marketing Management: Analysis, Planning, Implementation and Control*, Englewood Cliffs: Prentice-Hall, sixth edition.

Kotler, P. and Armstrong, G. (1993) *Marketing: An Introduction*, Englewood Cliffs: Prentice-Hall, third edition.

Kotler, P. and Levy, S.J. (1969) 'Broadening the concept of marketing', *Journal of Marketing* 33, January: 10–15.

Kotler, P. and Zaltman, G. (1971) 'Social marketing: an approach to planned social change', *Journal of Marketing* 35, July: 3–12.

Kotler, P., Haider, D.H. and Rein, I. (1993) *Marketing Places: Attracting Investment, Industry, and Tourism to Cities, States, and Nations*, New York: Free Press.

Kowinski, W.S. (1985) *The Malling of America*, New York: W. Morrow.

Kroker, A. and Cook, D. (1986) *The Postmodern Scene: Excremental Culture and Hyper-aesthetics*, Montreal: New World Perspectives.

Kroker, A., Kroker, M. and Cook, D. (1989) *Panic Encyclopedia: The Definitive Guide to the Postmodern Scene*, Basingstoke: Macmillan.

Kropp, F. (1993) 'Postmodernism and value change: a new approach to examining changing values', Miami: Academy of Marketing Science, May.

Kuhn, T.S. (1970a) *The Structure of Scientific Revolutions*, Chicago: University of Chicago Press, second edition.

Kuhn, T.S. (1970b) 'Reflections on my critics', in I. Lakatos and A. Musgrave (eds) *Criticism and the Growth of Knowledge*, Cambridge: Cambridge University Press, 231–78.

Küng, H. (1991 [1990]) *Global Responsibility: In Search of a New World Ethic*, trans. J. Bowden, London: SCM Press.

Kvale, S. (ed.) (1992) *Psychology and Postmodernism*, London: Sage.

Lacan, J. (1977 [1966]) *Écrits: A Selection*, trans. A. Sheridan, London: Routledge.

Laczniak, G.R. and Michie, D.A. (1979) 'The social disorder of the broadened concept of marketing', *Journal of the Academy of Marketing Science* 7, 3: 214–32.

Lansley, S. (1994) *After the Goldrush. The Trouble With Affluence: "Consumer Capitalism" and the Way Forward*, London: Century.

Lasch, C. (1979) *The Culture of Narcissism*, New York: Norton.

Lash, S. (1990) *Sociology of Postmodernism*, London: Routledge.

Lash, S. and Urry, J. (1987) *The End of Organised Capitalism*, Cambridge: Polity.

Lash, S. and Urry, J. (1994) *Economies of Signs and Space*, London: Sage.

Latour, B. (1993 [1991]) *We Have Never Been Modern*, trans. C. Porter, Hemel Hempstead: Harvester Wheatsheaf.

Latour, B. and Woolgar, S. (1986) *Laboratory Life: The Construction of Scientific Facts*, Princeton: Princeton University Press, second edition.

Lavin, M. and Archdeacon, T.J. (1989) 'The relevance of historical method for marketing research', in E.C. Hirschman (ed.) *Interpretive Consumer Research*, Provo: Association for Consumer Research, 60–8.

Leavis, F.R. (1930) *Mass Civilisation and Minority Culture*, Cambridge: The Folcroft Press.

Leavis, F.R. and Thompson D. (1933) *Culture and Environment*, London: Chatto and Windus.

Lefebvre, H. (1991 [1947]) *Critique of Everyday Life*, trans. J. Moore, London: Verso.

Leong, S.M. (1985) 'Metatheory and metamethodology in marketing: a Lakatosian reconstruction', *Journal of Marketing* 49, Fall: 23–40.

Levitt, T. (1960) 'Marketing myopia', *Harvard Business Review* 38, July–August: 45–56.

Lewis, P.F. (1975) 'To revive urban downtowns: show respect for the spirit of the place', *Smithsonian* 6, 6: 32–41.

Linstead, S.A. and Grafton Small, R. (1990) 'Theory as artefact: artefact as theory', in P. Gagliardi (ed.) *Symbols and Artifacts: Views of the Corporate Landscape*, Berlin: de Gruyter, 387–419.

Linstead, S.A. and Grafton Small, R. (1992) 'On reading organisational culture', *Organisation Studies* 13, 3: 331–55.

Little, J.D.C. *et al.* (1994) 'Commentary', in G. Laurent, G.L. Lilien and B. Pras (eds) *Research Traditions in Marketing*, Dordrecht: Kluwer, 44–51.

Locke, D. (1992) *Science as Writing*, New Haven: Yale University Press.

Lodge, D. (1988) *Nice Work*, London: Secker and Warburg.

Lodge, D. (1990) *After Bakhtin: Essays on Fiction and Criticism*, London: Routledge.

Lorenz, A. and Alexander, G. (1994) 'Brands fight back', *The Sunday Times*, 3 April, 3: 3.

Lorenz, C. (1993) 'A meeting of minds', *Financial Times*, Monday 25 October: 15.

Lovelock, J. (1982) *Gaia: A New Look at Life on Earth*, Oxford: Oxford University Press.

Luck, D.J. (1969) 'Broadening the concept of marketing – too far', *Journal of Marketing* 33, July: 53–5.

Lukács, G. (1971 [1923]) *History and Class Consciousness*, London: Merlin.

Lutz, R.J. (1989) 'Editorial', *Journal of Consumer Research* 16, June: unpaged.

Lynch, J.E. (1994) 'The end of marketing?', in O. Westall (ed.) *British Academy of Management Annual Conference Proceedings*, Lancaster: Lancaster University, 322–4.

Lynch, J.J. (1992) *The Psychology of Customer Care: A Revolutionary Approach*, Basingstoke: Macmillan.

Lyotard, J-F. (1984 [1979]) *The Postmodern Condition: A Report on Knowledge*, trans. G. Bennington and B. Massumi, Manchester: Manchester University Press.

Lyotard, J-F. (1988 [1971]) 'Discourse figure', in G. Bennington, *Lyotard: Writing the Event*, Manchester: Manchester University Press, 56–102.

Lyotard, J-F. (1989) 'Acinema', in A. Benjamin (ed.) *The Lyotard Reader*, Oxford: Blackwell, 169–80.

Lyotard, J-F. (1991 [1988]) *The Inhuman: Reflections on Time*, trans. G. Bennington and R. Bowlby, Cambridge: Polity.

Lyotard, J-F. (1992 [1986]) *The Postmodern Explained to Children: Correspondence 1982–1985*, trans. D. Barry *et al.*, London: Turnaround.

Lyotard, J-F. (1994 [1991]) *Lessons on the Analytic of the Sublime*, trans. E. Rottenberg, Stanford: Stanford University Press.

Macann, C. (1993) *Four Phenomenological Philosophers: Husserl, Heidegger, Sartre, Merleau-Ponty*, London: Routledge.

Macey, D. (1993) *The Lives of Michel Foucault*, London: Hutchinson.

McCloskey, D. (1985) *The Rhetoric of Economics*, Madison: University of Wisconsin Press.

McCracken, G. (1988) *Culture and Consumption: New Approaches to the Symbolic Character of Consumer Goods and Activities*, Bloomington: Indiana University Press.

McCracken, G. (1990) 'Culture and consumer behaviour: an anthropological perspective', *Journal of the Market Research Society* 32, 1: 3–11.

McDonald, M.H.B. (1992) 'Strategic marketing planning: a state-of-the-art review', in M.J. Baker (ed.) *Perspectives on Marketing Management, Volume 2*, Chichester: Wiley, 25–59.

McDonald, M.H.B. (1994) 'Marketing – a mid-life crisis?', *Marketing Business* 30, May: 10–14.

McHale, B. (1987) *Postmodernist Fiction*, London: Routledge.

McHale, B. (1993) *Constructing Postmodernism*, London: Routledge.

McKenna, R. (1991) 'Marketing is everything', *Harvard Business Review* 69, 1: 65–79.

McKitterick, J.B. (1957) 'What is the marketing management concept?', in F.M. Bass (ed.) *The Frontiers of Marketing Thought and Science*, Chicago: American Marketing Association, 71–82.

McMurdo, L. (1993) 'Chasing butterflies', *Marketing Week*, 21 May, 28–31.

McQuarrie, E.F. and Mick, D.G. (1992) 'On resonance: a critical pluralist inquiry into advertising rhetoric', *Journal of Consumer Research* 19, September: 180–97.

McQuitty, S. (1992) 'An examination of chaos theory and its relation to marketing', *Marketing Theory and Applications, Volume 3*, Chicago: American Marketing Association, 474–83.

McRobbie, A. (1994) *Postmodernism and Popular Culture*, London: Routledge.

Maffesoli, M. (1988) 'Jeux de masques: postmoderne tribalisme', *Design Issues* 4, 1/2: 141–51.

Magnus, B., Stewart, S. and Mileur, J-P. (1993) *Nietzsche's Case: Philosophy as/and Literature*, New York: Routledge.

Magrath, A. (1990) 'Differentiate by design', *Marketing News* 24, 23: 19–20.

Majaro, S. (1993) *The Essence of Marketing*, Hemel Hempstead: Prentice-Hall.

Marion, G. (1993) 'The marketing management discourse: what's new since the 1960s?', in M.J. Baker (ed.) *Perspectives on Marketing Management, Volume 3*, Chichester: Wiley, 143–68.

Markin, R. (1982) *Marketing: Strategy and Management*, New York: Wiley.

Marshall, B.K. (1992) *Teaching the Postmodern: Fiction and Theory*, London: Routledge.

Martin, C.L. (1985) 'Delineating the boundaries of marketing' *European Journal of Marketing* 19, 4, reprinted in G.E. Greenley and D. Shipley (eds) *Readings in Marketing Management*, Maidenhead: McGraw-Hill, 19–26.

Mead, G. (1993) 'Charity in fashion', *Financial Times*, Thursday 28 January: 18.

Merton, R.K. (1938) 'Science and the social order', *Philosophy of Science* 5: 321–37.

Merton, R.K. (1973) *The Sociology of Science: Theoretical and Empirical Investigations*, Chicago: University of Chicago Press.

Mick, D.G. (1986) 'Consumer research and semiotics: exploring the morphology of signs, symbols and significance', *Journal of Consumer Research* 13, September: 196–213.

Mick, D.G. and Buhl, C. (1992) 'A meaning-based model of advertising experiences', *Journal of Consumer Research* 19, December: 317–38.

Mick, D.G. and DeMoss, M. (1990) 'Self-gifts: phenomenological insights from four contexts', *Journal of Consumer Research* 17, December: 322–32.

Miller, C. (1990) 'Nostalgia makes boomers buy', *Marketing News* 24, 24: 1–2.

Miller, C. (1992) 'P.F. Flyers relaunch targets nostalgic baby boomers', *Marketing News* 26, 4: 2.

Miller, C. (1993) 'Software that's fun and educational – that's "edutainment"', *Marketing News* 27, 9: 2.

Miller, D. (1987) *Material Culture and Mass Consumption*, Oxford: Blackwell.

Mintzberg, H. (1989) *Mintzberg on Management: Inside our Strange World of Organisations*, New York: Free Press.

Mitchell, A. (1993) 'The transformation of marketing: the challenge of technology', *Marketing Business* 25, November: 9–14.

Mitchell, A. (1994a) 'Hard on the tail of the copycats', *The Times*, Thursday 9 June: 35.

Mitchell, A. (1994b) 'The transformation of marketing: new marketing vision', *Marketing Business* 26, January: 12–17.

Moore, E.W. (1985) *The Fairs of Medieval England: An Introductory Study*, Toronto: Pontifical Institute of Medieval Studies.

Moore, S. (1993) 'On the ads that drive us mad', *The Observer Magazine*, Sunday 30 May: 5.

Morgan, Glenn (1992) 'Marketing discourse and practice: towards a critical analysis', in M. Alvesson and H. Willmott (eds) *Critical Management Studies*, London: Sage, 136–58.

Morgan, Gareth (1993) *Imaginization: The Art of Creative Management*, Newbury Park: Sage.

Morris, M. (1992) 'The man in the mirror: David Harvey's "condition" of post-modernity', in M. Featherstone (ed.) *Cultural Theory and Cultural Change*, London: Sage, 253–79.

Morris, M. (1993a) 'Future fear', in J. Bird *et al.* (eds) *Mapping the Futures: Local Cultures, Global Change*, London: Routledge, 30–46.

Morris, M. (1993b) 'Things to do with shopping centres', in S. During (ed.) *The Cultural Studies Reader*, London: Routledge, 295–319.

Morrison, A. and Wensley, R. (1991) 'Boxing up or boxed in?: a short history of the Boston Consulting Group share/growth matrix', *Journal of Marketing Management* 7, 2: 105–29.

Mort, F. (1989) 'The politics of consumption', in S. Hall and M. Jacques (eds) *New Times: The Changing Face of Politics in the 1990s*, London: Lawrence and Wishart, 160–72.

Mourrain, J.A.P. (1989) 'The hyper-modern commodity form: the case of wine', in T.J. Childers *et al.* (eds) *Marketing Theory and Practice*, Chicago: American Marketing Association, 318–22.

Mueller-Heumann, G. (1992) 'Market and technology shifts in the 1990s: market fragmentation and mass customisation', *Journal of Marketing Management* 8, 4: 303–14.

Mulvagh, J. (1993) 'Back to the past at Laura Ashley', *Financial Times*, Saturday 3 April: xii.

Murray, J. and O'Driscoll, A. (1993) *Managing Marketing: Concepts and Irish Cases*, Dublin: Gill and Macmillan.

Murray, J.B. and Ozanne, J.L. (1991) 'The critical imagination: emancipatory interests in consumer research', *Journal of Consumer Research* 18, September: 129–44.

Murray, R. (1989) 'Fordism and post-Fordism', in S. Hall and M. Jacques (eds) *New Times: The Changing Face of Politics in the 1990s*, London: Lawrence and Wishart, 38–53.

Naisbitt, J. (1994) *Global Paradox: The Bigger the World Economy, the More Powerful its Smallest Players*, London: Nicholas Brealey.

Narver, J.C. and Slater, S.F. (1990) 'The effect of a market orientation on business profitability', *Journal of Marketing* 54, October: 20–35.

Nason, R.W. (1985) 'The misdirected capitalistic paradigm', in N. Dholakia and J. Arndt (eds) *Changing the Course of Marketing: Alternative Paradigms for Widening Marketing Theory*, Greenwich: JAI Press, 119–31.

Nava, M. (1992) *Changing Cultures: Feminism, Youth and Consumerism*, London: Sage.

Nencel, L. and Pels, P. (eds) (1991) *Constructing Knowledge: Authority and*

Critique in Social Science, London: Sage.

Nevett, T. (1991) 'Historical investigation and the practice of marketing', *Journal of Marketing* 55, July: 13–23.

Nevett, T. and Nevett, L. (1987) 'The origins of marketing: evidence from Classical and early Hellenistic Greece', in T. Nevett and S.C. Hollander (eds) *Marketing in Three Eras*, East Lansing: Michigan State University, 3–12.

Nicholson, L.J. (ed.) (1990) *Feminism/Postmodernism*, New York: Routledge.

Niethammer, L. (1992 [1989]) *Posthistoire: Has History Come to an End?*, trans. P. Camiller, London: Verso.

Nietzsche, F. (1977) *A Nietzsche Reader*, ed. R.J. Hollingdale, Harmondsworth: Penguin.

Nilson, T.H. (1992) *Value-added Marketing: Marketing Management for Superior Results*, Maidenhead: McGraw-Hill.

Nisbet, R. (1980) *A History of the Idea of Progress*, New York: Basic Books.

Norman, B. (1989) *Talking Pictures*, London: Chapmans.

Norris, C. (1990) 'Lost in the funhouse: Baudrillard and the politics of postmodernism', in R. Boyne and A. Rattansi (eds) *Postmodernism and Society*, Basingstoke: Macmillan, 119–53.

Norris, C. (1991) *Deconstruction: Theory and Practice*, London: Routledge.

Norris, C. (1992) *Uncritical Theory: Postmodernism, Intellectuals and the Gulf War*, London: Lawrence and Wishart.

Norris, C. (1993) *The Truth About Postmodernism*, Oxford: Blackwell.

Nyeck, S. (1992) 'Postmodernity and consumer pattern: a cognitive analysis', in K.G. Grunert and D. Fuglede (eds) *Marketing for Europe – Marketing for the Future*, Aarhus: EMAC, 1371–4.

O'Brien, L. and Harris, F. (1991) *Retailing: Shopping, Society, Space*, London: David Fulton.

O'Dohonoe, S. (1994) 'Postmodern poachers: young adult experiences of advertising', unpublished PhD thesis, Edinburgh: University of Edinburgh.

Ogilvy, J. (1990) 'This postmodern business', *Marketing and Research Today* 18, 1: 4–21.

O'Guinn, T.C., Lee, W-N. and Faber, R.J. (1986) 'Acculturation: the impact of divergent paths of buyer behaviour', in R.J. Lutz (ed.) *Advances in Consumer Research, Volume XIII*, Provo: Association for Consumer Research, 579–83.

Olins, R. (1992) 'Is it art? Probably', *The Sunday Times*, 13 September, 8: 5.

Oliver, G. (1980) *Marketing Today*, Hemel Hempstead: Prentice Hall.

Olson, J.P. (1991) 'Philosophical tensions in consumer inquiry', T.S. Robertson and H.H. Kassarjian (eds) *Handbook of Consumer Research*, Englewood Cliffs: Prentice-Hall, 533–47.

Ortony, A. (1979) 'Metaphor: a multi-dimensional problem', in A. Ortony (ed.) *Metaphor and Thought*, Cambridge: Cambridge University Press, 1–16.

Orwell, G. (1962) 'Politics and the English language', in G. Orwell, *Inside the Whale and Other Essays*, Harmondsworth: Penguin, 143–57.

O'Shaughnessy, J. (1992a) *Competitive Marketing: A Strategic Approach*, London: Routledge, second edition.

O'Shaughnessy, J. (1992b) *Explaining Buyer Behaviour: Central Concepts and Philosophy of Science Issues*, Oxford: Oxford University Press.

O'Shaughnessy, J. and Holbrook, M.B. (1988) 'Understanding consumer behaviour: the linguistic turn in marketing research', *Journal of the Market Research Society* 30, 2: 197–223.

Ostergaard, P. (1993) 'The broadened concept of marketing as a manifestation of the postmodern condition', in R. Varadarajan and B. Jaworski (eds) *Marketing Theory and Applications, Volume 4*, Chicago: American Marketing Association, 234–9.

Outhwaite, W. (1985) 'Hans-Georg Gadamer', in Q. Skinner (ed.) *The Return of Grand Theory in the Human Sciences*, Cambridge: Cambridge University Press, 21–39.

Paglia, C. (1992) *Sex, Art and American Culture*, London: Viking.

Parker, A.J. (1992) 'Retail environments: into the 1990s', *Irish Marketing Review* 5, 2: 61–72.

Passmore, J. (1985) *Recent Philosophers*, London: Duckworth.

Peattie, K. (1992) *Green Marketing* London: Pitman.

Peter, J.P. (1983) 'Some philosophical and methodological issues in consumer research', in S.D. Hunt, *Marketing Theory: The Philosophy of Marketing Science*, Homewood: Richard D. Irwin, 382–94.

Peter, J.P. and Olson, J.C. (1983) 'Is science marketing?', *Journal of Marketing* 47, Fall: 111–25.

Peters, T. (1992) *Liberation Management: Necessary Disorganisation for the Nanosecond Nineties*, London: Macmillan.

Peterson, R.A. (1992) 'Introduction to the special issue', *Journal of the Academy of Marketing Science* 20, 4: 295–7.

Pickering, A. (ed.) (1992) *Science as Practice and Culture*, Chicago: University of Chicago Press.

Piercy, N. (1992) *Market-led Strategic Change*, Oxford: Butterworth-Heinemann.

Pine, B.J. (1993) *Mass Customisation: The New Frontier in Business Competition*, Boston: Harvard Business School Press.

Platten, D. (1986) 'Postmodern engineering', *Civil Engineering* 56, 6: 84–6.

Pollay, R.W. (1986) 'The distorted mirror: reflections on the unintended consequences of advertising', *Journal of Marketing* 50, April: 18–36.

Pollay, R.W. (1987) 'On the value of reflections on the values in "the distorted mirror"', *Journal of Marketing* 51, July: 104–9.

Popcorn, F. (1992) *The Popcorn Report*, New York: Harper-Business.

Porter, R. (1990a) *The Enlightenment*, Basingstoke: Macmillan.

Porter, R. (1990b) *English Society in the Eighteenth Century*, Harmondsworth: Penguin, second edition.

Poster, M. (1984) *Foucault, Marxism and History: Mode of Production Versus Mode of Information*, London: Polity.

Poster, M. (1988) 'Introduction', in M. Poster (ed.) *Jean Baudrillard: Selected Writings*, Cambridge: Polity, 1–9.

Poster, M. and Venkatesh, A. (1987) 'From Marx to Foucault – an intellectual journey through critical theory', in R.W. Belk *et al.* (eds) *Marketing Theory*, Chicago: American Marketing Association, 20–6.

Powers, T.L. and Martin, W.S. (1987) 'A historical examination of the marketing concept: profits or progress?', in T. Nevett and S.C. Hollander (eds) *Marketing in Three Eras*, East Lansing: Michigan State University, 169–80.

Pullinger, K. (1994) 'Moving sidewalks to Heaven and Hell', *The Observer Review* Sunday 7 August: 2–3.

Randall, G. (1993) *Principles of Marketing*, London: Routledge.

Rapp, S. and Collins, T.L. (1990) *The Great Marketing Turnaround: The Age of the Individual and How to Profit From It*, Englewood Cliffs: Prentice-Hall.

Rapp, S. and Collins, T.L. (1994) *Beyond Maxi-marketing*, New York: McGraw-Hill.

Rassuli, K.M. (1988) 'Evidence of marketing strategy in the early printed book trade: an application of Hollander's historical approach', in T. Nevett and R.A. Fullerton (eds) *Historical Perspectives in Marketing: Essays in Honour of Stanley C. Hollander*, Lexington: D.C. Heath, 91–107.

Rassuli, K.M. (1991) 'An interpretation of events in the recent history of consumer research: implications for paradigms and theories', in C.R. Taylor *et al.* (eds) *Marketing History – Its Many Dimensions*, East Lansing: Michigan State University, 50–66.

Ray, L.J. (1993) *Rethinking Critical Theory: Emancipation in the Age of Global Social Movements*, London: Sage.

Readings, B. (1993) *Introducing Lyotard: Art and Politics*, London: Routledge.

Reekie, G. (1993) *Temptations: Sex, Selling and the Department Store*, St Leonards: Allen and Unwin.

Relph, E. (1987) *The Modern Urban Landscape*, London: Croom Helm.

Renfrew, C. (1978) *Before Civilisation: The Radiocarbon Revolution and Pre-historic Europe*, Harmondsworth: Penguin.

Renfrew, C. (1988) 'The emergence of civilisation', in A. Cotterell (ed.) *The Penguin Encyclopedia of Ancient Civilisations*, Harmondsworth: Penguin, 12–20.

Roberts, W.A. (1984) 'A Kuhnian perspective on marketing science and the scientific method', in P.F. Anderson and M.J. Ryan (eds) *Scientific Method in Marketing*, Chicago: American Marketing Association, 14–17.

Robey, D. (1986) 'Anglo-American New Criticism', in A. Jefferson and D. Robey (eds) *Modern Literary Theory: A Comparative Introduction*, London: Batsford, 73–91.

Robin, D.P. (1977) 'Comment on the nature and scope of marketing', *Journal of Marketing* 41, January: 136–8.

Rogers, E.M. (1987) 'The critical school and consumer research', in M. Wallendorf and P. Anderson (eds) *Advances in Consumer Research, Volume XIV*, Provo: Association for Consumer Research, 7–11.

Rorty, R. (1980) *Philosophy and the Mirror of Nature*, Oxford: Blackwell.

Rorty, R. (1985) 'Habermas and Lyotard on postmodernity', in R.J. Bernstein (ed.) *Habermas and Modernity*, Cambridge: Polity, 161–75.

Rorty, R. (1989) *Contingency, Irony, and Solidarity*, Cambridge: Cambridge University Press.

Rorty, R. (1991) *Consequences of Pragmatism (Essays 1972–1980)*, Hemel Hempstead: Harvester Wheatsheaf.

Rose, G. (1991) *The Post-modern and the Post-industrial: A Critical Analysis*, Cambridge: Cambridge University Press.

Rosenau, P.M. (1992) *Postmodernism and the Social Sciences*, Princeton: Princeton University Press.

Rosenberg, L.J. (1985) 'Revisioning marketing management for the new paradigm era', in N. Dholakia and J. Arndt (eds) *Changing the Course of Marketing: Alternative Paradigms for Widening Marketing Theory*, Greenwich: JAI Press, 89–104.

Rostow, W.W. (1990) *Theorists of Economic Growth from David Hume to the Present*, Oxford: Oxford University Press.

Rothman, J. (1992) 'Postmodern research and the arts', *Journal of the Market*

Research Society 34, 4: 419–35.

Ruland, R. and Bradbury, M. (1991) *From Puritanism to Postmodernism: A History of American Literature*, Harmondsworth: Penguin.

Ryan, S. and Skipworth, M. (1993) 'Shoppers guillotine the "green" revolution', *The Sunday Times*, 4 April, 1: 7.

Rylance, R. (1994) *Roland Barthes*, Hemel Hempstead: Harvester Wheatsheaf.

Sachs, W.S. and Benson, G. (1978) 'Is it time to discard the marketing concept?', *Business Horizons* 21, August: 68–74.

Sack, R.D. (1992) *Place, Modernity, and the Consumer's World*, Baltimore: The Johns Hopkins University Press.

Said, E.W. (1978) *Orientalism: Western Conceptions of the Orient*, Harmondsworth: Penguin.

Samli, A.C., Palda, K. and Barker, A.T. (1987) 'Toward a mature marketing concept', *Sloan Management Review* 28, 2: 45–51.

Sangren, P.S. (1988) 'Rhetoric and the authority of ethnography: "postmodernism" and the social reproduction of texts', *Current Anthropology* 29, 3: 405–24.

Sarup, M. (1992) *Jacques Lacan*, Hemel Hempstead: Harvester Wheatsheaf.

Sarup, M. (1993) *An Introductory Guide to Post-structuralism and Postmodernism*, Hemel Hempstead: Harvester Wheatsheaf, second edition.

Schama, S. (1988) *An Embarrassment of Riches: An Interpretation of Dutch Culture in the Golden Age*, New York: Knopf.

Schlossberg, H. (1991) 'Health club TV targeting an audience that can't click back', *Marketing News* 25, 21: 1, 15.

Schlossberg, H. (1992) 'Packaged-goods experts: micro-marketing the only way to go', *Marketing News* 26, 14: 8.

Schlossberg, H. (1993) 'Category management can ease manufacturer-retailer friction', *Marketing News* 27, 10: 16.

Schonstrom, S. (1992) 'The merchant of Venice', *Scanorama* April: 10–16.

Schudson, M. (1984) *Advertising, the Uneasy Persuasion: Its Dubious Impact on American Society*, London: Routledge.

Schutz, A. (1967 [1932]) *The Phenomenology of the Social World*, trans. G. Walsh and F. Lehnert, Evanston: Northwestern University Press.

Scott, L.M. (1992) 'Playing with pictures: postmodernism, poststructuralism and advertising visuals', in J.F. Sherry and B. Sternthal (eds) *Advances in Consumer Research, Volume XIX*, Provo: Association for Consumer Research, 596–612.

Scott, L.M. (1993) 'Spectacular vernacular: literacy and commercial culture in the postmodern age', *International Journal of Research in Marketing* 10, 3: 251–75.

Scruton, R. (1994) *Modern Philosophy: An Introduction and Survey*, London: Sinclair-Stevenson.

Searle, L.F. (1994) 'New Criticism', in M. Groden and M. Kreiswirth (eds) *The Johns Hopkins Guide to Literary Theory and Criticism*, Baltimore: The Johns Hopkins University Press, 528–34.

Selden, R. and Widdowson, P. (1993) *A Reader's Guide to Contemporary Literary Theory*, Hemel Hempstead: Harvester Wheatsheaf, third edition.

Shapiro, M.J. (1992) *Reading the Postmodern Polity: Political Theory as Textual Practice*, Minneapolis: University of Minnesota Press.

Shaw, E.H. (1991) 'An historical analysis of the four utilities concept and its relevance for modern marketing thought', in C.R. Taylor *et al.* (eds), *Marketing History – Its Many Dimensions*, East Lansing: Michigan State University, 33–48.

Shay, D. and Duncan, J. (1993) *The Making of Jurassic Park*, London: Boxtree.

Shenk, D. (1993) 'Buy a hat, save the earth', *Hemispheres* May, 25–8.

Sherry, J.F. (1991) 'Postmodern alternatives: the interpretive turn in consumer research', in T.S. Robertson and H.H. Kassarjian (eds) *Handbook of Consumer Research*, Englewood Cliffs: Prentice-Hall, 548–91.

Sherry, J.F. and Camargo, E.G. (1987) ' "May your life be marvellous": English language labelling and the semiotics of Japanese promotion', *Journal of Consumer Research* 14, September: 174–88.

Sheth, J.N., Gardner, D.M. and Garrett, D.E. (1988) *Marketing Theory: Evolution and Evaluation*, Chichester: John Wiley.

Shields, R. (1989) 'Social spatialisation and the built environment: the West Edmonton Mall', *Environment and Planning D* 7, 2: 147–64.

Shumway, D.R. (1989) *Michel Foucault*, Charlottesville: University Press of Virginia.

Siegel, H. (1992) 'Relativism', in J. Dancy and E. Sosa (eds) *A Companion to Epistemology*, Oxford: Blackwell, 428–30.

Silverman, H.J. (ed.) (1988) *Philosophy and Non-philosophy Since Merleau-Ponty*, London: Routledge.

Silverman, H.J. (1990) 'Introduction – the philosophy of postmodernism', in H.J. Silverman (ed.) *Postmodernism – Philosophy and the Arts*, New York: Routledge, 1–9.

Silverman, H.J. (ed.) (1991) *Gadamer and Hermeneutics*, New York: Routledge.

Simintiras, A.C., Schlegelmilch, B.B. and Diamantopoulos, A. (1994) ' "Greening" the marketing mix: a review of the literature and an agenda for future research', in M.J. Baker (ed.) *Perspectives on Marketing Management, Volume 4*, Chichester: Wiley, 1–25.

Singh, J. (1990) 'A typology of consumer dissatisfaction response styles', *Journal of Retailing* 66, 1: 57–99.

Skinner, Q. (1985) 'Introduction: the return of grand theory', in Q. Skinner (ed.) *The Return of Grand Theory in the Human Sciences*, Cambridge: Cambridge University Press, 1–20.

Smart, B. (1985) *Michel Foucault*, London: Routledge.

Smart, B. (1992) *Modern Conditions, Postmodern Controversies*, London: Routledge.

Smart, B. (1993) *Postmodernity*, London: Routledge.

Smith, B.H. (1988) *Contingencies of Value: Alternative Perspectives for Critical Theory*, Cambridge: Harvard University Press.

Smith, D. and Lynn, M. (1993) 'Price wars', *The Sunday Times*, 26 September, 3: 3.

Smith, R.A. and Lux, D.S. (1993) 'Historical method in consumer research: developing causal explanations of change', *Journal of Consumer Research* 19, March: 595–610.

Smyth, E.J. (1991) *Postmodernism and Contemporary Fiction*, London: Batsford.

Soderlund, M. (1990) 'Business intelligence in the postmodern era', *Marketing Intelligence and Planning* 8, 1: 7–10.   *p 5* 10-4

Soja, E.W. (1989) *Postmodern Geographies: The Reassertion of Space in Critical Social Theory*, London: Verso.

Solomon, M.R. (1983) 'The role of products as social stimuli: a symbolic interactionism perspective', *Journal of Consumer Research* 10, December: 319–29.

Solomon, M.R. (1986) 'Deep-seated materialism: the case of Levi's 501 jeans', in

R.J. Lutz (ed.) *Advances in Consumer Research, Volume XIII*, Provo: Association for Consumer Research, 619–22.

Soper, K. (1993) 'Postmodernism, subjectivity and the question of value', in J. Squires (ed.) *Principled Positions: Postmodernism and the Rediscovery of Value*, London: Lawrence and Wishart, 17–30.

Sparks, L. (1990) 'Spatial-structural relationships in retail corporate growth: a case study of Kwik Save Group PLC', *The Service Industries Journal* 10, 1: 25–82.

Sporre, D.J. (1989) *A History of the Arts: Prehistory to Post-modernism*, London: Bloomsbury Books.

Squires, J. (ed.) (1993) *Principled Positions: Postmodernism and the Rediscovery of Value*, London: Lawrence and Wishart.

Stacey, J. (1990) *Brave New Families*, New York: Basic Books.

Stafford, M.R., Asquith, J.A.L. and Daugherty, P.J. (1993) 'Electronic zipping: ad agency views', in M. Levy and D. Grewal (eds) *Developments in Marketing Science, Volume XVI*, Miami: Academy of Marketing Science, 450–6.

Stalk, G. and Hout, T.M. (1990) *Competing Against Time: How Time-based Competition is Reshaping Global Markets*, New York: Free Press.

Staunton, W.J. (1984) *Fundamentals of Marketing*, Tokyo: McGraw-Hill, seventh edition.

Stern, B.B. (1989a) 'Literary explication: a methodology for consumer research', in E.C. Hirschman (ed.) *Interpretive Consumer Research*, Provo: Association for Consumer Research, 48–59.

Stern, B.B. (1989b) 'Literary criticism and consumer research: overview and illustrative analysis', *Journal of Consumer Research* 16, December: 322–34.

Stern, B.B. (1992) '"All the world's a stage": drama and consumer research', in J.F. Sherry and B. Sternthal (eds) *Advances in Consumer Research, Volume XIX*, Provo: Association for Consumer Research, 450–1.

Stern, B.B. (1993) 'Feminist literary criticism and the deconstruction of ads: a postmodern view of advertising and consumer responses', *Journal of Consumer Research* 19, March: 556–66.

Sturrock, J. (ed.) (1979a) *Structuralism and Since: From Lévi-Strauss to Derrida*, Oxford: Oxford University Press.

Sturrock, J. (1979b) 'Roland Barthes', in J. Sturrock (ed.) *Structuralism and Since: From Lévi-Strauss to Derrida*, Oxford: Oxford University Press, 52–80.

Sturrock, J. (1993) *Structuralism*, London: Fontana, second edition.

Suerdem, A. (1992) 'What are you doing after the orgy? or does the consumer really behave ("well")?', in J.F. Sherry and B. Sternthal (eds) *Advances in Consumer Research, Volume XIX*, Provo: Association for Consumer Research, 207–12.

Summers, D. (1993) 'Ban Regal cigarette ads, says watchdog', *Financial Times*, Wednesday 29 September: 10.

Tauber, E.M. (1974) 'How market research discourages major innovations', *Business Horizons* 17, June: 24–7.

Taylor, M.C. and Saarinen, E. (1994) *Imagologies: Media Philosophy*, London: Routledge.

Taylor, W.J. (1965) 'Is marketing a science?', *Journal of Marketing* 29, July: 49–53.

Tedre, R. (1993) 'Shock of the old', *The Observer Life*, Sunday 24 October: 24–5.

Terry, S.H. (1869) *The Retailer's Manual: Embodying the Conclusions of Thirty Years' Experience in Merchandising*, Newark: Jennings Brothers, 1978 reprint.

Tester, K. (1993) *The Life and Times of Post-modernity*, London: Routledge.

The Economist (1989) 'Management brief – still trying', *The Economist*, 313, 7623: 112–3.

The Higher (1993) 'Business needs a philosophy', *The Higher*, Friday 26 November: 13.

The Modern Review (1993) *The Revival Handbook*, London: The Modern Review.

Thomas, M.J. (1993) 'Marketing – in chaos or transition?', in D. Brownlie *et al.* (eds) *Rethinking Marketing*, Coventry: Warwick Business School Research Bureau, 114–23.

Thomas, M.J. (1994) 'Do marketing educators have a future?', in J. Bell *et al.* (eds), *Marketing: Unity in Diversity*, Coleraine: Marketing Education Group Conference Proceedings, 939–47.

Thompson, C.J. (1993) 'Modern truth and postmodern incredulity: a hermeneutic deconstruction of the metanarrative of "scientific truth" in marketing research', *International Journal of Research in Marketing* 10, 3: 325–38.

Thompson, C.J., Locander, W.B. and Pollio, H.R. (1989) 'Putting consumer experience back into consumer research: the philosophy and method of existential-phenomenology', *Journal of Consumer Research* 16, September: 133–46.

Thompson, C.J., Locander, W.B. and Pollio, H.R. (1990) 'The lived experience of free choice: an existential-phenomenological description of everyday consumer experiences of contemporary married women', *Journal of Consumer Research* 17, December: 346–61.

Thorne, T. (1993) *Fads, Fashions and Cults – The Definitive Guide to (Post) Modern Culture*, London: Bloomsbury.

Toffler, A. (1990) *Powershift: Knowledge, Wealth and Violence at the Edge of the 21st Century*, New York: Bantam.

Tomlinson, A. (1990) 'Introduction: consumer culture and the aura of the commodity', in A. Tomlinson (ed.) *Consumption, Identity and Style: Marketing, Meanings and the Packaging of Pleasure*, London: Routledge, 1–38.

Tornroos, J-A. and Ranta, T. (1993) 'Marketing as image management – a postmodern reformulation of the marketing concept', in D. Brownlie *et al.* (eds) *Rethinking Marketing*, Coventry: Warwick Business School Research Bureau, 166–75.

Toulmin, S. (1990) *Cosmopolis: The Hidden Agenda of Modernity*, Chicago: University of Chicago Press.

Touraine, A. (1971) *The Post-industrial Society*, New York: Random House.

Trevor-Roper, H. (1983) 'The invention of tradition: the Highland tradition of Scotland', in E. Hobsbawm and T. Ranger (eds) *The Invention of Tradition*, Cambridge: Cambridge University Press, 15–41.

Troy, L.S. (1993) 'Consumer environmental consciousness: a conceptual framework and exploratory investigation', in D.W. Cravens and P.R. Dickson (eds) *Enhancing Knowledge Development in Marketing, Volume 4*, Chicago: American Marketing Association, 106–14.

Turnbull, P. (1987) 'A challenge to the stages theory of the internationalisation process', reprinted in P.J. Buckley and P. Ghauri (eds) *The Internationalisation of the Firm: A Reader*, London: Academic Press, 1993, 172–85.

Turner, B.S. (ed.) (1990) *Theories of Modernity and Postmodernity*, London: Sage.

Tyler, S.A. (1987) *The Unspeakable: Discourse, Dialogue and Rhetoric in the Postmodern World*, Madison: University of Wisconsin Press.

Ulmer, G.L. (1985) 'The object of post-criticism', in H. Foster (ed.) *Postmodern Culture*, London: Pluto Press, 83–110.

Updike, J. (1984) *Hugging the Shore: Essays and Criticism*, Harmondsworth: Penguin.

Updike, J. (1991) *Odd Jobs: Essays and Criticism*, Harmondsworth: Penguin.

Urry, J. (1990) *The Tourist Gaze: Leisure and Travel in Contemporary Societies*, London: Sage.

Uusitalo, L. and Uusitalo, J. (1985) 'Which sense of paradigms makes sense in marketing?' in N. Dholakia and J. Arndt (eds) *Changing the Course of Marketing: Alternative Paradigms for Widening Marketing Theory*, Greenwich: JAI Press, 69–85.

van den Bulte, C. (1994) 'Metaphor at work', in G. Laurent, G.L. Lilien and B. Pras (eds) *Research Traditions in Marketing*, Dordrecht: Kluwer, 405–25.

van Rossum, R. (1984) 'Is the theory of life cycles pure humbug?' *Financial Times*, Thursday 23 August: 14.

Veeser, H.A. (ed.) (1989) *The New Historicism*, London: Routledge.

Venkatesh, A. (1989) 'Modernity and postmodernity: a synthesis or antithesis?', in T.L. Childers *et al.* (eds) *Marketing Theory and Practice*, Chicago: American Marketing Association, 99–104.

Venkatesh, A. (1992) 'Postmodernism, consumer culture and the society of the spectacle', in J.F. Sherry and B. Sternthal (eds) *Advances in Consumer Research, Volume XIX*, Provo: Association for Consumer Research, 199–202.

Venkatesh, A., Sherry, J.F. and Firat, A.F. (1993) 'Postmodernism and the marketing imaginary', *International Journal of Research in Marketing* 10, 3: 215–23.

Verschaffel, B. and Verminck, M. (eds) (1993) *Zoology on (Post)modern Animals*, Dublin: Lilliput Press.

Vidal, G. (1993) *United States: Essays 1952–1992*, London: André Deutsch.

Wagner, P. (1994) *A Sociology of Modernity: Liberty and Discipline*, London: Routledge.

Waldrop, M.M. (1992) *Complexity: The Emerging Science at the Edge of Order and Chaos*, Harmondsworth: Viking.

Wallendorf, M. and Brooks, M. (1993) 'Introspection in consumer research: implementation and implications', *Journal of Consumer Research* 20, December: 339–59.

Walsh, Keiron (1993) 'Marketing and the new public sector management', in D. Brownlie *et al.* (eds) *Rethinking Marketing*, Coventry: Warwick Business School Research Bureau, 124–33.

Walsh, Kevin (1992) *The Representation of the Past: Museums and Heritage in the Post-modern World*, London: Routledge.

Walters, C. (1988) 'Ancient Egypt', in A. Cotterell (ed.) *The Penguin Encyclopedia of Ancient Civilisations*, Harmondsworth: Penguin, 22–44.

Warnock, M. (1970) *Existentialism*, Oxford: Oxford University Press.

Waterman, R.H. (1990) *Adhocracy*, New York: W.W. Norton.

Watkins, A. (1991) 'Mr Heseltine may get his secret wish', *The Observer*, Sunday 20 October: 21.

Weber, M. (1971 [1904]) *The Protestant Ethic and the Spirit of Capitalism*, London: Unwin University Books.

Weber, M. (1993) 'The "anything goes" philosopher', *The Higher*, Friday 10 December: 15.

Webster, F.E. (1988) 'The rediscovery of the marketing concept', *Business Horizons* 31, 3: 29–39.

Webster, F.E. (1992) 'The changing role of marketing in the corporation', *Journal of Marketing* 56, 4: 1–17.

Wells, W.D. (1993) 'Discovery-oriented consumer research', *Journal of Consumer Research* 19, March: 489–504.

Wensley, R. (1990) '"The voice of the consumer?": speculations on the limits to the marketing analogy', *European Journal of Marketing* 24, 7: 49–60.

Wernick, A. (1991) *Promotional Culture: Advertising, Ideology and Symbolic Expression*, London: Sage.

White, H. (1989) 'New Historicism: a comment', in H.A. Vesser (ed.) *The New Historicism*, London: Routledge, 293–302.

White, S.K. (1988) *The Recent Work of Jürgen Habermas: Reason, Justice and Modernity*, Cambridge: Cambridge University Press.

Whittington, R. and Whipp, R. (1992) 'Professional ideology and marketing implementation', *European Journal of Marketing* 26, 1: 52–63.

Williams, R. (1977) *Marxism and Literature*, Oxford: Oxford University Press.

Williams, R. (1980) 'Advertising: the magic system', in R. Williams, *Problems in Materialism and Culture*, London: Verso, reprinted in S. During (ed.) *The Cultural Studies Reader*, London: Routledge, 1993, 320–36.

Williams, R. (1983) *Keywords: A Vocabulary of Culture and Society*, London: Fontana, second edition.

Williamson, J. (1978) *Decoding Advertisements: Ideology and Meaning in Advertising*, London: Marion Boyars.

Williamson, J. (1986) *Consuming Passions: The Dynamics of Popular Culture*, London: Marion Boyars.

Willis, S. (1991) *A Primer for Daily Life*, London: Routledge.

Willmott, H. (1993) 'Paradoxes of marketing: some critical reflections', in D. Brownlie *et al.* (eds) *Rethinking Marketing*, Coventry: Warwick Business School Research Bureau, 207–21.

Willsmer, R. (1984) *The Basic Arts of Marketing*, London: Business Books.

Wilson, E. (1990) 'The new components of the spectacle: fashion and postmodernism', in R. Boyne and A. Rattansi (eds) *Postmodernism and Society*, Basingstoke: Macmillan, 209–36.

Wilson, M. and McDonald, M. (1994) 'Marketing at the crossroads – a comment', *Marketing Intelligence and Planning* 12, 1: 42–45.

Wolpert, L. (1992) *The Unnatural Nature of Science*, London: Faber and Faber.

Wong, V. (1993) 'Marketing's ascendency and transcendence: is this what it takes for business to succeed?', in D. Brownlie *et al.* (eds) *Rethinking Marketing*, Coventry: Warwick Business School Research Bureau, 71–85.

Wong, V. and Saunders, J. (1993) 'Business orientations and corporate success', *Journal of Strategic Marketing* 1, 1: 20–40.

Wood, D. (ed.) (1992) *Derrida: A Critical Reader*, Oxford: Blackwell.

Wood, L. (1990) 'The end of the product life cycle', *Journal of Marketing Management* 6, 2: 145–51.

Woodward, A. (1993) 'Just one last puff', *The Sunday Times*, 22 August, 9: 6–7.

Woolgar, S. (1988) *Science: The Very Idea*, London: Routledge.

Workman, J.P. (1993) 'Marketing's limited role in new product development in one computer systems firm', *Journal of Marketing Research* 30, 4: 405–21.

Wright, T. (1989) 'Marketing culture: spectacles and simulation', in T.L. Childers *et al.* (eds) *Marketing Theory and Practice*, Chicago: American Marketing Association, 326–8.

Wyver, J. (1989) 'Television and postmodernism', in L. Appignanesi (ed.) *Postmodernism ICA Documents*, London: Free Association, 155–63.

Young, R. (ed.) (1981) *Untying the Text: A Post-structuralist Reader*, London: Routledge.

Zagor, K. and Mead, G. (1992) 'Illumination from the stars', *Financial Times*, Thursday 5 November: 18.

Zagorin, P. (1990) 'Historiography and postmodernism: reconsiderations', *History and Theory*, 29: 263–74.

Zikmund, W.G. (1982) 'Metaphors as methodology', in R.F. Busch and S.D. Hunt (eds) *Marketing Theory: Philosophy of Science Perspectives*, Chicago: American Marketing Association, 75–7.

Zikmund, W.G. and D'Amico, M. (1986) *Marketing*, New York: John Wiley, second edition.

Žižek, S. (ed.) (1992) *Everything You Always Wanted to Know About Lacan (But Were Afraid to Ask Hitchcock)*, London: Verso.

Zurbrugg, N. (1993) *The Parameters of Postmodernism*, London: Routledge.

Made it ma, top o' the world!